A WRITER'S TIME

Also by Kenneth Atchity

You Know You Still Alive If It's Costin' You Money: Cajun Household Wisdom

The Mercury Transition: Career Change Empowerment through Entrepreneurship

Critical Essays on Homer (editor)

In Praise of Love

Homer's Iliad: The Shield of Memory

Sleeping with an Elephant: Selected Poems

Italian Literature: Roots and Branches (coeditor)

Eterne in Mutabilitie: The Unity of the Faerie Queene (editor)

A WRITER'S TIME

TIME Making the Time
to Write

KENNETH ATCHITY

Revised Edition

W·W·NORTON & COMPANY · NEW YORK · LONDON

An AEI book

The poem "Writer to Source" is reprinted with the kind permission of May Harding. The poem "The First Step" is from *C. P. Cavafy: Collected Poems*, edited by George Savidis, Edmund Keeley and Philip Sherrard, trans. Translation copyright © 1975 by Edmund Keeley and Philip Sherrard. Reprinted by permission of Princeton University Press

Illustrations by permission of Norton Wright.

The text of this book is composed in 11/13 Janson
Composition and manufacturing by the Maple Vail Book Manufacturing Group.

Library of Congress Cataloging-in-Publication Data

Atchity, Kenneth John.
A writer's time : making the time to write / Kenneth Atchity.—
Rev. ed.
p.   cm.
Includes bibliographical references.
1. Authorship.   I. Title.
PN145.A83   1995
808'.02—dc20   94-15014
ISBN 0-393-03693-6
ISBN 0-393-31263-1 (PBK)

W. W. Norton & Company, Inc.
500 Fifth Avenue, New York, N.Y. 10110
www.wwnorton.com

W. W. Norton & Company Ltd.
Castle House, 75/76 Wells Street, London W1T 3QT
6   7   8   9   0

For Vincent and Rosemary

Contents

Acknowledgments

For ideas and suggestions about the structure and content of this book I am grateful to Rebecca Rivera, Charlene Solomon, Chuck Jensvold, Ruth Ballenger, A. J. Panos, and especially Doug Price. I learned much about the creative process from my mother and father, Fred and Myrza Atchity; from my son Vincent and daughter Rosemary; and from Alex Cord, Norman Cousins, Edward DeBono, Benedict Freedman, A. John Graves, Kathy Jacobi, Marsha Kinder (my coeditor at *Dreamworks*), Denise Levertov, Mark McCloskey, Mort Ransen, Carl Sautter, and Norton Wright. My students and colleagues at Occidental College, UCLA's Writers' Program, the University of Houston, the Beverly Hills Library Wednesday Writers Workshop, and my clients and private students at L/A House and Atchity Editorial/Entertainment International have been a constant source of ideas and responses without which this book would never have been. I'm grateful to my "allies" in my new show business career: David Adashek, Susan Cooper, Sid Kiwitt, Bob Lawrence, Stu Robinson, Sandy Watt, Steve Weiss, Ellen Weston, and Warren Zide. For my own writing, John Gardner, Bart Giamatti, Tom Huff, and Lowry Nelson, Jr., have given me inspiration and guidance over the years, and I feel fortunate to have Carol Houck Smith as my editor at Norton. I also owe much to the books listed in the bibliography, and most of all to Chi-Li Wong for understanding, loyalty, and support "above and beyond."

Author's Note

The advice in this book draws from the problems that writers have presented in individual consultations, private and university classes, and development meetings—as well as from my own experience as writer, editor, publisher, and independent producer. The system described in *A Writer's Time* has helped thousands of writers to overcome problems at one stage or another of their professional careers, from beginners to hardened professionals. The system isn't based on preconceived or philosophical notions about what writing ought to be, though it reflects my lifelong interest in the way the imagination works through myth and story. *A Writer's Time* has little to do with romantic concepts of the suffering writer.

Neither is it based on my belief in myself as a writer. It's hard to think of yourself that way, especially if you're spelling "writer" with a capital W. I find it much less intimidating to think of myself simply as a person who, among other activities, writes in order to speak his mind. I write nearly every day, but I know better than anyone that most of the time I'm not writing. I'm doing something else: lecturing, editing books and screenplays, connecting them with agents, producing for film, television, or video, talking on the phone, holding meetings—and taking many vacations. *A Writer's Time* explains how you can manage to write and publish in the same lifetime that demands your involvement in a multitude of other activities.

A writer, after all, is only a person who loves writing, and believes in it strongly enough to want to do it well. A person who writes about something that's not of interest is not, by my definition, a writer (there are students, of course, but their goal should be to finish being students at the earliest opportunity, so they can begin writing only about what they love). Having to write about things other people tell you to write about invariably leads to writer's block. If you concentrate on your own interests, you've licked most of the problem.

Norman Cousins, author of *Anatomy of an Illness* and *The Healing Heart*, divides the human race into "positive" and "negative" people: The positive people work miracles, accounting for the evolution of human performance. I have another division, productive and nonproductive people: those who can *do* things and those who only *talk* about things (especially talk about why they can't do things). As far back as I can remember, I was determined to contribute something, to be productive, and I've always questioned those who—though they may know much—go through life without making a mental contribution to the species: "If I live, I ought to speak my mind."

Productive people have a love affair with time, with all of love's ups and downs. They get more from time than others, seem to know how to use time much better than nonproductive people—so much so that they can waste immense quantities of time and still be enormously creative and productive. One of my favorite examples is John Peabody Harrington, the great anthropologist of the American Southwest. At the time of his death, Harrington's field notes filled a basement of the Smithsonian Institution in Washington, D.C., and several rented warehouses in the Washington suburbs were needed for the overflow. Yet Carobeth Laird, Harrington's biographer, called him one of the greatest wasters of time she'd ever known—and said he felt the same way about himself.

In the section of this book dealing with time, we see how

discrepancies can occur, and how you can get onto the right track, becoming productive in your use of time to achieve your writing and publishing goals. I firmly believe that anyone can be productive once the decision is made to master time and the necessary skills. This book shows you how to do both.

Aristotle said that the most characteristically human activity is planning your life, yet it's amazing how few people take life planning seriously. Those who do are the productive people; those who don't disappear under the surface without leaving a bubble behind to brighten the world. So strongly did the Greeks believe in planning that they literally planned their lives, dividing them into seven-year periods and deciding what they wanted to accomplish during each of those periods. It's not time that's scarce: It's planning. The Italians say, "there's more time than life," suggesting that you'll have plenty of time to do all you want to do if you take the time to plan.

During the next year or the next few years, plan to lay the foundation for your writing career. Immerse yourself in the planning process and build the foundation, and take your satisfaction from the doing of it, not from the having done it. The poet, as e. e. cummings reminds us, cares not for things made but only for the making. Your career, you'll discover, will take the shape of your foundation. To those who understand the relationship between craftsmanship and architecture, this will not be surprising.

The plan begins with a dream, a dream so strong that it must become true. Then you put the dream in order, in your head, allowing it to develop as any living being develops before its birth; next the dream is sketched on paper, in the step known as "first draft." Vacation comes next, removing yourself from the newborn object, building perspective toward it (another type of gestation). Finally you return to the process of revision, knowing what to take out, what to leave in. You've made your dream come true by risking the realization of the sketch: writing the book, building the wall.

A life should be as carefully planned as a work of art so

that it takes on the characteristic shape of your mind (the true meaning of "lifestyle"). You set goals for yourself by asking what you envision yourself doing in seven years. What image of yourself have you been secretly entertaining? Bring the image out of the closet, entertain it consciously (in the privacy of your own workroom). Examine it carefully. Ask yourself if it's realistic. Goals that are too high are counterproductive, just as goals that are too low are unworthy of your efforts.

Once you've focused on the image in your mind, you begin asking yourself what steps are needed to make that image—your dream—a reality. Then you learn the steps in all the ways human beings learn anything: by imitation, by self-education, by schooling. This book helps you take the first steps. From there, you have to continue on your own.

In Hollywood, it is said that four things guarantee success, in this order:

> *Perseverance (or determination, or stamina)*
> *Connections*
> *"Being fun to work with"*
> *Talent*

Successful writers all agree that success consists of writing, submitting your work for publication, and continuing to write and submit until you're accepted. Meanwhile, your primary attention is on the work, not on the submitting process—and certainly not on the rejection. But this book also shows you how to make the necessary split between the pragmatic "publishing" side of your mind and the artistic side from which true satisfaction derives. Once the split is made and the work begun in earnest, nothing but your own lack of faith and discipline can stop you from achieving success.

Discipline is the key to all that follows, the bedrock of productive writing. Talent is not a rare commodity. Discipline is. It requires determination more than self-confidence, the commitment of your will to the dream. *A Writer's Time* shows you how the mechanics of discipline work, but only you can will yourself to develop those mechanics in your own writing.

I haven't mentioned the Muse, the mythic word for "inspiration." She is the last person you want to depend on. Professional writers generally speak of her with a mixture of affection and tolerance: Discipline, not the Muse, results in productivity. If you write only when she beckons, your writing is not yours at all. If you write according to your own schedule, she'll shun you at first, but eventually she won't be able to stay away from your workshop. If you deny her urgings, she will adopt your discipline. Nothing attracts her more than a writer at work on a steady schedule. She'll come around. In other words, you become your own Muse, just as you make the clock of life your clock.

I'll have much to say about the "product" throughout the book, some of which may surprise those who are convinced that the product itself brings satisfaction. The product is what readers value. But writers love the work: It's the producing that satisfies, the daily work itself, and the knowledge that you've found a craft which will profit infinitely from a consistent application of discipline and attention.

A Writer's Time is based on the principles of vision, responsibility, productivity, and professionalism. *Vision* has to do with the power of the writer's dream, of the mental illumination that moves you toward self-expression. Write from the heart about things that matter to us all, and let nothing deter you from writing what only you can write. *Responsibility* means responding to your vision; if you have talent, inspiration, and something to say, you *must* write or all your life will be "bound in shallows and in miseries." *Productivity* comes from learning the mechanics of discipline and time management, of routine work on a program focused on accuracy and the refinement of technique. *Professionalism* is the harmonious combination of vision, responsibility, and productivity that occurs as experience leads to self-confidence. Happiness and security will come if you can embrace your work and dedicate your life to it.

Good work habits will produce the works that change our lives and make them, if not happier or better, always more interesting. Most successful writers have adhered to these simple guidelines:

Write with a purpose. "My purpose," wrote one person, "is to make what I write entertaining enough to compete with beer." What you're competing with is everything in the world—and nowadays that's more than ever before.

Write to make a difference. Write because you have something to say to us all. In dramatic writing, fiction, and nonfiction, this means knowing exactly what your work is about and being able to tell the publisher in ten words or less. The writing must demonstrate its premise in a convincing, persuasive way.

Keep your audience in mind, their needs and their desires. Journalists do this by focusing on the 5 W's (Who, What, When, Where, Why) because they know what their readers look for.

Convey emotion, break out of your academic inhibitions and psychological barriers. William Faulkner hints at this when he says, "Writing is a craft consisting of pen, paper, and whiskey." The purpose of the whiskey is to rid the author of inhibitions.

The first paragraph must, like the first page, hook the attention of the reader. One of your first readers is the editor who judges your manuscript. Brian Vachon said, "if that first and most important paragraph does not slap and sparkle like the sun in water, then we editors can't bother unduly with the rest." That may sound tough, but it's the exact same standard you apply when browsing in a bookstore.

Writing must have an element of magic to it. When that magic takes over, the writer himself loses track of time during the writing—and the reader will lose track of time during the reading. If you're happy at work and think of it as your own private briar patch—a place of escape from the world in which time is your time—the clock of life becomes your clock, and even the thorns in that briar patch are of your own choosing.

Remember that publishers are interested in your public voice. "Publish" means to make public, and the public primarily understands language that is related to a conventional norm of structure and style—even if that norm is employed merely to depart from it. The writer who insists on speaking in a "private voice" finds it difficult to join the network of publishers and readers. Private writing is often good therapy. It makes you feel better by helping you deal with feelings, by helping you discover your own patterns of thought and behavior, or by helping you find out what you think in the act of writing it down. Private language is, in many cases, natural to private groups like families and useful to the individual. A diary is one example of useful private language, Mission Control's directions to the shuttle astronauts another.

Since publishers want to hear your public voice, your letters to editors should be businesslike and direct. If a publisher becomes interested in your public voice, and establishes a professional relationship with you which endures over a period of time, then he might be interested in your private language and life as well. But that comes later.

This new edition reflects what I've learned in my new career as writer-producer for film, television, and video. Producing films for video, television, and the theaters, as well as working with an increasing number of both experienced and "first-time" novelists, screenwriters, and nonfiction writers, has taught me new ways of crisis management, and of "stealing time" from that clock on the wall. When you don't have the luxury of a regularly scheduled existence, the "stopwatch" system outlined at the end of chapter 3 may help you find the time you need to make an accelerated transit to *your* new career in writing.

Finally, in order to become productive and professional, your philosophy must be optimism. Unswerving optimism. Or at least optimism with a built-in swerve override. Self-respect and self-confidence must sustain you against those who might take a long time recognizing the value of your writing. The road is long, even though the journey becomes a pleasure once it is embraced. The length of the journey depends on faith, in yourself and in the work you've undertaken. You need to become one of the positive people in order to pursue a career in writing and remain human at the same time. Once your will is engaged, press on resolutely and you can do anything you dream of, decide upon, and plan to do. When others distract you, tell them you're doing important work and can't come down.

Kenneth Atchity
Los Angeles, 1994

ONE

Getting to Know You

What a Writer Does

Writers write. A writer feels uncomfortable when someone uses the word "writer"; it always sounds presumptuous. Once at a party the hostess introduced me to a producer as her friend "the writer." "Oh," said the producer, "say something in writing."

His joke overcame the uncomfortable label. "Writer," like "Muse," "inspiration," and "talent," is a mystical buzz-word calculated either to impress or intimidate. Most of the time, especially at the beginning of your career, such words are likely to intimidate you.

Most writers are more comfortable saying, "I write things—that's all." One of the first questions I ask when a writer needs help to become productive is, "When is the last time you sat down and wrote?" I don't mean sat down and stared out the window, but actually moved your hand across the page or your fingers on the keyboard. Generally the response is, "What do you mean?" You know what I mean! You'd be surprised how many such people haven't written a thing for weeks! If you simply define a writer as someone who is writing, clarity sets in. You're truly a writer when you're writing; and if you don't write regularly, don't pretend to give yourself that title. "Start writing more," Ray Bradbury tells would-be writers at conferences, "it'll get rid of all those moods you're having." Work, not contemplating work, brings satisfaction to the writer, and the ultimate satisfaction is not in having your work published (that's some satisfaction, but one usually mixed with equal parts of frustration). "If a poet is anybody," said e. e. cummings, "he is somebody to whom things made matter very little—somebody who is obsessed by Making." The ultimate, continuing satisfaction is in writing itself.

More than the craft of writing, this book is devoted to helping you unlearn all the things—about yourself and about writing—that you've been brainwashed with since fourth grade: excessive language, structural rigidity, confusion of analysis with creativity, reliance on vocabulary instead of clarity, the myths about contractions or the use of the word "one" as an impersonal pronoun, the belief that inspiration is all that's needed, the belief that you should revise the last sentence before you write the next, reverence for Roman-numeral outlines, and many others. Let go of the heavy burden of bad habit, lack of self-confidence, and unnatural usage. After that, you can be yourself, writing naturally about what matters to you.

Once you have survived your education (essential as far as it goes) your task is to recover your prekindergarten mentality and to look at writing as a question of "filling in the blanks." Now they will be blanks of your own choosing, filled in at your own pace. Exactly what those "blanks" are is one of this book's concerns, and how you fill them in for yourself is another. How you get rid of everything else is partly described here, but is largely a matter of willpower and decisive introspection.

Writing is a craft. A craft not only can be learned, it must be learned. Only the inclination to write—and the talent—come naturally; all the rest is a result of training, the trustiest form of which is self-imposed discipline on a routine basis.

What about Anxiety?

If the mere thought of writing—not to mention actually sitting down to write—causes you anxiety, don't be surprised or dismayed. Anxiety comes with the territory. By its very nature, writing is an anxiety-producing activity. Writing is reexamining values, and nothing produces more anxiety for the human being than reexamining widely accepted values and searching for a way of justifying and articulating the reexamination. The secret of becoming productive and retaining your own peace of mind lies in learning how to harness the anxiety and transform it into "productive elation."

Most of us hate to think. Five minutes of thought can be more terrifying, more energy-draining than days and days of routine or habitual activity. Your mind is intrinsically thrifty, and prefers to do things the way it has done them before. It sees its primary business as establishing effective channels for action, and resists altering a channel that has become established, to say nothing of constructing a new one that causes anxiety.

Yet writers hate routine. They hate all habits they haven't developed for themselves. They associate themselves more with intuition than with that thrifty old grandmother Reason.

So you begin by recognizing that anxiety comes with the profession of writing; how you manage your anxiety becomes a mark of distinction—no matter how annoying or downright painful it can be in the meantime. It's easy to think of great writers who have not survived their love-hate relationship with anxiety—from Hemingway to Sylvia Plath, at one extreme; to Coleridge and Faulkner, whose addictions (to opium or alcohol) place them at the milder extreme. The challenge of surviving as a writer lies in learning not to avoid anxiety but to cope with it and make its energy positive.

To conquer anxiety and make it productive, nothing can replace understanding your own mind, getting to know both how the mind works in general (the subject of chapter 2) and how your own mind, with its peculiar quirks and particular dreams, works. If you dream of making the clock of life your clock, you must understand the mind that controls your perception of time and of reality. Before anything reaches paper, the business of being a writer is the business of developing self-awareness and honest introspection. Keats called the profession of writing "soul-making," and the first step toward success is recognizing the psychological discipline that writing requires.

Anxiety is the enemy only at the beginning of your career. If you challenge the creative stress of anxiety on a routine basis, you turn it into a helpmate. Productive elation, initiated and shaped by your own will, becomes, side by side with time, your most faithful collaborator. You make your own pressures, and suddenly anxiety is now a blessed spirit rather than a destructive fury: You've transformed it into your onboard Muse.

In coping with the anxiety known as "writer's block," one of the first rules is *Never sit down to write until you know what you're going to write.*

When it comes to the physical act of writing (not preparing to write, thinking about writing, researching, or any other definition that may lead you to associate writing with staring at a blank piece of paper), you decide you'll never sit down to this work without having planned it out in advance. The blank piece of paper produces a "block" because it's flat and your mind isn't. When your mind wants to come up with something to write, it draws from storehouses and storehouses of ideas and images. You can't pry an idea from a flat piece of paper: Flatness is almost the worst model for the multistorehouse mind bursting with ideas!

Therefore it makes more sense to do the prying in your head and to sit down to the paper only when you know exactly what you're going to write. If sitting down to write is intimidating, get away from the intimidation—go sit outside, giving yourself a time limit and a word count to write in your head for fifty minutes: "I'll give myself fifty minutes to write fifteen words." Now allow yourself to waste a chunk of that time without even looking at the paper.

Once that "waste" time has passed, perhaps twenty minutes, tell yourself you have thirty minutes left in which to compose a single fifteen-word sentence. Say to your mind, "Take your time, I know this is tough for you—don't hurry." When you actually employ this technique, the mind usually responds instantly, fed up with your pronouncements about its capacity. You'll find there's plenty of time left in the thirty minutes to move beyond the first sentence.

All that you've done is remove the intimidation. By alleviating the rational part of your mind's anxiety, you've managed to mine the intuitive part and to bring its treasures up onto your internal viewing screen so that you can go back to your workshop at the appointed time and transcribe that intuitive vision onto paper. *A Writer's Time* will show you how to make the act of writing the act of transcribing what is already clearly formed and therefore clearly viewed inside your mind.

How the Mind Works in Time

You probably won't be able to convert instantly to this method of time discipline. But here's how you start the conversion. You learn how to program your consciousness to give you what you need: something to write on the blank page.

You begin with a decision. Almost any decision will do. You decide today, for example, "Here's what I'm going to write tomorrow: 'Mary walked down the street and never came back.' " Almost any decision will do because the purpose of the decision is simply to get the process started, and the process doesn't start until some decision has been made. Don't forget that the creative mind works through negation, one part of the mind denying another in an ongoing dialogue. The initial decision activates the process, which begins by contradicting the decision!

The minute your rational mind has made that first decision, you relieve it of its responsibilities for the day and thank it for its loyal and brilliant executive ability. (It is, after all, amazing that the rational part of your mind, the logical and conventional part we all share in common—what I describe as the "Continent of Reason" in the next chapter—can come up with something on demand. The Continent is a much more efficient thinking machine than are any of the areas of intuitive consciousness, those countless idiosyncratic centers of perception that are different for each of us. I call these "the islands.") What happens instantly is that the Continent's opening decision is written in the sky above all those islands in the back of your mind.

The "back of your mind" can't believe Reason's sentence about Mary. It's the most stupid thing the islands have ever heard. They say it's a ridiculous way to start your story—too weak! The dialogue between Reason and the islands has begun. The islands have a million better ideas and each and every one of them starts thinking about better sentences.

As the day wears on, ideas from the strongest islands begin announcing themselves to that part of your mind I call "the Managing Editor." The rational mind has programmed the intuitive islands to reject its arbitrary decision because it knows what the islands have to say is likely to be more powerful than anything it can come up with through sheer intellectualizing.

At this point, as ideas begin to announce themselves, the Managing Editor listens politely—then tells them to go back where they came from. "We write in the morning," the Editor tells them, "so thank you very much, I appreciate your interest and find your suggestion stimulating, but bring it back in the morning."

The programming of the islands has now turned into creative pressure. Elation is the feeling you have when the pressure produces results. One natural result of this denial on the part of the Editor is to sort the stronger island suggestions from the weaker. The Editor knows it will have the final word, so it can afford to put pressure on the island sources.

When the islands start shouting, if you write down their first suggestions you'll have a wide selection of, at worst, nonsensical gibberish; at best, you'll have a supply of relatively weak suggestions. And you'll be left making your final selection solely on the basis of the Continent of Reason.

However, by initially denying the islands, you end up extinguishing the weaker suggestions. Your mind is just testing you to see how serious you are about your desire to be disciplined and to get the best from the suggestions. Darwinian forces come into play. By the time you begin writing the next morning, only the strongest suggestions—often by that time the result of combination and negotiation among the islands and between them and the Continent—will have survived.

Ninety-nine times out of a hundred, what you'll write down will not be the original sentence you decided on yesterday morning. The new sentence will be better, the result of your entire mind's activity.

If the dialogue has produced nothing by the next morning, you have two choices: Either go with your original sentence or decide you're not ready to write yet. Take a vacation! The benefits of vacations are immeasurable. The longer an idea "percolates" in the mind the greater its chances of being expressed clearly and powerfully when the time is right.

Avoiding Negative Reinforcement

It's crucial to adopt the rule of not writing until you're ready to write. Doing otherwise creates a massive negative reinforcement which, if it accumulates over days and years, can be fatal to your writing. You must develop the habit of producing positive reinforcement, of only writing when you know you have something to write.

Don't worry about excessive vacations, provided you've adopted an agenda and are working according to the guidelines in chapter 4, "Writing in Time." Every time you sit down and realize you're not ready to write, then get up and consciously declare a holiday, your anxiety level goes up another notch until it reaches the point of productivity. This is how you force work from the islands, by using the Continent's pressure. Understanding that this process works and how it works is what converts anxiety to elation.

The Continent can't tolerate lack of productivity, even in the areas of work it normally shuns; once it gets the idea that something is wrong with an agenda it agreed to enforce, it will enlist its energies to save that agenda—even though this may be acting against its initial urge to ignore this whole business of writing. It's up to your Managing Editor to set up the pattern for enlisting the Continent this way.

Once the habit has been established, the situation becomes even more manageable because you can now use the principle of linkage (discussed in chapter 3) to make sure you know what you're going to write tomorrow.

Slumps

Slumps are different from general depression. I used to think slumps were natural phenomena, a reaction to the highs of productivity, and that the progress of a productive life was a cycle of ups and downs. I thought then that the slumps were the price you paid for the triumphs.

I no longer completely believe that. Instead I think you can do without the slumps if you have enough willpower (discipline) and introspection (which allows you to trick the mind into behavior your dreams demand).

Here's an example from my own experience.

One day I was sitting at my desk writing, when I suddenly felt a depression coming on. I could almost feel it, moving liquidly around in my head. At the same moment I also realized that I had a choice: I could either allow the depression to overcome me or not.

This time I decided not. I stood up, left the house, and ran around the block. When I got back, I was out of breath but otherwise fine. No depression. This got me to thinking:

Depressions are physical, and something the mind may require. I'm not talking, of course, about deep depressions caused by unresolved traumas. I'm talking about the ones writers refer to as "slumps." In conversations with Norman Cousins, I found that he'd also concluded that creativity is physical, a matter of hormone secretion that produces that special "high" familiar to writers who lose themselves in the time of their writing.

I decided to see if there was something I could do to make the depressions enjoyable, since I theorized that they were necessary. Some people advise doing research during the slumps, but research is too much like work and the depression that stops the writing will probably stop the research. Instead, I looked around for things I didn't have time to do when I wasn't depressed. I found three: (1) video games, (2) autobiographies, and (3) magazines (stacks of which constantly reminded me of my inability to keep up with my subscriptions).

In other words, this was my "depression list": activities I'd look forward to doing next time I allowed myself to get depressed.

A strange thing happened. As a result of this decision made years ago, I haven't been functionally depressed since. I haven't had recurring slumps. Also, to my regret, I haven't played many video games, read many autobiographies, or caught up on my magazines—the stack is higher than ever.

Crutches

Another personal breakthrough occurred as a result of my decision, on July 14, 1972, to stop smoking. I was boarding a plane for Italy, to spend the summer in Florence, and I had two cartons of Tareytons in my suitcase to tide me over until I learned how to ask for cigarettes in Italian. As I seated myself, I said, after years of trying to quit, "I'm not a smoker any longer." For some reason I haven't yet figured out, this time the resolution stuck.

On board the train to Florence from Rome, the Italian soldiers in my compartment asked me if it was okay for them to smoke. I nodded, then proceeded to have my lungs filled with awful Italian tobacco. I asked the soldiers if they'd like some American cigarettes. They responded eagerly and I gave them my two cartons, explaining that I'd brought them along for a friend in Florence who no longer smoked.

When I settled myself on Costa di San Giorgio a day or so later I found, to my horror, that I was no longer able to write. I'd been writing something or other nearly every day of my life as far back as I could remember. I stared at my favorite ashtray and the gold lighter with leather skin as though they were gods who had failed me.

This condition went on for a month, until I was really down in the dumps despite the magnificence of my situation in Florence. I did various things to cheer myself up, including reading Virgil's *Aeneid* on the splendid terrace of Forte Belvedere, and more mundane things like spending money on exotic gewgaws. The nadir of the experience occurred the day I went down to the Ponte Vecchio to pick up the new Italian sunglasses (prescription, and extravagantly expensive) I'd ordered to make myself feel better.

I was staring down into the Arno through the sunglasses. They fell off and quickly disappeared among the muddy goldfish in the river. Filled with suicidal resolution, I headed across the bridge for my apartment. Things couldn't be worse, I thought.

Then a pigeon flew over and deposited worst on my shoulder.

Now I understood. The gods hadn't failed me: They had expelled me from their graces, showing me their ruder devices. My Muses had turned into harpies.

As I reached the long steps leading up to Costa di San Giorgio from Lungarno, the news vendor thrust *The International Herald Tribune* into my hand as he had daily for the past weeks. I barely glanced at it as I went up the steps toward the cobblestone street on which, long ago, Galileo discovered his own kind of productivity.

At the door of the apartment I noticed, on the back page of the paper, that Russell Baker's column was appearing again. It had been missing for the past three weeks because, as Baker explained in this column, he'd stopped smoking. He went on to describe how his doctor and shrink told him he had common withdrawal syndrome and that he could either return to his column and smoking or kiss his daily column goodbye until the syndrome spent itself.

I felt better immediately and decided then and there (a) not to commit suicide—which, in any case, hadn't been a very serious resolution, despite the pigeon's insistence; and (b) to forget about writing.

I decided that if my Muse was nicotine and my writing came from that source, it wasn't worth pursuing at all. And maybe, in fact, that was why the writing I'd done until then wasn't so great.

I concocted an unforgettable pasta from leftovers, and washed it down with a fine bottle of Chianti Classico.

The next morning, I couldn't remember the pasta but, without further ado, began writing again—and haven't stopped to this day.

What I learned from this experience, in retrospect (the way we learn everything), is that the mind is "trickable." Its division into islands and Continent, as described step by step in the next chapter, can be used to move the whole show forward.

The minute I decided not to write, I began writing.

The Continent made a rational decision, and the islands revolted. They weren't ready to revolt until a counterdecision had been made that gave them something firm to revolt against. Then they said, "Hey, he's gone too far—we're not letting him get away with this." And then they took over, to begin writing. My career took a positive turn, because my writing was now coming from the islands primarily, channeled through the Continent, instead of the other way around. My Managing Editor had been born.

Another example of this kind of self-trickery is a technique for remembering things on the "tip of your tongue." Tell yourself firmly that you can't remember them: Within microseconds, the islands cough them up, and you remember. The Editor, forcing the Continent to admit its shortcomings and limitations, causes the brain to allow voice to the islands.

The more you know about yourself, the more productive your writing will be.

So your first step is a resolution: From this point onward, I'm going to start figuring myself out, so that I—and not "they"—can be in charge of my writing and of my writing career.

TWO

How the Mind Works

"What's Going on in There?"

Whether they ask the question aloud or not, people always want to know what makes a writer's mind work. They're really asking: Is your mind different from mine?

It is, and it isn't. The well-adjusted productive writer has the same resources as everyone else but exploits them more thoroughly and more stubbornly. At the risk of emotional turmoil, the writer is more in touch with the whole mind, taking better advantage of its natural shape. Because of this self-exploration the writer's mind does work differently from that of the person who doesn't come to understand himself. Learning to write is learning your own mind. By explaining "what's going on in there," this chapter sets the stage to help you understand theories and practices to be developed in later chapters.

The imagination functions like the feelers of an ocean-floor crustacean. As we make our way across the sea of life, the imagination helps us scout out where we're going to be before we actually go there. It's set up to do the advance work for us—feeling on all sides, trying to determine the best path before the rest of us becomes committed to, and endangered by, the multiple choice of available perils.

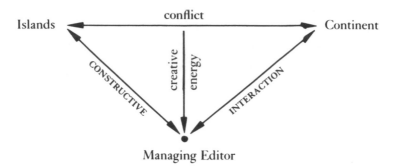

Managing Editor

I've found a useful metaphor for describing the mind: Inside our heads, we have what I think of as many "islands of consciousness," "the Continent of Reason," and "the Managing Editor." The islands are free-floating and changeable, but the Continent is relatively stationary and immovable. Like the Continent, each island perceives life entire, with its own fully developed viewpoint. Each island, in other words, has its own unique vision of reality and makes no comparison. Originality and individuality are island characteristics; the Continent is the consensus of society and culture, and is constructed by our education. The Continent operates by analogy, comparing the new to what it knows already. While a new island can be formed instantly from a new impression—both instantly and "all at once"—the Continent is slower, having to search its warehouse of memory to find a category to which to relate the new impression so that it can use that new impression in dealing with the world outside the mind. During sleep, the Managing Editor reviews all new impressions, both of new islands (accounting for "nonsense" dreams) and ones added to the Continent's ever-expanding web of analogies (reasonable dreams).

The writer wants to hear the winds from all the islands, seeing clearly and being willing to cope with the holographic, three-dimensional, reduplicating, multifaceted nature of consciousness. The writer's awareness of himself and his consciousness of the interaction between islands and Continent is the third element of the creative mind. I call this element "the Managing Editor."

The interaction of islands and Continent—the tension between them—causes the productive energy identified with the Editor's creative awareness. Once it has been formed from the island-Continent tension (and the acceptance of that tension as the natural state of things), the Managing Editor focuses like a spinning laser beam to illuminate activities on the islands and on the Continent, moving slowly or quickly depending on the writer's energy level. Awareness of superimposed images from the spinning illumination forms the first concept or dream that starts a specific creative process.

Writing is the Editor's ordering of materials from all the islands into the language and structure of the Continent, managing the analytical mind to have it organize images from the nonanalytical mind. No wonder writing causes anxiety. With such an activity as its start and such a process as its focus, how could it not? When an island sees an object as one thing and at the same instant the Continent declares it another, most people choose the Continent's way of seeing and repress the island's "crazy" viewpoint. Not the writer. The writer engages willfully in the one activity most people hate above all others: reexamining values, then searching for clear expression of new vision. Others call new vision "weird" or "strange" until it achieves wide acceptance; then they call it a "breakthrough"; finally they call it "classical." But the writer, from the outset, accepts both ways of seeing as routine. The writer's controlled ambivalence allows the sharing of a dream with us. If you want to be a writer, don't hope to displace your anxiety. Instead, find ways of coping with it, tricking it, transforming it. To make anxiety productive you transform it to "productive elation."

Whether you name the splits in your consciousness "right brain" and "left brain," "id" or "ego," "superego" or "libido," "father" and "daughter," "mother" and "son," "self" or "society," "intuitive" and "rational," what's important to recognize is that we're working with a divided mind. Non-artists cope with the pressures of division by allowing one part of the mind to dominate, that main Continent constructed by our interaction with and education by society. The writer refuses to allow one division to dominate; confusion may result, or even depression. Neat solutions are no longer acceptable. The writer is an explorer wanting to investigate and keep in touch with all the islands, no matter how depressing one might be, no matter how terrifying another.

So you can expect contradictions in the pages that follow. As a writer, you won't be startled. Walt Whitman was speaking for all artists when he wrote,

> *Do I contradict myself?*
> *Very well, then I contradict myself,*
> *(I am large, I contain multitudes.)*

The contradictions occur because, for the writer, opposing feelings or situations are often equally true at the same time. Contradictions and confusions, to a greater or lesser extent, are the natural companions of the writer, following the writer as goslings follow the mother goose. You expect them, welcome them as signs of your vocation, and learn to live with them without letting them nag you to death.

We dream before we do. All creative people dream first, whether they've developed their Managing Editor to allow them to be aware of this or not. Later chapters will detail this dreamwork process. But to begin with, it's helpful to outline the steps by which the mind moves from dream to creative and created work: (1) dream, (2) "doodling," (3) assembly, (4) gestation, (5) agenda, (6) vacation, (7) first draft, (8) vacation, (9) focused gestation, (10) agenda for revision, (11) revision, and (12) product. Though you may not realize it, you, too, go through a similar experience whenever you embark on and complete a successful project. Being fully aware of the steps leads to both productivity and peace of mind.

Dreamwork: Doodling, Assembly, and Gestation

Whether we examine a total writing career or an individual project, we find that it all begins with a dream: the writer's vision that presses for expression, or a "brainstorm," an image of what the writer feels compelled to write. In a general sense, the initiating dream—what we call "vocation"—is seeing yourself as having something to say that others will want to hear or need to hear. It's the image of yourself writing, of being someone who has written, and who is recognized as someone who has written.

In like fashion, the particular writing project may begin as a dream that occurs during sleep or as a daydream that won't cease until your Editor has forced your Continent to admit delegates from the islands loaded down with miscellaneous materials. It may start as a vivid hallucination that fills in the image of what you must write so precisely that all you finally have to do is transcribe what you see when you close your eyes. The hallucination leads to obsession; productive obsession becomes the compulsion to write the vision down.

You speak the dream out loud: "I think I can see myself doing that," you say at first. Then: "I can see myself doing it." The dream comes into focus, the image coalesces. The process known as inspiration has occurred, like lightning striking clay to bring it alive. The lightning may continue to strike as the clay takes shape, but the professional writer at this early stage ceases to depend on it: He takes the new life into his own hands. The next step in "dreamwork" separates the doers from those who are merely "dreamers" in the passive sense of the word. It takes place in two stages.

The first stage marries desire with will—saying, "I will do it!" The commitment of your will is the true beginning of creation, the necessary ingredient of productivity. Without it, creation will remain only a dream. The desire is formed in the imagination, but the will must be enlisted to give birth to desire through expression. When the will is enlisted, the Managing Editor is born—only the Editor can bring the islands and the Continent together in productive dreamwork.

Of course, the mind will resist that enlistment because expression makes the writer vulnerable, removing the defenses that protect the inner self from the world's attack, misunderstanding, jealousy, and indifference. This inevitable vulnerability is another source of the writer's anxiety. Desire must be strong, or the will will not serve. "Ambition" is one word for the combination of desire and will, "determination" another. Those who have the desire but in insufficient degree to command will remain pseudoartists, would-be writers. They are the ones who always seem to be writing a book that never appears.

The writer moves from commitment of the will to the second vital stage: decision to act.

For many writers, the dream leads quickly and decisively to doodling, the first tentative expression before the subsequent commitment of craft that will make the final expression fixed or concrete. This step is like testing the waters or preliminary sketching, including many false starts. Whatever you call it, it's an extremely important step because it allows the Editor to engage the energies of the whole mind—both islands and Continent—in the initial steps of the creative process.

The step proceeds either by invention or learning. Some people begin doodling, sketching out a path, testing it completely on their own. Others prefer to go to school for this portion. Either way, this is the predraft stage, the exploration of possible shapes for achievement. It is the first product of the dream.

Assembly of the elements comes next for some writers, but for others precedes the doodling. The assembly stage itself consists of expansion followed by contraction. Expansion is the time when you follow "follow your nose" to ideas, concepts, materials, images related to the original dream of your project. You allow no preexisting structures to prejudice the direction of your search during this part of assembly. Your instincts, if allowed freedom, will lead you to discovering the ingredients of what will later appeal as the "natural shape" of your fiction or nonfiction.

During the contraction stage of assembly, you discard materials that upon examination seem unworthy of inclusion in your project. You follow the "Yes or No" method: "Is this a good element?" Answer: "Yes," or "No." Discard the "No's" on the premise that a project consisting of "No's" is bound to be less effective than one consisting of "Yes's." Contraction is a necessary final stage of assembly because your mind is different after expansion than it was before you began. It contains knowledge and images which had they been present at the start would have prevented the collection of elements which, at the end, can be seen as clear "No's."

When assembly is done (and you know it's done because you feel you've collected enough to make something from), the time has arrived for gestation to begin in earnest.

The third stage of dreamwork begins when the decision to write has been made. You leave your doodles behind and take a vacation, ranging in duration from a half-hour walk to a two-week retreat depending on the project. During this period of gestation you allow the dream to become even more definite by denying your sketches, criticizing them. This stage begins with the Continent's rational analysis of the doodle, but ends with an involvement of the islands as well.

Faulkner said his novels began with an image (the "dream") that haunted him. He kept it in his mind, allowing the haunting to take its course until questions formulated themselves about the image. Then he answered the questions until the story found what I've called its "natural shape." The process can work in a similar way for you. When all the parts are in place, you're ready for the third stage: making the agenda.

In the film industry, gestation often takes the shape of one or more story conferences. The conference is held to discuss an idea (the doodle or sketch). No one takes notes; the process, like the story itself, is dynamic and organic. When the story takes a living shape, it becomes vivid and memorable and the notes serve to transcribe rather than to record. Writers spend far too much time recording when they should be brooding. You work toward a point in your craft when the story needn't be drafted until its action line is fully established in your mind. The card system to be described later is a crutch that helps you reach that point, but it's a crutch you'll leave behind once you have mastered the process of gestation.

Agenda

Now you're ready to ask the craftsman's first questions: How would I go about doing this work in a specified period of time? What materials will I need to do it with? Once these questions are asked and the writer begins answering them, the first gestation period moves quickly toward the birth process.

As gestation gives way to birth, we realize the importance of planned parenthood. Happy births are planned births! A plan, by definition, is the organization of materials toward an objective: putting the elements together in order to finish the project within a given time frame. The agenda for doing so includes elements such as pen and paper, typewriter and ink, as well as time and work space.

The doodling, assembly, and gestation processes have assured the writer that realization of the vision is possible. The next step is to reduce the project to a step-by-step agenda. The psychological result of good planning is to allow the mind, once the actual work begins, to concentrate on details and to forget about the intimidating general picture. The general picture is the original, amazing dream; the agenda is the Editor's blueprint for the dream. Writing a book, once the initial fever has subsided, is a terrifying prospect. But it's not terrifying to think of writing two or three pages a day, even day in and day out.

The agenda relates the parts to the whole, and must begin with the craftsman's inventory of needed parts (detailed in chapter 4, "Writing in Time"). The agenda makes the dream come true. An agenda relates "what's to be done" with "when will I do it," and deals both with individual compartments of time and the overall time from start to finish. A plan isn't productive until a working calendar is set up. The calendar will direct the project.

Obviously, a calendar must be realistic with regard to the project and the writer's abilities. How can you know in advance that the calendar you plan is realistic? You can't— until you've gained enough experience from successful and unsuccessful calendars of the past. Therefore it's essential from the outset that you build into your calendar periods of review in which the productivity of the calendar to date is measured and assessed. The calendar is fine-tuned until it becomes effective and self-reinforcing. It's also essential that you work hard to live up to the calendar's demands. Treading on your own dreams is truly insane.

Vacation

After you've completed your agenda, give yourself a well-deserved vacation. You need to be "psyched up" and ready to make the calendar work. The next step (the first draft) is action, and action requires energy. When you return from vacation, physically refreshed and filled with renewed resolve, you'll be prepared for a workmanlike attack on the project. You'll have prepared your work space and you'll be eager to get down to work, primarily because your well-made agenda will have reduced the task to suitable daily proportions. You'll no longer have to worry about anything except working during the daily compartments of time that make things happen for you (see chapter 3).

First Draft

The first draft is the time when you let your imagination flow through the materials you've collected so far, using a "road map" rather than a rigorous outline as a starting point. Ray Bradbury has a sign on his typewriter for first drafts: "Don't

Think." Your islands will speak most freely during the first draft, after the Continent has constructed the agenda for their speaking. Always head for drama at this point in the process: Choose the more dramatic alternative at every crossroads. Writing yourself "into a corner" guarantees drama as much as it does anxiety: The reader will relish watching you write yourself out of the corner.

Your objective now is to get that draft on the table. The first draft should involve no more than typing transitions where they are necessary between scenes (fiction or drama) or units of information (nonfiction). Later, during revision, the time will come for painstaking work on style, transition, logic, editorial decisions.

Use the time-management techniques in chapter 3 to ensure that writing the first draft won't defeat you. Don't stop to revise, don't stop to look up words, don't stop to look back. Just keep going at all costs, from the beginning right straight through the middle to the end. Then stop.

Vacation

It would be crazy to begin revising immediately after finishing the first draft, and counter to the way the mind likes to create. You're exhausted. You deserve a vacation. Go away from the project for at least a week.

Focused Gestation

When the week has passed, get ready for an even longer vacation by asking yourself this question: "What was my book about?" or "What is its natural shape?" Focusing the islands on a problem brings the pressure to bear: They'll solve it for you. Now enjoy a real vacation, waiting for that moment of inspiration in which the purpose of your book is revealed to you. Once it occurs, you're ready to begin revising; now you know what to take out. After all, how can you revise a book without knowing what it's about?

Revisionary Agenda

On the last day of the extended vacation, make an agenda for your revision, scheduling compartments of time in which you can comfortably and alertly do your very best to polish style and search out clear meaning.

Revision

The revision itself involves the principles of good editing, the primary one being cutting. This means removing everything that doesn't serve the natural shape of your novel or nonfiction book. Revision is an easy process if you know what you're aiming for, if you have that natural shape clearly in mind. If you can't bring yourself to throw away your deletions, keep them (I suggest misfiling them on purpose). Just to get them out of the way of your book's natural shape.

Now is the time to polish, to check every word for accuracy and economy, following Strunk and White's *The Elements of Style* and W. W. Watt's *An American Rhetoric.* Your book should be revised, with a vacation after each revision, at least twice but no more than four times without specific directions from a publisher.

The islands and the Continent work together through the stages of creation, vying with one another for voice and articulation. Writing is the conscious ordering of unconscious material, with the Continent of Reason applying its logic to the intuitive logic of the islands so that their alternative visions of the world can be expressed in a language the world can understand. In all stages, the third element—the Managing Editor—acts as referee and arbitrator. The writer who wishes to become productive, and to remain relatively sane as well, must learn how islands and Continent work together effectively and without killing one another.

Remember that there's a distinction between "public" and "private" voice. You may be interested in your private voices (as Joan of Arc was); but unless you find a way of allowing us to hear them, you're probably too caught up in the voices from your "islands" and you're in for trouble as a writer. Your Continent controls the medium of communication; it has been shaped and created by language (through education). Writers have always recognized that language is insufficient for perfect communication of their private vision. The vision of the islands cannot be expressed except through the wordless language of feeling, which the writer experiences in isolation. That experience must be translated into words that express the writer's island vision, so that we can share it. The chosen structure triggers a response in us similar to the writer's creative vision. The words themselves are not the vision. The words are in a sense arbitrary: It's the shapes of feeling, the form of thought, the images that words convey that move us to see as the artist sees.

The Continent also controls the structures by which the words are given whole form: action line, character, setting, tone of voice. The writer's dream is to return to the freedom of dream—and to take us along by means of a reasonable use of language and form, even when the effect is to make us recognize the limits of our Continent. In this way the writer refashions the Continent for us all.

The Editor, mediating between Continent and islands, understands that the agenda gives the Continent, which demands total control (to ensure our physical survival, for one thing), the assurance that the act of writing won't jeopardize its responsibility. The agenda is the Editor's promise to the Continent that the writing will be limited to certain times of day, leaving plenty of time for the routine business of living which is the Continent's primary occupation. The Editor knows that the dream can be expressed only through cooperation with the Continent. Chapter 4, "Writing in Time," explains the ground rules that make that cooperation productive.

THREE

Finding Time: The Elusive Collaborator

WRITERS, hoping to mitigate the loneliness, long for collaborators. The Managing Editor knows that the strongest, most faithful collaborator is time. Talent and discipline combined with time can make your dreams come true.

"Where do you find the time?" people ask. They suspect that a special dispensation has granted you more time than they have. But time becomes amazingly productive for those who look for it: Finding time is the key to a life filled with happy work. Yet only a fixed amount of time, if you measure it by the Continent's clock on the wall, seems available—the same amount available to everyone. That paradox makes time the strangest element of all . When you make the clock of life your clock, you discover the truth of the Spanish saying, "Life is short, but wide."

Finding time begins with an act of the will. You also have to look for time in the right places. Knowing about time's characteristics will make you comfortable with the way it works best so the two of you can work together effectively. As soon as you've had some success at time finding, you discover something wonderful: Time, unlike money (but like generosity), comes back to those who give it freely. Perhaps that's what people mean when they say that one person seems to have more time than others. Time expands for those who court it: "If you want something done, find a busy person." This may sound odd to those who are always saying, "I wish I had more time to do all the things I want to do." There is more time available than most people realize. For those who "have time on their hands," boredom is the great enemy. Finding time to do what *only you* can do—and what *you love to do most*—distinguishes happy productive people from the unproductive and the unhappy.

The time you find for writing is the most valuable time of your life because it belongs to no one but you. This is the time of your islands, the time when you see what only you can see, and when you labor to make us see it as well. No wonder time flies when you're working well; you look up to discover yourself entirely out of sync with the Continent's clock on the wall. You've lost yourself in your work, back there among the islands, happy and free. You've experienced timelessness while still in time. From the beginning, writers have been accused of justifying their art as the search for immortality. But no writer I know would feel for an instant that being remembered after one's death is adequate compensation for dying, much less an efficient motivation for the willful madness of artistic discipline. The immortality associated with writing lies in the writer's daily visit to an internal eternity.

How is your relationship with time going? Do you recognize your optimal patterns of time-work management, or have you allowed yourself to be dominated by the Continent's time? This checklist is a starting point toward making the clock of life your clock instead of the Continent's.

- You never seem to find the time to start that writing project you've been dreaming of.
- When people say, "What makes you think your time is so valuable?" you feel guilty.
- You ask other people, "Where do you find the time?"

- You hear yourself saying, "I don't know where the time goes."
- You spend most of your time responding to external pressures instead of to your inner vision.
- You can't seem to figure out the relationship between your motivation to write and the demands of your personal life.
- Your whole life seems to have become "one big interruption."
- You've been planning to "get started" all your life.
- You're proud of your talent, but don't understand the technical discipline required to make it productive.
- You keep attending creative writing classes and do no writing on your own.

Let's Get Started!

Every human being has exactly the same amount of time, and yet consider the output of Robert Louis Stevenson, John Peabody Harrington, Isaac Asimov, Ray Bradbury, William Goldman, Neil Simon, Joyce Carol Oates, Agatha Christie, and John Gardner. How did they accomplish what they have? They weren't deflected from their priorities by activities of lesser importance. The work continues, even though everything else may have to give. They know that their greatest resource is themselves. Wasting time is wasting themselves. When people ask them, "Where do you find the time?" they wonder, "Where do you lose it?"

The following principles will help you to find the time you're losing—and to begin shaping your own life. You must wake up your Managing Editor and ask him to make a deal with your Continent of Reason: "I'm going to spend one hour—no more, no less—every day working on my writing and you can take a break during that hour." Your deal with the Continent continues: "During that hour, I'm going by island clocks. But, before you go off in a huff, remember that

I'm asking for only an hour. You should be able to handle that—you're so big and smart, surely you've got that much self-confidence!"

Generally, with this kind of sweet talk, the Continent will respond favorably and allow you the hour. What it dreads are interminable threats: "I'm going to write this book if it kills me. I'm going to write this book if it takes the rest of my life." Inspiration and the Muse have nothing to do with your deal; the deal depends on discipline and craft. Whether you feel like it or not, you sit down to do the writing. The Muse will come, don't worry. A writer seriously at work is irresistible to her. But you don't wait for her. It's a question, as Humpty Dumpty told Alice, of who's to be the master.

Another warning of a bad attitude toward time is the question, "What makes you think your time is so valuable?" People who ask you that question are enemies to your shaping of your own life. Your response should be, "I don't *think* my time is that valuable; I *know* my time is that valuable. It's all the time I have." Feel sorry for them that they don't think of their time that way.

In a productive, well-ordered life two elements must be managed: time and work. Poor time managers fail to recognize the difference between the two elements: Work is infinite; time is finite. Therefore you must manage your time, not your work. Work expands to fill whatever time is allotted to it. If your work is successful, it generates more work; as a result, the concept of "finishing your work" is a contradiction in terms so blatant and so dangerous that it can lead to nervous breakdowns—because it puts the pressures on the wrong places in your mind and habits. Time, on the other hand, is finite, though there's much more of it available than people who manage it poorly think. The real problem is that we don't have enough disciplined energy to use all the time that's given to us.

Instead of trying to finish your work, you need merely find time to do your work; then simply concentrate on doing it the best you can. The satisfaction will come from knowing that each day you've allotted time for the work you love, the work you want to do.

When I began consulting with students and clients with time-management problems, I came to realize that I was recalling my Jesuit education, which stressed self-discipline more than the managing of external factors. Management expert Harold L. Taylor agrees: "All we can ever hope to do is to manage ourselves with respect to time." Time-work management must be based on self-management (Aristotle's sense of planning your life).

Your will power is the barrier to overcome, just as it is also the starting point for the overcoming.

Time can't be accumulated, but it can be bought. It can't be stockpiled, but it can be controlled. You buy it financially and psychologically—the one by exchanging income for free time, the other by shielding yourself through advance thinking against unexpected incursions into your time.

My brother used to say that time is money. I, an other-worldly professor who cared little about money, ignored him. That's because I'd done poorly in high school algebra, or geometry, or whatever it was that dealt with equations. A few years ago he observed that I was overextending myself. My own successes had ganged up on me. He said, "Haven't you realized yet that money is time?"

I was startled. "What did you say?"

"Time is money," he repeated.

"I thought I heard you say money is time." I looked at him, beads of perspiration on my brow.

"Same thing," he said, "don't you remember that equations are reversible?"

I hadn't remembered, but from that moment on I applied what my brother pointed out. With money you can buy time: time to do the things you *want to do*, instead of merely doing the things you merely *can* do. Aim to do what *only you* can do, and stop doing what you — as well as others—*can* do. Simply being able to do a thing is not a good reason for doing it if you want to be in control of your own time.

Like everything else in life, the process of revising your view of time begins with a decision. It's a matter of willing to change your life by starting today to manage your time and understand its relationship to work and personal satisfaction.

Here are some starting points, gleaned from my own experience and that of other time-management experts:

- Stop doing things no one needs to do.
- Stop doing things someone else will do if you stop doing them.
- Stop doing things that aren't the kind only you can do.
- Recognize the difference between activities only time can do and those you can actually do something about. Start the former—like popping in the toast or putting the water on to boil—on their tracks, and move on to the latter. Don't waste time trying to change physical laws.
- Start doing the things you want to do, the things only YOU can do.
- Start acting instead of reacting.

The First Step

Decision is a giant first step because it leads automatically to focus and perspective. Psychologists call the process "selective perception." Selective perception means that once your mind has focused on an object, you'll begin seeing that object—or its absence—everywhere. Once you decide you want to write a book, you start noticing books more, noticing them in a more craftsmanlike way, noticing what must go into writing them, and noticing that you're not doing anything about writing your own book.

In other words, a simple pressure begins building into a grand momentum from the first moment of decision, provided that the decision is a sincere commitment of the will.

Taking Time to Schedule Time

Even thinking takes time. Some people spend much of their active lives daydreaming, without living to see their dreams come true. Examine the attitude you have toward your own thinking. Even a person who can think of twelve things at a time can still only think of twelve things at a time. Which means that thinking about the negative things, the gloomy things, the depressing feelings of impossibility is a waste of prime thinking time.

You break that self-destructive habit by saying to yourself: "Next time I catch myself driving along and thinking dark thoughts, I'll switch to a positive channel and think about a writing project that forms part of my dreams. If it doesn't work at first, I won't be surprised, since I know that it's hard to change habits. But I also know it can be done, so I won't worry about it. I'll just try it again each time I catch myself thinking dark thoughts." Once you've tried this a few times, the technique will work. The positive reinforcement set up by this habit-formation process is so strong that you'll start looking forward to positive rather than negative daydreaming. What happens next tells even more about the mind. You'll start looking forward to the next stray dark thought, just so you can practice your new technique of turning from negative to positive; in the process, your mind will purge itself of the dark thoughts.

Thought control may be the ultimate in time management, because it allows you to invoke and exploit your own positive emotions and make them work to shape your will into a lifelike resemblance to your dreams.

No time is more important than the time used to examine and schedule your time. You're doing that already by taking the time to read this book. Then you'll make time scheduling a regular part of your daily routine.

Some time consultants suggest planning the day's activities in the evening, before retiring, and again in the morning, before beginning the day. The important thing to remember is that time planning doesn't take much time—a few minutes—but results in immense amounts of time saved, including time to waste if and when you feel the need for it.

Yes, it's important to schedule leisure time, and time to do nothing; isn't it much more comforting to know that you've allowed that kind of time for yourself than to live in a constant state of anxiety partly because you're not sure you'll ever find time to relax? And when you are in leisure time, isn't it better to know that you're supposed to be relaxing and enjoying "free time"—and that you've scheduled yourself so carefully you needn't spend your free time worrying or nursing anxiety?

Begin by actually answering that question you've been asking yourself: "Where does the time go?"

Make an inventory of your time over the span of a week. Figure out where the hours go by making a list of activities in pencil and estimating the number of hours spent after each activity. Don't worry about accuracy at this stage. Just put down estimates:

Activity	Hours Spent
1 Sleeping	56 (7 × 8)
2 Working	etc.
3 Writing	
4 Eating	
5 Commuting	
6 Entertainment	
7 Personal hygiene	
8 Errands and shopping	
9 Housework	
10 Reading	
11 Exercise	
12 Spiritual time	
13 Phone time	

Now go back and add up the hours, recalling that there are 168 hours in a week. You'd be surprised at how many people will make this list and be missing 20 hours or more—or end up with 20 hours more than there are in a week.

The second step is to recalculate your list, still in pencil, being more honest with yourself this time.

Once the list is as accurate as you can make it (leaving out nonroutine events such as vacations or sicknesses), add two columns to the left of each item. In the first column, estimate how much you like this particular activity (on a scale of one to five). By "like" I mean how much pleasure an activity affords you—physically, psychologically, or in any other way you measure pleasure. You're asking: "How much do I really like this activity?" (Sleep is in parentheses because good sleep is necessary to good living, and you don't barter it.)

In the second column, rate how much potential each activity has for enhancing your ability to "buy time."

For example:

Like (a)	Benefit (b)	Composite (a + b)	Activity	Hours Spent
—	—	—	(Sleeping)	48
5	0	5	Eating	16
3	5	8	Working	42
5	5	10	Writing	11
0	2	2	Housework	10

—and so on.

Eating brings you maximum pleasure, but does little or nothing to add to your financial status or material gain (unless you're a restaurant critic). On the other hand, working rates a "5" on the material scale but, since you're bored with your job, only a "3" on the pleasure scale.

All items that rate a combined score of five or more are items you'll want to retain in your life (since the purpose of this remanagement is not to reduce your pleasure, but to increase it along with increasing your time for doing things you want to do). You'll retain eating, but try to drop housework because it falls below the five (the housework will be handled by hiring someone to do it with your extra income from more working). With working, you'll try to find ways of improving the pleasure in your present job, or finding another job which remains a "5" on the earning scale but reaches a "5" on the pleasure scale as well. With each activity you drop, you gain hours for writing.

Attention Span and "The Right Compartment"

This is the point where goal setting is crucial. You're going to revamp your allotment of time so as to accomplish what you now think are your priority goals. You know that the difference between accomplishment and self-recrimination is willpower, so you put the pencil away and take out your pen. You're calling your own bluff, something that only those with determination can and even want to do. You've engaged yourself in the bravest of human activities, testing your potential in order to offer the rest of us the results. Of course you risk failure by doing so. That's what makes life exciting. Of course risk also produces anxiety, but rename the anxiety "productive elation" or "stimulating challenge" or "controlled inspiration" and you're on your way to coping with it.

The principles for time management are similar to those for writing. Program activities in the mind before it's time to do them, and you'll discover that doing them becomes easier and infinitely more productive. You can't imagine yourself addressing a group of four hundred? You *have* to imagine yourself doing it, or you'll never be able to do it. That's what imagination is for: to go in advance so action can follow.

You'll need to identify your concentration span for each activity you undertake. This is the only way to find the exact, productive compartments of time for particular projects. How long at one time can you give your absolute and undivided attention to writing a novel? Thirty minutes? Eight hours? You're not sure? You need to be sure, because it is counterproductive to stay at your desk beyond your attention span. Bad habits build up immense negative reinforcement; the longer they dominate your behavior, the stronger the negative reinforcement.

Knowing the moment to quit is the key to reorganizing your writing time.

So let's go on. The symptoms of "too short," "too long," and "just right" compartments are familiar to all of us:

Compartments of time that are too long leave you with feelings of guilt or disgust (depending on your upbringing), frustration, and more than a vague anxiety about the validity of your writing ambitions. You say to yourself, "Omigod, I spent three hours and got nothing written. What kind of writer am I?"

A black cloud begins to form in your mind when you think about working again tomorrow. Worse, these feelings create a monster of negative reinforcement that quickly becomes a whole tribe of monsters when the "too long" compartment becomes a habit or a regular occurrence. You feel guilty about not having done anything yesterday, and that guilt makes it even more difficult to begin tomorrow. You solve this "too long" anxiety by reducing the compartment of time—spending less time on the project at each sitting.

"Too short" compartments are marked by a different kind of unproductive anxiety. You feel that the time limit you've set is unnecessarily short—in fact, too short to make beginning worthwhile. If you tell yourself, "Tomorrow I'll start writing for five minutes every day," the proposed period seems ridiculous and you simply don't start at all. Even if you set aside fifteen minutes to get into a project, you know at the outset that nothing satisfying will happen in fifteen minutes and you'd have to stop precisely when the islands' energy begins flowing into the project. You solve this feeling of frustration by expanding the compartment of time, making the work period longer.

Compartments that are "just right" show none of these symptoms. Instead, you have a feeling of incipient exhaustion overbalanced by satisfaction, the satisfaction of getting into your work and forgetting the Continent's clock for the time being. You conclude these time compartments when you feel exhaustion coming on (if you continue beyond that moment, exhaustion begins constructing a negative reinforcement).

Here's what happens when your Managing Editor has found the proper compartment of time in which to write. When you notice that such a compartment is nearly over—it's 9:50 A.M., and you want to stop at 10:00—you feel you've accomplished something positive. But you also feel a bit frustrated that this wonderful involvement is coming to an end for the day. (If you feel exhausted and not elated as a result, then you're experiencing an overlong compartment.)

So you're looking forward to the next session, but you'd also love to continue this one. Continuing is a mistake because it breaks your discipline; the tension between your longing to go on and your awareness of discipline creates a peculiar sense of frustration. The moment of stopping creates its own special energy (easily confused with frustration, because it seems you hardly started and you're upset you have to stop). I call this special energy "restart energy" because it can be applied immediately to "linkage," the pivotal principle of good time-management theory.

You use this special energy, that combination of elation and frustration, to form a "linkage" to tomorrow's compartment. Instead of continuing your writing for the last ten minutes, you stop and use those ten minutes to decide what you're going to write tomorrow: "I feel great today. What I'm going to start with tomorrow is. . . ." Hemingway called this "leaving water in the well." Depending on your personality and needs, this restart decision will take different forms. It can be purely mental, or you can write down a hasty outline to yourself and tape it next to the computer. This pattern of action gives you the reassurance that tomorrow you'll experience the same positive reinforcement you've experienced at your writing session today.

It takes a week or so to set up the pattern, so don't expect it to work perfectly on the first two days. Once it's established, you'll know: You'll be counting the pages you've written. At the same time, you've programmed the islands to be "working" exactly as outlined above, but even more effectively because your program is based on the positive experience of a successful session.

The pattern forces you to realize that you are the one who creates the compartment—by making up your mind that you're going to write at a certain time, for a certain time each day. You're in control of the success of that time compartment.

Now you understand Norman Mailer's observation that writer's block is a failure of the ego: It's a matter of not being in charge of your own mind. You're the only one who can say, "At seven o'clock I'm going to sit down to write until eight." When you sit down tomorrow to write, good things will happen. The islands will have been busy coming up with even better ideas of what to write first—and on the way to your session you review their suggestions and decide which you'll go with when you start. Don't forget to do this, otherwise you'll be sitting in front of the blank piece of paper during the review. Do it in the shower, while you're putting out the trash, or when you take your early morning walk. (Remember the rule: Don't sit down to write without knowing what you're going to write.) Never waste your writing time deciding what to write. Writing time is for writing, not for the gestation of writing.

My first order as a writing instructor is to tell students they can't write without my permission. Sometimes I won't let them start writing until the last quarter of the term. What they *are* allowed to do is to think of their stories, of their structure—and to tell me and the class about them until we're convinced that the story is clear enough and the pressure is strong enough so that when they finally do sit down to write the writing will come without hesitation.

It's all a question of putting pressure on the mind to make the mind behave, of finding the right degree and shape of tension for creativity. The mind doesn't like to behave if it doesn't have to, so your Managing Editor finds ways of tricking the islands and Continent into doing what you want them to do.

Once you've identified the right compartments of time, you won't have to worry about anything except what you're doing during those compartments. You don't worry about accomplishments, what you've done or haven't done. You concentrate on what you're *doing* to make each compartment as satisfying and involving as possible.

Linkage

Every time you finish a productive compartment of time, you construct your linkage to the next one. Drawing on the energy that urges you to continue, you say instead: "Okay, I've got to stop in ten minutes. Instead of writing for the next ten minutes, I'm going to use that time to decide how I'm going to begin tomorrow." You've made the linkage. This technique isn't peculiar to the writing profession. You go on a first date and you really like the person. What do you do to make sure you see him or her again? You might make another date on the spot, or you might leave an object behind—one way or another, making a linkage. "At what time next week," asks Peter Sellers in *The Party*, "might I be able to come and retrieve my hat?" If you get your hat back by messenger the next day, the linkage has failed.

But in your writing, there's no one but you. The linkage becomes your Muse. No cold starts, in other words. You decide today what you're going to do tomorrow.

You can use a mechanical restart technique to create an automatic linkage between your writing sessions. Let's say you're almost finished with your session for the day, having already determined the right time compartment for this particular activity, and you're going to take the last ten minutes to clean up your shop like a good craftsman, and also to restart for tomorrow. So you're typing along. When you reach the middle of a page in the middle of a sentence—at a point when you know what comes next—you stop typing. If you find yourself completing the sentence out of pure habit, start the next one and stop yourself halfway through it when you know how you want to end it.

Then take the page out of the typewriter, with that sentence dangling in midair. Or save the file, with the sentence half-written.

You see how this builds up a linkage? You know that when you start the piece again, the start won't be traumatic. When the next session begins—and it can be the next day or a year later, the method works in either case—you put a new piece of paper in the typewriter (or recall the file in your word processor, print out the half-page, delete the portion you just printed from your screen) and copy the previous half-completed work.

It's inevitable that by the time you've copied your previous work down to where you left off, your mind will be back on the same track and flowing along, ready to complete the half-sentence and to continue writing without interruption or without sign of the break. As an added dividend, your work will appear seamless! You've overcome the restart problem with a mechanical linkage. When you try this technique, you'll discover that you don't often end the original sentence the way you planned to end it. But that doesn't matter because the important thing was to keep going. In other words, this writing business is not a moral contest of keeping your vows to yourself. It's a contest in which you ask: Can I express my mind? Will I find ways to do that? Writers have long recognized that words really aren't the greatest vehicles for expression, which means, for one thing, that there are many ways of expressing the same thought. Especially in the first draft, which word you use doesn't often matter that much.

Everyone who achieves what others consider large works has developed a system similar to this one; no one writes a book or builds a wall. You write one page at a time, you lay one brick on top of another. Everything great is done in small segments, and the more carefully the individual segments are crafted the greater the whole work will be. The trick is to develop a method that will connect the segments as though they'd never been apart. The glue that holds everything together is the fluid constancy of the mind, technically expressed through "linkage." Techniques like this one translate that constant mental energy into the external materials of the craft: tricks of the trade. Once you begin being productive, you'll develop tricks of your own.

Linkage-making has consequences far more profound than overcoming daily restart anxiety. The habit of linkages causes the creative mind to move into chronic productive action. Between today and tomorrow, the islands and Continent will be holding a grand debate about the decision the Editor made about tomorrow's time. They may have better ideas than the one the Editor announced, and they may try to force those ideas on you during the day. If you ignore the voices after listening to them—that is, if you resist the temptation to start tomorrow's activities before they're scheduled—the voices will become stronger and stronger until, when it's actually time to begin writing tomorrow, the strongest voices will be there to insist that you do it their way.

Which is exactly what the Editor planned.

At that point, you've succeeded in activating your mind's full potential. You've also removed the anxiety of having to deal with cold starts. The decision is made at the end of today's positive energy, while the motor is still warm.

The Kinds of Time: First Time, End Time, and Middle Time

Everything you can learn about setting deadlines and making schedules won't be effective unless you also recognize that there are three different kinds of time. Each has its own physical characteristics, each demands that it be scheduled and thought about differently from the others. The three kinds of time are:

First Time
Middle Time
End Time

The failure to recognize the difference among the three kinds of time leads to confusion, exhaustion, and, at worst, depression and total inertia.

First Time is the hardest, the time that goes by most slowly, the time that seems to drag on with fewest results. Because First Time is the mind's initial confrontation with a new experience, its degree of intensity is highest, causing the Continent maximum stress. Therefore First Time is the time in which concentration span may thin down to two minutes even if, later in the project, it might thicken to five hours. You must allow more time at the beginning of a project to accomplish less work—because that's the nature of First Time. Laying new tracks is harder at the railhead than it is after the first two rails have been laid.

When you begin scheduling, then, you don't take the total amount of time available between start and deadline and divide it equally over the days available. If you do that, you'll be disappointed and—worse—frustrated. You won't understand why you couldn't accomplish even the daily average of two pages on the first day of your project if you don't realize that the first two pages are going to take longer, and will be harder to compose, than any other two. Until your mind becomes accustomed to this new task, it moves more slowly just as your feet do when they learn a new dance.

You can solve the problem in one of two ways:

First, you can break First Time down into smaller units, setting less ambitious first goals, objectives that are smaller than those you will aim for during the middle or end of your project. In First Time, your goal is simply to accomplish the minimum satisfactory unit, regardless of how small that unit might be.

If you should feel like writing more than the first scntence, for example, by all means do so. But if one sentence is all you accomplish the first day, congratulate yourself for having done good work. The first sentence *should* take longer; that's the natural structure of First Time, whether it applies to going out on a date or writing a novel. It's the "getting to know you" stage.

The second solution is more drastic: Eliminate First Time!

When a writer comes for help about a project he's worked on for years but for some reason can't start writing, I often discover that what's blocking him is the fear and difficulty of First Time.

"Could you begin in the middle—with the section on gallbladders?" I ask. Usually the answer is an ecstatic, "Yes!"

"Then begin in the middle, and forget about the beginning for the time being." Doing so, you're doing exactly what Aristotle praised Homer for: beginning with "the middle things." In other words, solution number two tames First Time by disposing of it altogether.

Even the reader isn't always happy with First Time (when he's adjusting to the author's vision and style), so why in the world should the writer have to go through that unneeded anxiety? If your book demands an introduction because all books of its kind have an introduction, isn't it better to write the introduction after you've written the book? Then you know what you're introducing, and can write a concise, one- or two-page introduction that tells clearly and authoritatively what this book is about. The writer's alternative is to struggle through an introduction that's complicated and artificial because it's trying to introduce a book that hasn't yet been written.

Because of the painful characteristics and afflictions of First Time, we've developed at Atchity Editorial what we call "the fish-head theory" of editing (see the section on revision in chapter 4). Editing a manuscript generally starts with cutting out the indigestible opening pages and looking for a beginning in the more exciting and complicated middle of the action.

You can understand why we do this. First Time is difficult for the producer, and it's generally unsatisfactory for the product as well. Skip it whenever you can, and everyone will be happier.

Last Time or *End Time* is characterized by high energy flow and pressure to finish (psychologists call it "closure"). Think of the slow-moving horse, after an exhausting day in the field, who hears the whistle and gallops at high speed for the barn. That's how I learned about End Time, when I was seven, on that horse's back in the cornfield. My uncle, not knowing I was riding, gave the whistle. He watched in horror as we rounded the corner heading for the barn and closed his eyes so he wouldn't see me decapitated. Fortunately, I had the good sense to fall off the horse. But I've never forgotten the surprising power of End Time.

When you recognize End Time, you should make sure that you could, physically, finish the project if you relinquish yourself to its pressure and continue beyond your routine compartment. If the answer is "Yes" (e.g., "I could, theoretically, type thirty pages at one sitting"), then by all means go with it because the energy to conclude, though it ends with exhaustion, provides its own special kind of flow. Lock yourself up if necessary, turn off the phone, leave home, anything to allow End Time its way once you're sure its way can lead to the end. William Saroyan, sitting down when he knew what he was going to write, was using End Time entirely to type out *The Human Comedy* in a few days. Experienced journalists know how to use it well, when they put off writing until an hour before deadline. Not everyone has this kind of nerve.

There's a danger to End Time. In your obsession to work in this nonroutine intensity, you can lose track of linkage. That means if you experience its pressures prematurely, you endanger your routine by submitting to them. Generally End Time should be ignored when it announces itself; when true End Time is upon you, the announcement is generally so strong that it's automatic. You don't stop and think about it,

because it just happens. "Something comes over you." You
become possessed by the project. The rule then is: If you're
wondering whether you're experiencing End Time, you're
not. True End Time displaces all other thoughts.

In *Middle Time* most writers have problems maintaining
perspective toward their work. Middle Time's greatest pitfall
is exhaustion, and its most common side effect is confusing
that exhaustion with depression or with a dismal reevaluation
of the work at hand. Writers, during Middle Time, begin to
think their projects aren't worthwhile. When you talk to
them, you realize that exhaustion is what's really happening,
natural and predictable exhaustion.

During Middle Time you need vacations, as many as you
can fit into your routine. Middle Time agendas break down
work sessions into clumps of productive compartments,
between which the energy needed to make them productive
can be regenerated. In planning your calendar for Middle
Time, for example, don't schedule your hour or two hours
every day. Plan to take weekends off, and you'll do better
during the week. The off-time puts pressure on the on-time
to make it productive.

Middle Time seems endless. Another way of handling it
is to further divide it into beginning, middle, and end. All
large units that seem unmanageable should be dealt with this
way. Instead of looking at the entire cross-country route at
once, break the route down so that you're looking at one day
or one week—or one scene—at a time. Continue breaking it
down until the parts no longer intimidate you.

What Only Time Can Do: Percolation

Time accomplishes some things that you simply can't do
yourself, and worrying about them is a waste of time. My
favorite example is the toaster. Even though I preach this principle, I don't apply it to my toaster (though I do to boiling
water, except in the case of pasta). I still pop the toast up
before it's ready, or stare at the pasta water wishing it were

ready. I know it's a stupid habit, and every morning I laugh at myself and hate the toaster for being so slow.

I'm unhappy that the toaster is wasting my time. I'm dawdling around the kitchen, looking for things to do while the bread is toasting, and this makes me impatient. But it isn't the toaster that's wasting my time: it's me and my failure to apply my own knowledge of the time-work interaction in the case of toast.

That's totally counterproductive, unless your real purpose is relaxation during toasting (then you shouldn't worry). If you have a project on the table and go away from it, when you come back to edit or continue it, the longer you've been away the better the revision is going to be (there's a point of diminishing returns, but for all practical purposes it's not worth considering). The point is, you can edit objectively after three days have passed and you cannot edit objectively after three minutes have passed. So the attempt to edit instantly is negating the natural process, not allowing time to do its job.

The professional, productive writer concentrates on a number of projects—getting them out, one at a time, and paying attention to the one at hand—letting time handle most of the editing and most of the marketing and, ideally, all the worry.

Letting time do most of the work is the real secret of productive people. They start things going down the right tracks, and let time's engineering bring the train to its destination.

Time and Energy

When people say, "I don't know where he finds the time and energy," I wonder whether they understand the relationship between time and energy. Energy level is the key to determining attention span. You need to know whether a given activity takes away or gives energy; then you need to schedule the activity at a time when your energy level is at its most productive level for the job. If reorganizing your child's life takes away energy, make sure you do it when your energy is highest; otherwise the conversation is likely to turn into a shouting match because you won't have the extra reserves for patience. If jogging produces energy, don't do it at a time when your energy is already high.

Your daily agenda should take account of your varying energy levels. You'll alternate activities that take energy with activities that give energy until you find your most productive cycle. As you experiment with introspection and scheduling, realize that each day may be different according to your routine for that day. Don't be discouraged if it takes some time to figure out your most effective schedule. The payoff is worth a few frustrating setbacks. Once you've discovered your natural cycle, your personal satisfaction will increase by leaps and bounds. You will have become a productive writer.

You'll even discover that your attitude toward various activities changes. An activity you hated suddenly becomes manageable and enjoyable, because you've started doing it at "the right time" and for "just the right compartment." You've taken control of the clock!

Another useful time-management compartment is a physical one: the box. The many closed boxes in my offices allow me to concentrate on the project at hand while other projects are in the same room. Once the top is on a box that project is, for the time being, out of the Continent's concern. At the same time, inside the box, the islands are percolating.

Box management may sound bizarre to those who haven't tried it, but those who have know that it works. Putting the lid on the box is like consigning a thought to "the back of your mind," where it continues to gather momentum without help from the Continent. You should even have a box of "unimportant" things to do, things you'll get to eventually but not worry about until "eventually" arrives. Think of this box as a "later" box. If you make a habit of putting as much as you can into this box, the quality of your activities—and your productivity—will inevitably improve because you'll be doing more important things before you turn to the "later" box.

Plan to review the contents of the "later" box at some regular interval, once a month, or, at first, once a week. You'll discover that many of the items in it no longer have to be done by anyone, even by you. Others items should be handled, but it's too late to do them now, and the world hasn't ended because you didn't get to them.

Your workroom itself becomes a box, one that should be closed when you're not working so the Continent can rest. The work will continue, but on the relaxed islands instead of on the more rigid Continent. The closed door allows the "vacation."

Dreams vs. *Goal Setting*

When you set your goals, remember this rule: Don't step over a million pebbles if, with directed effort, you can take one step over a mountain range. In other words, don't set your goals too low; if you do, you won't have an effective incentive to move toward your dream. And, when it comes to dreaming, remember that we rarely exceed our dreams.

Goals are the stepping stones to dreams. The dream is on the horizon, the stepping stone directly in front of you.

On the other hand, be careful not to set goals and dreams too high. If you do, you're creating negative instead of positive reinforcement. You know you really can't win the Nobel Prize for literature by the end of next year, so that isn't a sound goal. The Nobel Prize may be your dream, but no date should be attached to it. Attach deadlines to your goals, not to your dreams.

Goal setting, like the other aspects of time management, requires self-knowledge. Examining your goals, like examining your activities, means knowing what you want. Since your "wants" change, goal setting requires constant attention and revision. That shouldn't upset you; taking care of plants, animals, and people requires no less. Why shouldn't taking care of yourself be the same way? The system you set up must include revision of the system itself; a time when you look at your own progress and ask if this particular version of the system is working for you. Every management system does the same. If, when time for revision arrives, the goal you set yesterday is no longer valid, change it. The object is to control the shape of your life, not just to achieve a goal for the sake of achieving.

Adjust your system on a regular basis. I'd suggest a period of two weeks before the first adjustment. With practice in the discipline of self-management, you'll know how often you need to reassess your goals and the system you've constructed to achieve them.

Once your goals have been set, start heading in their direction. One way of beginning the process is to start with the minimum you can imagine doing without feeling intimidated, exhausted, or in any other way negatively affected by the goal.

That might be only twenty minutes. If so, set your clock for twenty minutes and start. If twenty minutes works the first day, and you've actually begun your project, you'll soon discover the natural pressures exerting themselves, causing you to want to go beyond the twenty minutes the second day. If that happens, don't resist; just make sure that you've allowed time in your schedule for this kind of desirable overflow. Slowly increase the time compartment until you discover its maximum comfortable length.

The "Gordian-knot" approach is another way to start. Accomplish your first priority and let everything else you think you have to do fend for itself. For example, if you decide you should spend twenty hours a week writing, spend the twenty hours—broken down into useful compartments—as early as possible in the week, and let the rest of the week's activities take care of themselves. Activities naturally readjust to the time available. Even without conscious fine-tuning and rearranging, things will work out pretty well if you simply make sure you're taking care of "number one."

Either way, it begins with the plan: the decision translated into a formal statement of will.

General Time-Work Management Tips

Here are some hints from my own experience. Many of them have been confirmed by other time-management experts. Some may work for you, but only you can be the judge:

- Group tasks. You can often save time by consolidating tasks. For example, check writing and household budgeting can be done two or three times a month, rather than every day or week. Napoleon read his mail once a month; he discovered that most of the problems it contained had already been solved.
- If you commute, use that time productively. If you're on a train or bus, read or write; if you're driving, mull over the scene you'll be writing at your next work session, listen to an instructive tape, or relax—without feeling guilty!
- Stop procrastinating. Putting off unpleasant tasks makes them pile up and also creates a mental block against doing them. Try discarding them in the first place, or doing them immediately. Delegate all you can but don't delegate things that don't need to be done.
- Avoid unnecessary "business" lunches. Not only do they take hours, they make the rest of the day less productive. Instead of a cocktail at lunch, hold it for your end-of-the-day reward.
- Put Carl Jung's sign above your desk: *"Yes ~~No Maybe~~."* This is to remind you to say "No" more often.
- Take care of correspondence immediately—with a note, postcard, letter, or telephone call.
- Keep your phone calls as short as possible, and have a list of each item you want to discuss before you make the call, along with whatever background information you need.
- Carry a small notebook with you, to jot down ideas and lists of things to be taken care of. Put only one idea on each page.

- Analyze your activities, using some of your time each day to look for new ways to save time and cut down on work.
- Take advantage of short cuts. If something costs more, it's usually worth more. Some people shop around for six months trying to get the "best price" for an appliance or a piece of furniture—and end up saving, at best, less than 20 percent of the price. All the time it took to save that 20 percent is invaluable, at least to me. Shop by phone if possible, asking for prices and availability in advance.
- Keep the Pareto Principle in mind: that 20 percent of your activities account for 80 percent of the value of all your activities. In fact, 80 / 20 is the general rule:

  > Twenty percent of your writing projects account for 80 percent of your writing income.
  > Twenty percent of your time accounts for 80 percent of your satisfaction and self-esteem.
  > Eighty percent of your phone time is spent with 20 percent of your callers. And so on.

- Instead of buying another bookshelf or filing cabinet, weed out your shelves and your files. Your library and your filing system will improve, and so will your productivity and the quality of your work. The same principle can be applied to your office space, your reading, and even your network of contacts.

Telephone Management

When it comes to the telephone, remember it's your telephone: Use it as you want and need to use it. Don't respond to it as it wants you to respond to it. Some people think disconnecting the phone is immoral, but they're crazy for thinking that if there are constant interruptions.

In the old days, a friend who wanted to talk with you would drive his wagon across the countryside to your house.

You'd see the dust cloud in the distance, and go inside to put on a pot of coffee. Then you'd sit on the porch in your rocking chairs and take the time for a good talk because you knew your friend needed to talk badly enough to make the trip. Now we're living in a world when anyone—from carpet salesmen to your most distant relative or European drinking buddy—can interrupt you at the most intense moments of your writing life.

If you truly care about the activity you're engaged in, you have to make interruptions impossible, or at least postponable. Here are some specific techniques that might help:

- If you have a phone-answering machine (and I recommend this), don't be afraid to turn it off when you don't feel like returning home to a whole list of calls. Many people, when the machine is on, will leave a message that doesn't require a call-back. Machines like this save a great deal of time, as long as the owner remembers that he or she, not the machine, is in charge here. Answering services aren't nearly as effective, unless you have that rare one that actually finds out what the call is about. Make a habit of not returning calls from strangers who don't state their business.
- Keep a call-back book, listing the names and numbers of people who've called you, or whom you've decided to call. Merely having such a book reduces your phone time because, after a few weeks, the planning aspect of writing down the names reduces your desire to call most of the people on your list. Another thing happens: By the time you get around to calling, the problem that caused the call may have been solved or you've seen the person. Eventually you outgrow the need for the call-back, because you've established new telephone habits.
- Disconnect the telephone whenever you want peace and quiet.
- If possible, have someone else answer the phone for you and politely query the callers. You may be able to dis-

courage those who are trying to sell you something you don't want.

Daily Priority Checklist

Some management experts recommend making a daily checklist of priorities in the evening, some recommend making it in the morning. I recommend both. Assess the coming day's goals before retiring and upon arising. Herodotus, in the very first history in Western culture, tells the story of a tribe who made decisions by the following steps: First, they decided in council in the afternoon; then they all got drunk, and made an intoxicated decision before going to bed; finally, in the morning they reviewed the previous decisions and made their binding decision.

What they were doing was taking advantage of all the parts of the mind—islands, Continent, and Editor. That's what occurs if you plan both in the evening and in the morning. The exhaustion of evening gives perspective to overly ambitious goals, but the perspective is corrected by the renewed energy of morning. Until you establish a new pattern based on the planning habit, I suggest you pencil in your next day's list before going to bed. In the morning, while having your coffee or tea, change the checklist from pencil to pen, reassessing the reasonableness of your goals for the day.

The list is basically the Gordian-knot approach to planning, and is most useful to people who don't like the discipline of scheduling hours. For those who prefer to live on a schedule, the same principle applies: Pencil in your schedule first, then ink it in after reflection.

I combine the list method with the schedule method. On the top of my daybook I list things I've decided must be attended to tomorrow. When the time for scheduling tomorrow's hours arrives, I make sure I've taken care of everything on the list before filling in the other hours. The list is important because it reminds me of my major goals and purposes; but it's useless unless it becomes a program. A program means allotting time to your goals on a regular basis.

Once you've formed this new habit, the process becomes automatically self-correcting and self-improving.

Deadlines (Don't Procrastinate)

Why is it so easy to put off the most important things in favor of doing dishes? Because we know how much anxiety we must confront to do the important things, so of course we want to put them off. When it comes down to daily activities, do the writing first and let the dishes pile up. Ask yourself, "Would it be the end of the world if I didn't sweep the patio?" If the answer is "No," do the writing instead.

When your day of meetings and responsibilities and people and phone calls and ups and downs—and even rejections—begins with four hours of your own writing under your belt, it's much more likely that it will be a good day.

As for deadlines, let's face it: Life itself has a deadline, the most arbitrary deadline of all. Everything we accomplish we accomplish because of deadlines, our fear of them, our awareness of them, our love of the challenge they bring.

There are two kinds of deadlines: "external" and "internal," those you set for yourself and those you allow others to set for you. When you start comparing them, you begin to see that the difference between them is also arbitrary. The purpose of the deadline is to make the writer stop writing, to get the writing done. Since an editor has been defined as "someone who tells a writer when he's finished writing," it's not surprising that one of your Managing Editor's functions is setting the deadline and then being as fierce about it as the relationship between Editor and writer demands.

From your viewpoint as a writer, the deadline allows you to plan your time. Working backwards from it, you can figure out how much time you need to spend on a given project each day in order to finish it. Of course, in the real world, the deadline can often be changed. But changing the deadline indicates lack of planning and lack of discipline.

Journalists rarely have writer's block. The pressure of deadlines forces the anxiety into work. They study their subject, think about it in perspective, search for a lead and a conclusion—and only then sit down to write (often an hour before the copy is due). This, of course, is a generalization about a profession that is anything but general. But if you listen to journalists discuss their methods of composition, it's clear that the islands and the Continent are at work, dissolving anxiety even as they use it to roll out the finished product.

Constantly extending a deadline is a symptom of a dangerous syndrome: perfectionism and a lack of self-confidence. If you're afraid to stop working on a manuscript, remember that no book, however long the time producing it, will be perfect. Strive instead to perfect the way you spend your writing time.

The Stopwatch Method of Time Management

Not everyone has a regularly scheduled life. From my writing clients I've learned that the calendar approach that I recommend most of the time, where a certain time (say, 9 to 10 A.M.) is set aside for writing each workday, isn't for everyone. Some people have no control over clock time. When the phone rings, they must answer it. Others simply don't want to discipline themselves by committing to a specific hour on the workaday clock. They've spent too much time toeing the line and need the freedom of refusing to be controlled by the wall clock. Yet I've discovered that they're willing and eager to commit to the stopwatch method whereby you spend an hour or two each day (with vacations!) on your writing career. With the stopwatch method you can "steal time" to write. While the clock on the wall, to which everyone's wristwatch is synchronized, is run by the Continent, the stopwatch belongs to your islands. The stopwatch allows you to call "time out." The stopwatch is your "creative clock."

Here's how it works: Contract with yourself (through the usual Managing Editor negotiation with Continent and islands) to spend "one hour per day" (or "five hours before the week is over") on the particular writing project you're concerned with—no matter where the minutes that comprise that hour will be found throughout the day. Your Managing Editor uses your stopwatch to keep track of the time you steal from the Continent's practical activities. When the stopwatch is running, you're writing. When you stop writing, you stop the stopwatch. Your two stopwatch hours may be gleaned over a six-hour period, or over a twelve-hour period. You "steal" them when you can: waiting at the doctor's, when an appointment hasn't shown up yet, when your phone goes out and no one can call you until it's repaired, when your date for the evening doesn't show up. I normally try to begin writing at 6 A.M., and commit myself to a minimum of three hours a weekday. Because I receive many phone calls from the East Coast and from Europe, I often complete my three stopwatch hours only by 10 A.M. and sometimes as late as noon. But I don't turn to my other activities until those three hours are secured. The stopwatch allows you to truly make the "clock of life" *your* clock! When students bring their stopwatches in to my weekly private workshop, the gleam in their eyes tells me even before I check their stopwatches that they've accomplished their goal: to make time to write, without being bound to the Continent's clock.

FOUR

Writing in Time

Now that we understand time and the mind's way with it, let's see how they move together through the steps of creation. What seems like an extremely intricate process can be broken down into manageable segments, as you'll see in this chapter. First, though, let's explore in detail the two stages involved in actually sitting down to write: first draft and revision.

First Draft: Vision

Whether you're writing fiction or nonfiction, poetry or drama, the first draft is the time for vision, the time to allow all the islands to say whatever they feel like saying, to say what they see. This is not the time for self-editing and analysis, not the time for revision. Your purpose at this stage is to get it all out so you can do something with it. This is the process of giving birth, not the process of surgical intervention.

It's the time, in other words, to explore the natural shape of your idea. You let the story unfold, let it "tell itself" by not restricting your ideas. Telling itself begins with your research (whether for fiction or nonfiction), and how you allow it to take form. Later in this chapter, we'll discuss the card system, a helpful technique in the assembly or research stage. For now, a summary of the system will suffice.

By the time you have progressed through all the steps of the creative process up to the first draft, you will have noted all your "assembly" or research on 5″ × 7″ cards. As your research progresses, you'll also decide which cards to keep and which to reject. This happens naturally, so don't worry about it here. The true creativity comes when you "sort" the cards to provide a cohesive flow, arranging them in the way you think best for the project. Once the cards are sorted in the order that seems natural to you, you're ready to begin the first draft (after a vacation, of course): You've created a "road map," a term I find more useful than the more rigid concept of the "outline."

When you sit down to write your first draft, your creative juices are already flowing; now it's simply a matter of following the cards. Your first step is to decide the order of the cards for each section of your project. The second step is to decide which cards are essential, which can be abridged, summarized, or discarded.

Make your decisions quickly, then type out the first card. After that, type a transition between the first and second cards. Transitions should be self-confident and straightforward. Don't waste time telling what you're going to tell us, and what you told us; forget the grade-school rules: Just tell us once, clearly. Your first draft is a kind of sketch, and the important thing is forward motion. The cards are to facilitate forward motion, not impede it. As soon as you feel you no longer need to consult the cards, set them aside until you start the next page.

The same process applies to the next page. As you become more confident, you'll rely on the cards less and less. That's what you are trying to accomplish. The cards are crutches. You'll be able to go back to them if need be during the revision process. Keep going for now, using the cards only as structure to help you through hesitations in the flow.

You're seeking at this point to discover the "natural shape" of the story or of your subject matter. Time-management principles are crucial here: Get anything down, because what you write first becomes the basis for what comes later, even though it may not be what you end up with when "later" comes. The first decision causes the process of negation to begin operating. Getting the first draft down is the first achievement that separates thousands of people who want to write a book from the few who actually do write books.

Once the draft is down, you have the rest of your life to edit and redefine it. Don't stop for corrections during the first draft. The first draft is the *visionary* process, not the *revisionary* process of editing.

Let me explain the difference. The visionary process is that moment when all the islands come together and can be heard. Your Managing Editor's job is to listen to the voices and let them speak as clearly as they can. His job right now is not to sort them. That comes later. The faster you work the better job you'll do of recording the diversity and strength of those island voices.

Imagine that a meeting of the United Nations is taking place on the Continent. The Continent is your assembly hall, because it takes the Continent's skills to actually write the syntax and vocabulary of your language and attend to the formal structure of your book. As the island delegates start pouring into the hall their exuberance makes the Managing Editor nervous. But if he's dedicated to your creative purpose, the Editor will not start telling people where to sit. His only concern is making sure they get in the hall. "Take a seat anywhere," he says, "just take a seat as soon as you can so we can get everyone in here."

The delegates, of course, start vying for the best seats—and the very fact that they want those closest to the Editor tells you something. They're aware of the Editor's ability to translate between them and the Continent: Without that, the outside world will never hear their voices. Unless they submit their vision to the Continent through the Managing Editor's arbitration, the islands are doomed to inarticulate solitude. They jostle and nudge one another, and generally the strongest ones will get the best seats—which is exactly what you want. The question of whether the seating makes sense is a secondary issue that will be clarified later.

During the first draft you lose yourself in your work, and the time speeds by. You're making sure there's room for all the delegates. Here's where time-and-energy management is especially important. Your energy keeps the delegates coming in; it attracts them like a beacon. If you stop work too soon, the flow is interrupted, and the delegates will get discouraged. If you work too long at one sitting, the cloud of exhaustion that hangs over the assembly hall makes the unarrived delegates feel the assembly isn't as exciting as it looked from a distance. They may turn back, and your inspiration will dry up. If you work just the right amount of time, you maintain the excitement and the attraction: The delegates line up, eager to get in the hall.

Close your session for the day by saying at the door: "Tomorrow, the delegate from Nightmareland will enter first." Or, "The delegate from Fantasyland comes first tomorrow." While they're waiting through the intervening night, the remaining delegates are assured that the entry flow will continue.

One more piece of advice about time during this draft— "go with the flow." The flow is something you'll recognize when it happens. This is what writers wait for: It's the book trying to get out. So if your daily session is scheduled for one hour, and you've already finished a good six pages, but the flow is going strong, continue to the point just before exhaustion, preserving only enough strength and energy to form the linkage to tomorrow's session. Keep in mind, of course, that you're still obligated to your agenda and the same minimum for tomorrow. The flow can't be allowed to jeopardize the discipline. Therefore it's dangerous to make a regular habit of extending your scheduled compartment. And don't think you're flowing when you're not.

Most people never reach the final version of a book for the very basic reason that they never do the first draft. They confuse the steps in the dreamwork process, thinking that the first draft should be perfect, revising as they go along. The first draft should simply be. You let it take the reins and follow its head; you keep plugging away until you come to a point where, as more than one novelist has expressed it, the characters rise up and take over the writing. Then the story or the book is dictated, and you end up transcribing. Your job, until that point is reached, is simply to keep going, using every possible trick to get your fingers moving on the keyboard.

Outline vs. *Road Maps*

Outlines, if their purpose is misunderstood, can derail the first draft process with their excessive zeal for Continental rationality. The writing is more important than the outline, just as the moving across the floor is more important than the shoes you move in. I prefer to use "road maps"—primitive outlines that simply tell you where you're starting, or where you're heading, and whose sole purpose is to get you started along the road.

The road map reminds me of the question, "Where did I think I was going?" For the writer, the *road* is the thing, not where the road is going, so it's important to give the first draft itself precedence over any mechanical aid. The road map is not as stringent as the outline, which asks, "Where do you think you're going?" and intimidates the island voices during the first draft.

Don't let this advice confuse you into thinking there's no place for "outlines." I object to the rigidity of the word—not the concept, but the misuse of the concept allows it to control rather than serve vision. An outline is useful during the revision process, just as it is during the marketing process. An outline differs from a road map because it's firm and objective, whereas a road map is fluid and negotiable. Slavish adherence to an outline during first draft will result in a first draft overwhelmed by the Continent of Reason and devoid of the bracing air of the islands, a first draft that is logical but without "life" (many textbooks are like this). So if you discover you've detoured from your original plan but are going strong, put the original plan behind you and keep going strong. You can consult the road map again when you've finished the draft and want to figure out what you've done and what it's all about.

If you don't understand this point yet, you may not have experienced the relationship between the form and the product, the shoes and the getting there. In that case, don't worry about the theory too much—just start writing; you'll sense what I'm talking about as you begin accomplishing your dreams.

Revision: After the First Draft

Productive writers know that the process of *revision* is entirely different from the visionary process of the first draft. "Write, rewrite!" is not a command based on repetition but a simple prescription for the two labors involved in the creation of literary products.

Free-lance editors (like those listed in *LMP*, *Literary Market Place*—see bibliography) are professional revisers. But good editors are also rare—and expensive—so it's wise to work on becoming your own editor. Self-editing is an acquired skill that comes only with practice, and with growing objectivity and confidence. At first it's extremely difficult to be objective about your own work. Time is the best ally in this respect. In time, a certain degree of objectivity sets in naturally.

Another excellent ally is reading your work out loud to yourself. It's harder to fool yourself when you actually hear what your words sound like.

Still another way of developing self-editing skills is reading your work to someone else, and watching the smallest expressions of revulsion, bliss, horror, delight, or indifference as you read. Make a note of these reactions, verify them with your listener, and revise appropriately.

Don't ask your best friend or spouse to edit or react for you. His or her role is primarily to support, an extremely important part of what you need. Your friend should read or listen to your work and say, "It's great—keep going!"—and, in all fairness, you should say that's what you want beforehand.

Richard Lanham's *Revising Prose* and Bruce Ross-Larson's *Edit Yourself* (see bibliography) are the best books I know of that actually take you through the steps of self-editing until you can master the skill yourself.

Professional editors are another matter. You want them to be completely honest with you, constructively honest but completely honest. Otherwise they can't really be of help. Finding an editor from whom you can take objective criticism is a rare discovery in a writer's career. When you find such a person, anger at suggested changes is your least appropriate response. If you still have problems dealing with criticism, don't take out your hurt or anger on your editor. Your editor's job is to tell you exactly how well your work reads, and to help you make it better. If your editor doesn't do both, find another editor! Another approach works with some people better than with others: If criticism angers you, allow yourself to be angry, but put your anger on hold until you have a chance to consider the criticism at a cooler moment. Then if you still feel your way is better than what your editor suggested, you can query the editor further about his or her reasons for suggesting a change. Often, after consideration and rumination, you'll find your editor's recommendations were appropriate.

The revision process should begin after some time has passed, because time will do more for the revision than any amount of conscious attention given too soon. Go away from the draft for as long as you can afford to—take a vacation—and when you come back most of your work will be done for you in the back country of the islands.

During the vacation, you do only one thing to aid the islands in their unconscious work. You ask them to percolate about the question, "What is the book I've written really about?" Tell them to let you know when one of them—or all of them together—come up with the exact answer to the question, in ten words or less. This sentence, of ten words or less, summarizes the structure and purpose of your book. It's a tough job to write that sentence, but when you succeed you will save yourself much time and effort, in marketing as well as in rewriting!

When you do sit down to revise, you know what you're going to do. You're going to cut and cut and cut. Ninety percent of revision is cutting, but now you're being objective, and ninety percent is objectivity, reading your work through the public's eyes. Cutting is a fine-tuning process that begins when you know what you're looking for: You need to know what you've already said before you can remove everything that confuses what you've said.

What do you cut? You cut everything that has nothing to do with "what the work is about." You need to have already identified your book's Sentence, the brief statement ("ten words or less") that summarizes its structure and purpose. Lajos Egri calls this the "premise," and applies the concept to dramatic writing in his excellent book, *The Art of Dramatic Writing*. The "premise" or "Sentence" is what Michelangelo was talking about when someone asked him if it was difficult to carve the David. Carving the David, he's said to have answered, wasn't the difficult part. It was finding the block of marble that contained the David (the visionary process: the first draft). After that, he simply chipped away everything that wasn't David.

In the revisionary process, you chip away everything that your book is not about. Discard the cuts, misfile them, or keep them in your "library" for future use. How you deal with the discarded material depends a good deal on your temperament and level of self-confidence.

A good example from Egri's book is his analysis of the premise of Shakespeare's *Macbeth:* "Ruthless ambition leads to its own destruction." In a well-made work of writing, every line, every paragraph, every page will relate to the controlling premise either directly or indirectly. If it doesn't, the experienced reader quickly recognizes that something's wrong.

Suppose that Shakespeare is finished with the first draft of his play and has got to churn out a second draft this evening in time for the first rehearsal tomorrow morning. He sharpens up his quills and sits down to write. What does he do first? In the time that's passed at the tavern between finishing the first draft and starting the revision, he's been thinking in the back of his mind: "What's this play really about?" Now he's got it. (In fact, like an experienced journalist, he won't sit down to revise until he "gets it.") The first thing he does this evening is to write, in his famous scrawl, his premise on a piece of parchment and tack it on the wall above his typewriter.

Next he reminds himself that the first hour (maybe, for Shakespeare, only the first few minutes) of the revision will be slower than the rest. It's important for any writer to remember this, because otherwise "First Time" will create negative reinforcement. Now Shakespeare is ready to begin revising in earnest. He goes through the play line by line, striking out the excess language (when he was sober; when he wasn't, Shakespeare left much excess), removing characters who weren't doing their job.

Halfway through, he's completely absorbed in his task, savoring the long speech Bottom makes when he awakens from the dream of being turned into an ass and loved by a fairy queen. "That's dynamite!" Shakespeare laughs to himself. Then, as he chuckles, his eyes go to the wall where the premise is staring down at him. "Oh-oh," he mutters, "what's this got to do with the ambition and self-destruction? Damn. Nothing."

What does he do with Bottom's hilarious speech? This is where the typical writer's neurotic retentiveness deserves a moment's notice. He can't bring himself to throw it away—it's too damned good. Those "too good" passages were the ones Samuel Johnson identified during revision, and always removed; if he liked them that much, they were suspect, and probably weren't doing their job properly. Dr. Johnson knew their job was to serve the whole; so he cut them out. Virginia Woolf took the same approach, practicing similar self-denial. She took out her favorite passages! The question is, "Which is more important, your ego or the work you've created?" Now that the work is virtually in existence, the disciplined writer will ensure that the work has its own heart instead of his ego for a heart. Otherwise what he's created won't have a life of its own.

The question, "What has this passage got to do with the Sentence of my book?" now has objective value and can be answered objectively. Accordingly, Shakespeare puts Bottom's dream report on the shelf, and later writes another play around it (*A Midsummer Night's Dream*).

Editing: The Fish Head

When you clean a fish, the first thing that goes is the head. Generally manuscripts should receive the same treatment because they, too, often have indigestible heads. This is especially true of fiction. The first thirty pages (beginning, "I was born on a cold winter's day in a small town in Louisiana . . .") may be background—a warming-up that's necessary for the writer—but uninteresting and not useful to the reader. Perhaps you find the true beginning of the book on page 31 ("My first reaction was disbelief. Then I looked into her eyes and saw the truth. She meant it. She'd been picnicking with him for months . . ."). Begin the book on page 31.

What about the background? How will the reader realize that the events on page 31 begin when the narrator has already reached the age of thirty? First, you must remember that fiction is based on your success in activating the reader's imagination, not in supplanting it. The reader needs little prompting to imagine the situation. For this reason, William Goldman recommends beginning as far into a scene as possible. Virginia Woolf explained that she inserted background only when needed, through a method she called "tunnelling."

You tunnel material into the story only when the absence of sufficient background would make it impossible for the reader to continue without confusion.

The important thing is to keep the story moving forward at all times. Every bit of background exposition must be earned by hooking our attention strongly enough to hold us through the exposition. After the first few pages of a book, once the story is in motion, the reader will stand for very little exposition.

Nonfiction has its own kind of "fish heads," generally overly long introductions that give the reader no credit for being able to figure out perspective or context. A 60-page draft introduction can often be reduced to 15 pages, 15 pages that clearly outline the importance of the book's subject matter and the direction by which the author will approach that subject matter.

The "Library"

Novelists are sometimes horrified at the thought of losing those thirty pages. After all, they represent the creation of the character, his birth, background, and maturity. Nevertheless, I urge you to follow Shakespeare's example. If you can't stand throwing anything away, don't: Put those "introductory" pages on the shelf—whether from your novel or nonfiction book—and use them for your "library." You can go to it any-time you need to borrow something, to tunnel into the story, or to present necessary information, and meanwhile you have the security of knowing that the material is always there.

How is the indigestible fish head created in the first place? The answer lies in understanding the psychology of the writer, and lies in how that psychology moves through time. The answer also lies in the writer's original lack of self-confidence, one of the characteristics of the anxiety we've been talking about. When you begin writing, especially on a project as intimidating as a book, self-confidence is low. You're psyched up to do this, but you more or less know you're faking it because you've never done what you're telling yourself to do. After all, a book is a mighty project and who could believe this writer's capable of carrying it off? Well, one of this writer's islands—maybe the whole passel of them—believes it. They're the guys who put you up to this in the first place. They got your Managing Editor's attention long enough to convince you to sit down and plan the writing. But the Continent, your rational mind, isn't so sure. The Continent feels it must take a heavy hand in order to carry this off. As a result, the beginning of a book is generally filled with air: padding, excess words, show-off scenes, in-jokes, revenge scenes, posturing, and all those other "purple passages" that express the Continent's determined attempt to fill up the required space. After all, the book has got to be long enough!

Suddenly on page 31, the situation changes. You're into the story (or into the exposition, if your book is nonfiction), and now the work has found its own impetus and moves forward with very little help from you. You've mined down enough to open the vein. From that point onward, the work is itself, an authentic object; and, ideally, your job during the visionary process is to continue following its dictation. When asked, in the *Purgatorio*, why he was greater than the other poets of his time, the pilgrim Dante replied, "I am one who, when love dictates, listens, and then goes forward signing what It says."

In the revision process, then, you remove those excesses from the fish-head portion of your work so we can enjoy the cleaned fillets through which the skeleton gleams. You can do that because, after all, now you've finished the book. There's no more self-doubt. You've done it, it's here, and no one can take it away from you (you've already made a copy of the first draft and put it in a safe place); moreover, now you're an "authority," no longer a "would-be author." It would be foolish at this point not to forget to go back and remove all traces of lack of self-confidence, wouldn't it? The discipline of writing is perhaps the most satisfying way of reconstructing a failed ego, or strengthening a weak one.

Removing the excess does take a special kind of discipline: the craftsman's discipline, which is to recognize that the work is more important than the workman. It is now so good it can speak to strangers, it has its own public voice. In editing, you take out the private voice.

Islands and Continent during Editing

To put the above in terms of the islands, here's what goes on during revision. All the delegates are now in the Continent's assembly hall, and the Managing Editor, with so many interesting voices in his power, feels two conflicting emotions: pride and excitement. He's also beginning to realize that his excitement is bordering on terror, because his next challenge is to put the whole group in order.

"In order" means translating the demands and voices of all the island delegations into the language of the Continent—issuing a proclamation that takes account of all island needs and visions and thereby, through the Continent's language, brings a new vision. As a result of the Editor's work—if it's successful—the Continent itself will be changed and will now include influences from all the islands.

The Managing Editor, who balances analytical consciousness with intuitive vision, is in charge of the revision process. The Editor's job is to make sure that in the final draft nothing remains that isn't comprehensible to the Continental audience; and to see that nothing of the islands' vision remains unexpressed. The Continental audience, as mentioned earlier, is your "public," and the mainland language is "public voice." The mainland audience understands only public voice, but that doesn't mean there can be no place for private voices or private language; it means only that the private languages must be introduced through the public language. In *A Clockwork Orange*, Anthony Burgess brings us a very special language by weaving it into the context of standard English until the "standard" reader (the "Continental audience") assimilates the special language and ends up knowing it as well as do Burgess's characters. The only way for the islands to attract visitors is for them to speak first in the visitors' tongues.

Does that mean that the Editor, during revision, has had no advice from the island leaders? Not at all. He soaked in their advice by allowing time to help him, that time he allowed to pass before undertaking the revision. As they entered the Continent's assembly hall, he allowed the island delegates to sit wherever they wished and to chat and chat and chat—to get acquainted, to get their mainland bearings—for a long while.

What was the Editor doing during that process? Nothing active, unless you recognize how active listening can be. The Editor was listening, monitoring the voices, both individually and all together, waiting for the moment when the main stream of communication became clear. Once the Editor figures that out, it's an easy job to rearrange what the islands wanted to say into the forms familiar to the Continent. When the Editor announces the order of reassembly, the islands are eager to cooperate, instantly recognizing the effectiveness of the Editor's decision. The Managing Editor is the successful compromiser who allows them all to be heard, which was, after all, their primary objective for coming. In the opinion of the island delegates, the good Editor is the one who tells them exactly what to do, with self-confident authority. The revisionary process is now in capable hands.

When to Stop Revising

Writers often claim they can't stop revising.

There's nothing wrong with a love for revising. What's wrong is allowing that love to impede the publishability of your writing. Contain your love in time compartments of proper size, and save some of it for later use.

You *must* stop editing—or you'll never finish anything. Begin with a time-management decision that indicates when the editing is to be finished: the deadline from which you construct your revisionary agenda. Ask yourself, "How much

editing time is this project worth?" Then allow yourself that
time. If it's a 1,000-word newspaper article, it's worth editing
for an hour or two. Allow yourself no more. Do all the editing
you want, but decide that the article will go out at the end of
the allotted time, in the form it then possesses.

Style

Style is what happens when characteristic energy shapes
mechanical precision. It's not something you create: Style is
what you are. Think first about accuracy, and style takes care
of itself. The most useful style is clear, objective, honest, and
direct, in keeping with the dictates of Strunk and White in
The Elements of Style. Style is the shape you give language when
you're concentrating on telling a good story dramatically or
when you're conveying important information clearly and
persuasively.

Because so many would-be writers confuse this issue and
have been misled by well-intentioned but poor teachers, it's
important to emphasize that style is not something you
develop consciously. It happens automatically and is the inevitable result of two combined forces: personality and precision.

When you try to develop style, you end up being artificial, and the artifice is obvious to anyone who reads the
results. The purpose of writing is not to impress, but to be
useful. Useful writing gets its subject or story across without
drawing undue attention to itself. Style is not content but
form, not what's in the channel but the channel itself. Because
it's *your* channel, it will be different from any other channel.

The writer who worries about style misunderstands what
craft is all about. Such preoccupation leads to affectation, a
despicable vice. The writer's business is to master language
and to make sure that ideas are expressed accurately, from the
structure of sentences to the structure of paragraphs and of the
whole project. Quintilian's warning applies here: You learn to
write quickly by learning to write well, not the other way
around.

To achieve style, then, first recognize that it's not *style* that you consciously develop but *accuracy*. When you're not sure of a word's spelling, stop and look it up (during the revision process); when you're not sure of the usage of "that," pull out your copy of Fowler's *Modern English Usage* and read pages 622–630 until you have a better idea of how the word is to be used. Each tiny decision you make in your daily practice of precision defines your own personality. That's all there is to style.

Meanwhile, you can do something to enhance natural stylistic development. You can read, and you can imitate.

Each day and each night before bed, read several pages of your favorite books—the plays of Shakespeare, the King James Bible, Mark Twain's essays, Hemingway's journalistic dispatches, Abraham Lincoln's letters—on an alternating basis. The authors you choose may be different from mine (the choice itself is a matter of individual style). This reading stokes your islands with powerful clear writing. The more they're stoked, the more difficult it will be for your Editor to produce bad writing. If his assembly halls are full of goodness, how can he not recognize when inferior stuff is coming out?

As another warming-up exercise you can actually copy good writing, physically experiencing it as you write it out in your own longhand. Or type the first pages of your favorite novel to "get the feel" of great writing. Body learning is a method at least as ancient as Homer who, in *The Iliad*, describes dancers dancing "on understanding feet," feet that, without intervention of the brain, keep time to the music. Anyone who's tried square dancing knows it's easier to learn by forgetting yourself and merging with the rhythm. Learning to dance from a book or from step-by-step instructions is much more difficult. There's no substitute for the real thing.

Copying great writing will put the motions of great writing automatically into your islands in such a way that they will notice—if you're in close enough touch with them—when your arm is not moving in "great" patterns.

Aside from these suggestions, don't worry about style.

Bend your energies toward being an accurate and forceful writer, and let style take care of itself.

Here's a list of style tips developed in my classes:

- Count every word. Reread each sentence and ask yourself if it contains unnecessary words. If it does, write it again, simplifying. Then reread to make sure it still says what you intended. Continue the process until you've written a clear, elegant sentence.
- Repetition is preferable to inaccuracy. Throw away your thesaurus.
- Watch out for your "crutch words" (words that kept you going during first draft): e.g., "very," "such," "according to," "so to speak," "as it were," "it is," "then," and so forth. Every writer has his own set of these words, which function well in first draft but must be removed in revision.
- "There are," "this is," "it is" are early warning signs of a fog attack. Turn on your parking lights immediately when you see one in your sentence, and rethink your route.
- Phrases such as "It can be seen," though often favored by academics, are stilted. Reverse constructions generally signal uncertainty.
- In American English, we generally use contractions like "you're," "don't," "can't," and so on, unless we're being emphatic. The habit of always spelling them out results in stilted and pedantic writing.
- Avoid "in that" and "as to." Both are symptoms of sloppy syntax.
- Avoid the impersonal pronoun "one." It creates distance—and it's silly.
- Don't be afraid of using "I"—and don't use "we" to replace it.
- Avoid contemporary clichés that indicate carelessness of thought.
- Sentences can't begin with "Too."

- If your writing attracts your reader's attention, your style probably needs editing. Suspect all your favorite sentences. Each sentence must serve the whole.
- "It makes sense in context," someone remarked about another's paper. Write so that context isn't needed for sense. Normally the reader should understand a sentence without going beyond it.
- If you have to choose between length and accuracy, choose accuracy. Much bad writing is caused by the "20-page" term paper. Don't let them do it to you! Write as much or as little as you need to do the job.
- Try to cut down on what Richard Lanham, in his book *Revising Prose*, calls your "lard factor." A 50 percent Lard Factor means half the words you're using are unnecessary. Lard factors of over 30 percent indicate real problems with your writing; over 50 percent and your writing is obese. If you can't figure out the percentage of your own lard factor, have someone estimate it for you.

Creativity and Time: The Agenda for Nonfiction

Vision and revision must be accomplished in time. You need to prepare yourself, as does any craftsman, with a plan to guide you. The foundation of your new discipline will be an agenda which applies the principles outlined in the last chapter to those describing the writer's mind and the steps of dreamwork. An agenda ensures you that the projected work will be completed. Completed, moreover, in time! Don't forget that you want to complete it by transforming anxiety into elation, without too much thinking; and, as you'll see, with plenty of vacations.

You construct the agenda twice, once in pencil, then—when you see the problems and resolve them—in pen. This will be the final version, aside from readjustments along the way. Here we will construct the agenda in its logical order, from beginning to end, in order to explain the details, but when you do your own agenda, construct it backwards from the deadline.

A word about the deadline. Whether it's one of your own making or that of a publisher, take it seriously. If you don't, you're truly wasting your time, and construction of an agenda will do nothing for your productivity.

Let's take a nonfiction project as our first example, a book about the great visionaries of our era (you've already queried publishers—see "Publishing in Time," chapter 6—and received an encouraging response). We're assuming that you work for a living, and therefore will need more time to finish this book than the writer who can write full time.

You begin by laying out the months for the project, with the last month (12) as the deadline (12/1) for submitting the book.

$$1\ 2\ 3\ 4\ 5\ 6\ 7\ 8\ 9\ 10\ 11\ 12/1$$

Next you make a most important pragmatic decision: How long will the book be—in manuscript pages? For the sake of our example, we'll decide on 250 pages.

The next step depends on what we call the card system. The writing of the first draft should be nothing more than typing transitions, where necessary, between segments of information (the cards). The question you now ask yourself is, "How many cards would I need per page in order to make that typing process painless and enjoyable? You'll need enough cards to give you more than enough material from which to choose for each page. Your Managing Editor has another rule to enforce discipline and create productive pressure: You can't carry cards over from one page to the next. In typing each page, your only decision will be which of these cards to use, and in what order.

Six $5'' \times 7''$ cards are far too many for one draft manuscript page. You'd be wasting time with that many cards per page. Five, for some people, is the ideal number. Others can do with four cards per page. For now, let's choose four.

Four cards per 250 pages comes to 1,000 cards for a complete first draft. But, because the sorting process will eliminate a number of "No" cards, you'll start with 1,300 cards and plan to eliminate approximately 300 even before you begin the first draft.

Once you've purchased your materials (1,300 cards and a ream of paper), you can make your agenda. What you're doing is scheduling time in terms of work and scheduling work in terms of time.

Assuming that you have some other regular form of employment, you can work on this project only five days each week, two hours per day, with any two days off. This means you'll be working with 20-day months throughout your agenda.

Here's a sample of the agenda.

1/1–1/10	First Vacation
1/10–3/31	Research: Part One
4/1–4/14	Second Vacation
4/15–7/1	Research: Part Two
7/1–7/10	Third Vacation
7/10	Sorting: Part One
7/11	Fourth Vacation
7/12	Sorting: Part Two
7/13	Mid-Agenda Vacation
7/14	Road Mapping
7/15–7/31	Fourth-Last Vacation
7/31	"Take a Deep Breath"
8/1–9/1	First Draft
9/1–9/10	Third-Last Vacation
9/10–10/10	Revision
10/10–10/15	Second-Last Vacation
10/15–11/15	Final Typing
11/15–12/1	Last Vacation
12/1	Deadline

1/1–1/10 FIRST VACATION

Since writing a book is no mean undertaking, you owe it to yourself to start the project with a vacation, let's say on

Maui. The only work you do during these ten days on Maui is fantasy: Envision yourself spending a year on this fascinating project—not writing a book, but spending a year. You'll work on it regularly, with vacations thrown in as rewards, but you'll stick to your agenda without fail, month in and month out. *Writing!* Once you can see yourself doing that, relax and spend the rest of the time snorkeling. One of the best beaches for this purpose is between the Wailea Beach Hotel and the Intercontinental.

1/10–3/31 RESEARCH: PART ONE

Research is a twofold process in time, consisting of expansion followed by contraction. The expansion is instinctual and involves a visit to your internal islands. The contraction is willful, the editorial assessment that takes place in the Continent's assembly hall.

The first step is to figure out how much material you'll need to construct your first draft comfortably. As mentioned earlier, four 5″ × 7″ index cards per page is a good rule of thumb. Multiply the number of cards by the number of manuscript pages of your book. Let's use our original example of 1,000 good cards, with "No's" to spare.

Now you're ready to start.

You've already decided that the proper balance between research in the literature (i.e., in previously published works on the subject) and field research is about 50/50. Books that are a general rehash of existing literature annoy you, and so do books that ignore the work of previous researchers. The 50/50 proportion allows you to divide your 100 days of research time into two sections of 50 workdays each, separated, of course, by a vacation.

The first half of your research, you decide, will be in the library to give you the necessary background before interviewing visionaries in the field. (In some projects, this process will be reversed because you'll want to do the field work first in order to form your own initial view before researching the published views of others.)

You have 1,300 cards to fill out before the actual typing time, so you begin by dividing the cards into two piles. Put 650 cards in the closet and forget about them. Divide the other 650 by 50, for a total of 13 cards that need to be filled out during each daily work period (still based on 20 days per month). Every day, when you go to the library, take only a manageable number of cards—say, 20 cards. You don't want to intimidate your Continent with too much effort spent away from its routine concerns.

Keep in mind that First Time is different from all other times and that you can expect it to take longer. Also remember that in the expansion phase of research, you cast your net as widely as you can.

On your first day at the library, don't go directly to the card catalogue. Remind yourself that you are (a) doing only what's enjoyable and (b) following intuition to discover the natural shape of your project. What makes every book original is the unique intersection in space and time of an author's mind with the subject matter: The intersection is what I mean by "the natural shape of the project."

So you begin by asking where the books on your subject are kept, and go there. Now you do something you had to stop doing sometime after fourth grade. Sit on the floor in the stacks, in front of the books on your subject. Choose the one that looks most interesting, that smells interesting, that your instincts and love for the subject tell you to read first. Never question this instinct, never allow the Continent to say things like, "Wait a minute, that's an old book. It's not likely to be as useful as the most recent one." You've already checked to see that there's nothing on bookstore shelves that treats the subject well. You allow the islands to control the expansion stage of research; the Continent is in charge of the contraction process.

Take your time with this first book, even if it's two hundred years old. Keep in mind that there's no time pressure because your agenda is already made. Dawdle. Savor. You have two hours each day to work in the library, and 50 entire days to collect your library research. You can afford to spend a day or two—even more—on a single book. Today all you have to do is fill your 13 cards, then you can go home. "Fill" should be interpreted loosely. Some cards will be quotations from the text you read, copied out word for word; others will be summaries of what you read; still others will be your own ideas that occur to you while browsing, ideas about your subject or your book's structure.

At first it's probably best to fill in the cards by hand. Something about the physical act of copying allows the brain to assimilate the structure of the subject being copied. But at a certain point this will seem burdensome to you. I suggest you then Xerox the passages you want, and, still at the library, tape them to the cards. This will speed up the research process.

Make sure you record on each and every card the text source, bibliographical data, and the date on which you added this material to your card collection. This kind of information is essential to the journalistic or scholarly credibility of your work; without it, you can't expect to be published. And it's much easier to record it as you go along than to attempt a reconstruction after the fact. It's the primary responsibility of nonfiction writers to give proper cognizance and attribution to their sources.

You needn't worry about your originality, even if your work is hugely based on that of others. What's original is your assembly, your discovery of the "natural shape" (which is, remember, the combination of your mind's interests and the shape of the subject itself): your perspective, your vision of the matter.

After you've been researching for a week or so, a natural pattern develops. The first book you read will take longer than the majority of subsequent ones; the second takes twice as long as the third; the third takes a third longer than the fourth; the fourth takes a little bit longer than the fifth—until finally you're going through most of the books quickly and settling into an average amount of time for each. This happens because your mind assimilates the natural shape of the subject matter. The process of assimilation begins even with the "outdated" book; structure is rarely outdated. Before long you are looking for essentials, seeing outlines at a glance and avoiding structures you've already taken in.

During the last few days of the expansion process, you'll be gobbling down eight or nine books in your few hours, quickly assessing points of vital interest to you. In other words, you don't have to *think* about the process too much: Just *do* it. The process has its own natural shape if you simply get out of its way.

It doesn't matter that you will inevitably have a larger number of cards for the first few books than for subsequent ones. These anxieties, too, will dissipate as you realize that you needn't keep adding cards with information that is repetitious.

Which brings us to the question, "What do you look for during this process?" You look for what interests you, without necessarily stopping to ask *why* it interests you. The natural pattern will become clear during the sorting process that follows research. Make it a rule to note only interesting things, following the principle that you don't want to write about anything that doesn't interest you.

After you've completed 80 percent of your library time—40 days—on the stacks, allow yourself the remaining 10 days to check out the card catalogue.

At this stage the expansion process is over. Card catalogue work begins the contraction process. Checking books you might have missed, using the catalogue as your guide, will either reveal agreement with the traditional structure of the subject or disagreement with it. In the first case, you've confirmed the accuracy of your own work without jeopardizing its enthusiasm. In the second, you've clearly established a niche for your work in the field of your choosing—or, more important, you've confirmed your initial instinct that a gap exists in the traditional way of looking at the subject. At worst, you've discovered a gap in your own research and you've allowed yourself a day or so to go back for those books you missed.

Now the contraction process of this stage is over, and you can take book cards, put them in a box, and proceed with the field observations.

4/1–4/14 SECOND VACATION

Now that you've finished the bookish part of your spadework, take a rest. How about 10 days of trout fishing or mountain climbing? If something related to the project occurs to you as you dangle from a cliff, stop rappelling long enough to jot it down. If nothing occurs to you, don't worry—just be careful with your ropes or your flies!

4/15–7/1 RESEARCH: PART TWO

Now for the most enjoyable part: interviewing the visionaries. The second half of your research time is given to field work, but also proceeds through expansion followed by contraction.

For a book such as this, you can anticipate the field work during research time. When you have enough "leads" from your library research and your initial thinking to know something about the visionaries within interview distance, write letters requesting interviews. The letters should be brief and persuasive, outlining the purpose of your project, your own background and motivation, and the manner in which you plan to incorporate material from the proposed interview. Assuming that you've received positive responses, you can now decide whom to interview when and where.

Your first interview, of course, will take longest with probably least satisfactory response (although beginner's luck may work for you here). But don't let that upset you; the individual interview will follow its own laws of time, so structure it to take advantage of this inevitability. Tell the subject that the interview will last 60 minutes (or whatever time you've previously decided on). Don't turn on the tape recorder until the subject is warmed up. Or, if that proves impractical (because some people won't even start warming up until the machine is running), at least record the moment when the subject starts getting into "the good stuff." That way you won't waste time later listening to the less important part of the interview.

During the interview, note on cards the major points of the subject's comments. There are the 650 cards you stashed in your closet. You'll discover later that these major points, recorded on your cards, will make continued reference to the tapes unnecessary.

Contraction and Last Time come into play as you see time running out in the interview. That's when you ask the pointed questions that haven't yet been answered, and when you give the visionary the opportunity to make an eloquent closing statement. Interviewing isn't an exact science and it is a science that improves with practice. The most important quality an interviewer can possess is sincerity; your first objective should be to put your interviewee at ease by communicating your love for the subject.

Outside, when the interview is over, take a few minutes to label the cassette carefully and also to check over the notes on your cards, making sure they're clear to you. Random thoughts will occur during this process. Write them on separate cards. Later, they'll provide transitions between pieces of information.

7/1–7/10 THIRD VACATION
During this vacation, your reward for having finished the research in time, think about only one thing when the book flashes into your mind: "What have I really found out about the great visionaries?"

7/10 SORTING: PART ONE
Set aside some good time for this—uninterrupted, solitary time—because this is one of the truly "creative" parts of the entire process, and one of the most enjoyable as well, as long as you follow the rule NO THINKING. Don't hurry through

this process: First, you'll ruin the fun; second, sorting will be less effective. You can afford to take your time because you already know that the urge to hurry is a false pressure. Your speed will automatically increase as you go along from First Time into Middle and End Time.

On this first day you take the entire stack of 1,300 cards (from your research and the interviews) and go through them asking yourself the question, "Yes or No?" Is this card good or not? Your aim is to throw away the ones that aren't (because you don't want a book made up of not-good pieces of information). Sometimes, until you gain confidence, you'll have trouble with this. In that case, save the "No's" on a shelf (or misfile them!).

If you insist on "Maybe's," form a third pile.

But keep in mind that you're aiming for a total of no more than 1,000 cards at the end of the process.

When you've gone through the entire pile of cards once, go through it again immediately to confirm or correct your initial decisions. Remember that the "person" who goes through this second sorting is a different person from the one who did the first sorting. Your mind has changed, and that calls for a second look (a kind of revisionary sorting).

During the sorting process, you're not dealing with the analytical question, "Why is this card good?" You're simply responding instinctively to the question: "Is it good or not?" Should it be a "Yes" or a "No"?

After the second sorting, you now have a pile of cards from which to write a good first draft. Put the "Maybe's" on the shelf. You can either ignore them or call on them for footnotes when you've finished the draft and entered the revision process.

7/11 FOURTH VACATION

Take a day off to think about the major effort to come, the rest of the sorting process. Where will you do it? How will you protect yourself from interruptions?

7/12 SORTING: PART TWO

This may be the most important and most creative day of your entire year, so decide to savor it by making it happen under ideal circumstances. Either ask the family to leave the house to you for the evening or morning; or *you* leave, and find a room with a view in which to do this most important sorting. One way or another, do your best to protect the time you need for this sorting.

Now that you have 1,000 good cards, your purpose is to sort them into piles according to their natural order. Make sure the sorting occurs on a surface large enough (a floor, for example) so that your final number won't simply be a function of a particular table's surface area. You need enough physical space in which the project's natural shape can be freely expressed. You're approximating the way in which the project is already freely expressed in your mind back there among the islands.

Look at the first card, asking yourself the question you'll ask through this entire process, "What pile does this card go in?" You're not dealing with analysis here, but response based on intuition. By this time, your intuition is well developed (you've been working on the project for months now).

The first card is easy: It goes in its own pile.

Reward yourself. Then take up card two.

Card two is a little harder. It either goes with card one or not.

Card three goes with two, or with one, or in its own pile. It's tougher than the first two.

And so on. Move as quickly as you can, remembering that intuition, not reason, guides you in this process.

Because you understand that First Time takes longer, you aren't discouraged if the first dozen or so cards take a while to sort. You know from experience that the pace quickens as you continue the process, and you fall into the rhythm of sorting.

When you've gone through all the cards, take a break.

Stand up, stretch, and walk out the door. Continue walking—around the block, or until you've gotten the blood flowing again. Come back in, and wash your face.

Now go through the cards again. This time your purpose is to correct or confirm your first impression of where each card belongs. At the same time, you're keeping in mind the elegance of simple structures—keeping an eye open for opportunities to lessen the total number of piles by combining those that really go together. You might discover, for example, that your two sections on "visionaries before our time" really aren't large enough to be two; therefore you collapse them into one pile.

When you've done this, put rubber bands around each of the combined piles that remain and quickly go through them to make your tentative decision about the order of the project, the order in which to arrange the piles themselves. The first pile will end up being chapter one, and so on.

Now you're done for the day. Reward yourself. Get a good night's sleep. What is sleep, after all, but a daily vacation that gives the brain a chance to sort all the incoming stimuli from your last waking period?

7/13 MID-AGENDA VACATION

Take a day off to celebrate making it to the midpoint of your agenda.

7/14 ROAD MAPPING

The day before you start on your next vacation (which is your fourth-last vacation), evaluate the order of the piles once again, and make your final decision.

This amounts to the "outline" of your book, the arrangement of your chapters in order from first to last (with the most dramatic one first, the middle ones arranged in logical order, and a conclusive one in last position). But note that it's not a fixed outline; it's a fluid one, one that allows both for the organic nature of the writing process and for the instincts needed to discover—then to express—the natural shape of your subject.

Pay particular attention here to the beginning, middle, and end. At the beginning you need a dramatic opening, a "hook" from which the middle can follow naturally. The end is where your conclusions will speak for themselves.

Once you're satisfied, after several reshufflings of the piles, that you have the three parts established, put the beginning and the end aside and work on the middle. Apply the same principles to it, making sure it has an intriguing beginning, a convincing middle, and a conclusive end. Do this as many times as necessary to reduce the middle to manageable proportions.

When you're through, stack the piles, each bound with a rubber band, in proper order and go through them one last time to fix the order in your mind.

Then put them in a safe place, and leave them there so you can take another vacation.

The whole process shouldn't take more than a few hours, assuming they're quality hours of uninterrupted work.

7/15–7/31 FOURTH-LAST VACATION

During this two-week vacation period, you are psyching yourself up for the first draft. You spend most of the time relaxing, and none of the time consciously thinking about the book: Instead, you imagine yourself in your work space so that, on the day before the first workday, you can make these changes and be ready to start in earnest.

7/31 "TAKE A DEEP BREATH"

Fresh with determination after your vacation, use this day as a transition to (a) arrange your work space exactly the way you imagined it and (b) take one last look at the separate card piles and rearrange them if a new order occurs to you. (As a result of your vacation, the new order may be even more effective than what you decided before.)

8/1–9/1 FIRST DRAFT

During this 20-day period, you'll do your first draft, which we're defining as "typing transitions, where necessary, between the cards." Your rule is going to be 15 pages minimum per three-hour workday, with no reward for doing more than 15. (You *can* do more than 15, but still must plan to do another 15 the next day. There's no carryover here.) On the other hand, if you do 15 pages early in your three-hour work period, you might want to take the remaining time off as a minivacation. Notice that we're increasing the hourly work period by an hour (because the first draft should be accomplished as quickly as possible); 15 pages may seem like a large number, but five pages an hour, without stopping to make corrections or changes, is a function only of your writing speed.

You'll have in front of you only the cards necessary for the day's work—i.e., roughly 60 cards for the 15 pages. When you sit down, make sure you still agree with the order of this particular set of cards. Once you've done this, you take the first set of four and review their order one last time; then decide what you need from the first card. Don't worry if you stop relying on the cards at any point; remember, they're only crutches: The real book is inside you, formed from the assimilation done back there among the islands and from the Editorial assembly done on the Continent.

On a longer project, with more time in the overall agenda, you might schedule a vacation when you reach the middle of the first draft—a week off to break the exhaustion or monotony and to dispel that Middle Time feeling that the project is somehow not worthwhile after all. Throughout all these steps, you are pursuing the natural concentration-relaxation cycle that exists in everything from heartbeats to athletic performance.

9/1–9/10 THIRD-LAST VACATION

This is an extremely important vacation period. With the first draft finished, you're asking yourself the question, "What is my book really about? What's it really saying?" The purpose of this question is to guide you through the process of revision so clearly that revision becomes fully mechanical and objective. Once you've come up with the answer, the ten-words-or-less "Sentence" of your book, formulate it in terms of "book jacket copy," write it down, and place it on the wall over your writing space.

9/10–10/10 REVISION

During this month you'll do the actual revision, based on the clear image you formulated on your vacation as to what the book is really about. At the rate of 15 pages per day, you're going to go through the manuscript (a) carving away everything the book is *not* about and (b) going back and polishing what's left. For this work period, choose a place where no one can disturb you; and, for three hours of pleasant work, go through the process of self-editing.

You must do 15 pages each day, but can do more if you feel like it, as long as the next day you still do a minimum of 15 pages. If you can finish the 15 pages at the beginning of your work period, you can give yourself a minivacation for the rest of that day's period as a reward for being efficient. Or you can go back to yesterday's revisions. Take your choice.

10/10–10/15 SECOND-LAST VACATION

Because typing is hard work, we know it's best begun with a little vacation. But on this second-last vacation, envision yourself at the typewriter for the next 20 days, with only those revised draft pages at hand needed for your daily quota of typing. You're psyching yourself up for the job.

10/15–11/15 FINAL TYPING

During this month of final typing allow yourself three hours for a working day (to give plenty of time for care and final polish). The rule is 12.5 pages minimum each day, ending on the half-page in midsentence as described in the "linkage" section (chapter 3). If you're feeling great, by all means go beyond the 12.5-page minimum, but no matter how many pages you do on any given day, you still need to do the minimum 12.5 the next day. As before, if you finish the 12.5 pages before the three hours are up, give yourself a minivacation.

11/15–12/1 LAST VACATION

To continue with vacations, we'll finish up the agenda by putting one in just before the deadline—from 11/15 to 12/1. We'll call this period a "buffer zone" during which your mind (islands as well as Continent) has the opportunity to make last-minute changes. Don't expect too many changes at this point: Consider this two-week period a genuine reward for your year's work.

If anything in this agenda intimidates you—any of the numbers of pages per day, hours per day, days on a given phase, and so forth—remember that *this* agenda is merely a model for general discussion (and general discussion is almost a contradiction in terms when it comes to the highly personal business of writing). You must construct your own agenda, to suit your own typing speed, available time, level of anxiety, and degree of ambition. You and only you can decide, by being honest with yourself, what agenda will work for you. And you can decide that accurately only after a period of trial and error. So build regular periods for reevaluation into your writing plans!

Now that you understand how the model will look when it's finished and presented in chronological sequence, construct your own agenda by starting with the deadline and working backwards in pencil—then making your adjustments, and rewriting your agenda in pen.

Now let's see how the agenda might work for a novel (a screenplay works much the same way), based on the same general approach and the same assumptions about your limited time and energies.

The Fiction Agenda

The principles for nonfiction are the same for fiction and drama, but they apply more loosely. Novelists and screenwriters tend to abandon or radically alter their agenda far sooner and far more frequently than nonfiction writers do, because of the organic nature of fiction writing. A work of dramatic fiction has a natural shape that tends to force itself upon the writer, starting a "flow" that often becomes sufficient impetus in itself, and there is no longer the need for an agenda.

You start with an agenda in fiction to give yourself confidence. But once the novel or screenplay is flowing, it may "take its own head" and scheduling time to revise your agenda may be counterproductive. If or when that occurs, get back to the agenda only if the project loses momentum or direction. As long as you always know what you're going to write at your next session, don't worry about an agenda. Rather than going through a detailed agenda for fiction and drama, therefore, let's see how agenda principles apply in general to fiction and drama.

A fiction agenda, no matter how tentative, begins with estimating the quantity of material you will need to complete a book or screenplay. Lay out the months for the project, with the last as the deadline for submission. Then, based on your research of published novels, estimate an approximate typescript length for your work of fiction—I recommend 250 to 350 pages if this is your first novel. Use the card system, asking yourself how many cards—each card consisting of a partial scene, character description, image, event, and so forth—you would need per typescript page, and fill out more cards than you need to fill the typescript. Some novelists find the card system an excellent way to work through the entire "road map" of a novel before committing anything to paper. They sort the cards, then "outline" the resulting stacks on a single sheet of paper. Others use the cards only to get started, and dispense with them once they're into the actual draft. Until you know which group you belong to, try using the cards throughout. You'll find out soon enough if you've made an unproductive choice.

The next phase of fiction and dramatic writing is Assembly, although dramatists have various views of how much assembly is necessary at what point in the creative process. Like "research" (described on pp. 76*ff.*) for nonfiction, assembly for dramatic fiction is a twofold process in time, consisting of expansion followed by contraction. The first step is to figure out if there is enough material associated with the subject you've chosen to get you through that daunting middle ground between your "hook" and your "conclusion." The beginning and end of a dramatic novel don't usually present problems; the difficulty is that endless middle, likened by one writer to the Serengeti Plain. If you fail to assemble enough materials, you'll never make it across the middle and will end up with a novel that looks more like a long short story. In the middle, you need obstacles and events that are naturally associated with your theme and character.

Divide your Assembly Time into two segments, with a rest between them. Within each segment, alternate periods when you spend time simply brainstorming with periods of "research," either in the library or among people (discussion or observation). Each day you'll brainstorm and observe alternately, following your instincts and guided by your own energy level. While you're assembling, the pressure to get started with the writing will build nicely. Hold that pressure in check.

First Time is of course different from all other times and you can expect it to take longer. In this expansion phase of assembly, cast your net as far as you can, not worrying where it might fall. For now, follow your nose into the character, action, theme, and setting of your novel. You don't have to have any of these dramatic elements firmly fixed in order to pursue this method. The fixing will come later after you've assembled enough to fix.

If you decide to use the library during part of your

Assembly Time, follow the suggestions for nonfiction, but allow yourself even greater freedom to browse and observe. Some writers sit in cafes for hours at a time, watching people, listening to conversations, looking for clues to their islands' vision; others actually "interview" people. The interviews for a novel are different from those for nonfiction. Primarily, what you look for here is emotion and insight about human behavior rather than information and perspective. You also search for what strikes you as dramatic and moving, without asking why. You allow your islands to control the expansion stage of assembly; the Continent is in charge of the contrac- tion process.

Take your time at the beginning of assembly, and let yourself feel that the process is aimless. Your agenda assures you that you're working on schedule; therefore the anxiety that comes naturally with this free-floating collection process can be exciting rather than intimidating. You can afford time tracing the history of fishhooks for your nautical novel by vis- iting that museum you've always wondered about. Each day all you have to do is fill your minimum number of cards, then you can go home. Some cards will contain a character's thought or a description of a setting, a single image; other cards might outline the structure of an entire chapter or sequence of scenes; still others will be the ideas that come to you while browsing, insights into your theme that may or may not find their way into the draft. If you decide that porce- lain dolls should be a recurrent symbol in your book, make six or seven cards with the word "dolls" on them (and nothing more), to use as markers when you reach the sorting process.

For fiction it's best to fill in the cards by hand, to take advantage of the brain's love for assimilation through the mus- cular act of copying. But use whatever works best for you, whatever method makes the process feel most comfortable. After a week or so, a natural pattern develops. You begin thinking along certain lines associated with one element or another of your project. When this happens, your instincts are in touch with the "natural shape" of your story. Expansion concludes when you've collected enough cards to convince yourself that you've chosen a rich subject, with endless detail related to it (revision is the time when you'll go after and / or verify the rest of that detail).

It's normal to allow this expansion process to take up about two-thirds of your first assembly period. In the last third, the concentration process, review the cards you've collected to see where you have "gaps"—holes in information that need to be filled before you can feel comfortable sitting down to write your draft. Make a preliminary sorting to see which elements require more assembly. Are your "setting" cards few in number compared to your "action" or "dialogue" cards? For that nautical novel, you might spend a few days checking out underwater flora and fauna (but keep in mind that it can deaden your creativity to collect *too much* information at this point; you want only enough to get your juices flowing and to overcome your fear of not being able to think of anything to write—as well as give your draft the sense of conviction that comes simply from knowing that you're talking about something specific). If you discover that you have more cards about your heroine than your hero, improve that balance during the last 30 days of the assembly process, the contraction period.

The second half of your Assembly Time should be used exactly as you used the first part, although this part will be even more enjoyable because you're returning to it refreshed. The excitement that comes with progress will add impetus and focus to your work. You'll actually start seeing the novel in detail in your mind's eye. This "half" can be foreshortened, however, if the urgency to write gets so strong that more assembly would be counterproductive.

The next phase of fiction writing is the sorting process, which should begin only after a proper vacation. On the first day of sorting, take the entire stack of cards and go through them asking yourself the question, "Yes or No?—Is this card dramatic or not? Will it create a memorable image or scene or thought in the reader's mind?" Throw away the ones that aren't dramatic (because you don't want a novel made up of undramatic material).

When you've gone through the entire pile of cards once, go through it again immediately to confirm or correct your initial decisions. You're not dealing with the analytical question, "Why is this card dramatic?" You're simply responding instinctively to the question: "Is it dramatic or not?" Should it be a "Yes" or a "No"?

After the second sorting, you now have a pile of cards from which to write a dramatic first draft. If there are any "Maybe's," put them on the shelf. You can either ignore them or call on them if you need them for background or detail. Most of what they contain is already in your mind and will come out automatically when it's needed.

Now that you have the predetermined number of good cards—say 500 to 1,000 for your 250-page draft—your purpose is to sort them into piles according to their natural order, the dramatic order of your story: a beginning that hooks the reader, a middle that keeps the reader involved through rhythmic ups and downs, and an ending that leaves the reader strongly moved. Work as quickly as you can, remembering that intuition, not reason, guides you in this process. There are more sophisticated ways to use these cards during the sorting process, but the techniques I have in mind will require further elaboration for the elements of fiction and drama, described at length in chapter 5.

Go through the cards again. This time you're correcting or confirming your first impression of where each card belongs. At the same time, you're trying to reduce the total number of piles by combining those that really go together. When you've done this, put rubber bands around each of the combined piles that remain and quickly go through them to make your tentative decision about the order of the novel, the order in which to arrange the piles themselves. Pile #1 will end up being chapter or scene one, and so on.

Go through the piles a third time. This final run-through produces what amounts to the "natural outline" of your novel, the arrangement of its segments in dramatic order from first to last. But please recognize that it's not a fixed outline; it's a fluid one.

Once you're satisfied, after several reshufflings of the piles, that you have the three parts established, put the beginning and the end aside and work on resorting the middle, the Serengeti Plain. Apply the same principles to it, making sure it has an intriguing beginning, an exciting middle, and a conclusive end. Later we'll discuss the various patterns that can be used to structure the middle of dramatic works. Do this as many times as necessary to reduce the middle to manageable proportions.

Preparing for the first draft requires reorganizing and once again estimating the number of cards you'll need daily in order to type the draft in a 20- or 30-day period, depending on how long you want your novel or screenplay to be. The goal will be to deal, each day, only with the cards required by that day's pages.

Take a day or so as a transition to (a) arrange your work space exactly the way you imagined it and (b) take one last look at the separate card piles and rearrange them if a new order occurs to you. Then take a vacation of a week or so to psych yourself up for the tough job of getting that draft done. After the vacation, you might find it helpful to draw the skeletal "road map," based on the sorted piles, on a single sheet of paper, to be placed above your desk—a kind of overview and ongoing guide through the cards.

If you want to take 20 days to type the first draft, your goal is going to be 15 pages minimum per 3-hour workday ($20 \times 15 = 300$ pages). Notice that we're increasing the hourly work period by an hour because the first draft should be accomplished as quickly as possible and, using the card system as a crutch, you should be able to concentrate for a longer time compartment than would have been productive during the assembly period. You'll have in front of you only the cards necessary for the day's work—30–60 cards, let's say, for the 15 pages. When you sit down, *if you feel like it*, make sure you still agree with the order of this particular set of cards. Once you've done this, take the first set of four and review their order one last time; then decide what you need from the first card. Don't worry if you begin writing madly and stop relying on the cards. The cards were only a crutch; the real novel's segments are inside you. Getting them down on paper is all that matters now.

The last major phase of fiction writing is Revision. With the first draft finished, take as long a vacation as you can afford, and ask yourself, "What is my novel really about? What's it really saying?" With this question you can guide yourself through the process of revision so clearly that revision becomes fully mechanical and objective. Once you've come up with the answer, the ten-words-or-less "Sentence" of your novel, formulate it in terms of "book jacket copy." Write it down and place it on the wall over your writing space. Your actual revision should be based on the clearest image you can construct: "Human beings are more important than causes," or, "Uncritical love will lead lover and beloved to catastrophe." With such a sentence in mind, it's easy to know what to cut. You cut whatever *doesn't* serve your sentence.

At the rate of 15 pages per day, you're going to go through the manuscript (1) taking out everything the novel is *not* about and (2) going back and polishing what's left. After each scene, each chapter, you should be able to clearly answer the question, "What did I establish with this scene?" If you can't answer the question, something's wrong with the scene.

You *must* do 15 pages each day, but *can* do more if you feel like it—as long as you still do a minimum of 15 pages the next day. Or, if you finish your daily 15 pages at the beginning of your work period, you can give yourself a minivacation for the rest of that day's period as a reward for being efficient. Or you can go back to yesterday's revisions. Choose, on a daily basis, what feels most comfortable (the Continent *loves* having this freedom of choice—the secret to setting up alternatives is to make sure that *all* the alternatives are positive).

In the successful revision, you make sure that your novel's natural shape controls your decisions, rather than allowing yourself authorial indulgence or editorial license. The sign of failure in the revision process is a published novel that includes passages which obviously serve nothing more than their own beauty or their author's opinion of good writing. These are the kind of passages that Virginia Woolf and Dr. Johnson sought to remove first. When these "purple passages" still exist in a dramatic work, they indicate a lack of discipline, lack of faithfulness to craft. They also demonstrate a failure to believe in your own book. During the revision process you must put on the hat of the objective reader—who considers the subject of the book first rather than the author's style or personality. When readers can't get through a story, they'll think the story was poorly written no matter how beautiful its style may be. Remove your own authorial ego so that the action of your drama is a self-contained entity. When that happens, you've created a drama with integrity and authority, ready to take its place on the public stage.

FIVE

The Elements of Fiction and Drama

How does the system of time-and-self-management described in this book differ from one kind of writing to another? In its essentials it doesn't. "Nonfiction" and "fiction" are terms invented to distinguish two branches of verbal expression. Both involve your Managing Editor pulling ideas out of the Continentally inarticulate but highly enthusiastic islands and putting them into the language forged by the Continent's cultural and grammatical conventions.

For each kind of writing, the process is similar, though subcharacteristics and terms used to describe it may differ. Any writer who writes both nonfiction and fiction knows that both forms are "creative." Biography and even history are, in many ways, as fictional as fiction; and fiction can be as informative as nonfiction. The academic term "creative writing" used to distinguish fiction, drama, and poetry from nonfiction is misleading. Those who understand the psychology of expression know that all self-generated writing is creative.

Fiction isn't identical with reality. Instead, dramatic fiction gives the *impression* of reality. Aristotle described it as an "imitation" of action. In many ways we prefer the imitation to reality. Fiction has a definable shape, a satisfying closure. When you read a good book or see a good play, you walk away with a feeling of having experienced something definite, something conclusive. Unfortunately, life itself doesn't often provide such a well-rounded feeling. We go to the theater or the bookstore to find fictions that are philosophically, morally, or dramatically more meaningful than those we encounter in the day-to-day consternation of modern life.

Dramatic fiction is a mechanism, something created; and consequently it has mechanical parts. New writers often make writing fiction too complicated, trying to put in more ingredients than are necessary. The result is usually bad stew, unsatisfying fiction. In good fiction, a character is constructed from only a few elements. Adding more makes for a faulty character. In life, you might argue, people often act in ways that don't make sense or that contradict their previous actions. This is precisely where fiction is not like life: When a character in fiction acts inconsistently, the reader says "he's acting out of character." In dramatic fiction, action is consistent with character. Fiction is always answering the question, "What would happen if a totally greedy man truly fell in love?" or "What would happen," as a famous writer once put it, "if I placed an imaginary toad in a real garden, or a real toad in an imaginary garden?" The creation begins, that is, with focusing mechanically on the necessary ingredients until they are few and until they are clear.

In my writing classes and consultations, students don't actually begin writing until they've worked out the elements of their stories in their heads, clearly and dramatically. When they do begin, they discover that writing is a matter of expanding and transcribing their clear vision of the dramatic story. Faulkner said he didn't write a book until things were well worked out in his mind. An image haunted him. First he brought it into focus, and he could see it clearly. Then he started asking questions about it. Then he started answering the questions. When all the answers were there, he was ready to write the story. The order in which you transcribe the events of your story doesn't even matter because it's not the writing process, but the dramatic retelling—the product of the writing—that must have a beginning, middle, and end.

Plot is a two-dimensional concept that, in most fiction (mysteries are an exception), hinders more than it helps. Readers prefer fiction to reality because, unlike reality, fiction has a definable beginning, middle, and end—and something to say. It's *about* something. Life, from what we can tell most of the time, is not clearly and dramatically *about* anything. Or, if it is, we usually haven't a clue to what that anything is. Fiction tells us, "Love makes the world go around," or, "People never change," or, "You can be what you dream." We're satisfied with fiction because it achieves what psychologists refer to as "closure," a rounding off and fulfillment—an ending. Of course, fiction does this mechanically. It's an illusion, a shared dream created carefully and consciously by the artist.

The visionary process in fiction begins with conceptualization in your mind, then moves to planning—using the cards, if you find them useful—or going through the gestation process without them once you've outgrown the need for them. When you're ready for the first draft, you use the notes or cards only as a crutch and return to the visualizing process, letting the story develop on its own.

The revisionary process is a matter of taking out and discarding or shelving as much as you can get away with removing. Some of the greatest practitioners of dramatic fiction, including Hemingway and Chekhov, achieve their greatness by how little they leave in. The less there is on a page, the more the reader's imagination is involved in recreating the fictional world. Through that involvement artistic communication is accomplished. The reader comes to share the writer's vision.

A writer should always follow the dramatic alternative. Audiences want action; they don't want verifiability. They want to see what happens when you as the writer have worked yourself or your characters into a corner (a corner of your own construction, of course). How will you get out? Obviously, you don't work your story into a corner, then resume it—after a few asterisks—a fictional month later. That's cheating the reader, who wants to see the "getting out" as much as the "getting in."

The greatest writers of fiction, like the greatest drama-tists, write for "the psychology of the audience" (i.e., dramatic action based on what the audience is expecting to occur), not for the internal psychology of their characters, and least of all for their own psychology. Fiction is not revenge for all those ills that life and relationships have caused you. *Revenge* is revenge. Fiction serves the reader's need as theater serves the audience's need.

You think, as you write, of how your audience wants to react, and write to their expectation. John Gardner told me he kept an imaginary photograph of his son above his typewriter, and looked up from his typing occasionally to see if his son was smiling. If his son wasn't smiling, he went back over what he'd done. Use your imagination to help you visualize your audience's response. Until you're able to do that, use the peo-ple you know, reading what you've written aloud to them and taking honest note of their body language and verbal reaction.

Don't forget that the audience doesn't want to be sur-prised any more than you do. It wants to know, in advance, that it's going to be surprised so it can worry itself to that point, imagining. The technique of foreshadowing comes into play here: giving the audience an inkling of what's to come, planting little time bombs that will go off later. But an inkling is an inkling, not a total preview. The less obvious the fore-shadowing, the better, because the reader watches for every clue. Too much causes suspicion or, worse, boredom. In fact, too much detail of any kind confuses the reader, then bores or angers him as he continues (if he continues at all). Once you've noted something in drama or fiction, to note it again is to make something of it.

An editorial client constructed several scenes in his novel showing an Italian family eating dinner because, he argued, "Italians eat a lot." But fiction isn't reality. When they eat the first meal, the reader is thinking, "Italian families are like that—they eat a lot." When they eat the second meal, the reader is thinking, "Am I missing something?" By the third meal, the reader is likely to lose appetite for the book. Something is wrong with the mechanics of the story; people are eating for no reason. In life people eat in order to eat. In fiction and drama, eating must advance the story or the scenes shouldn't occur.

In good drama and fiction, something must be happening at every moment. Action is always moving forward, never standing still. Every detail of characterization, gesture, description, and dialogue must contribute to the forward motion of the action. The story must never hesitate, any more than the reader may ever stop. If you make your reader stop, you risk losing him. When he stops the third time, it's no longer a risk—it's happened: He's no longer yours.

A good novel is dramatic. Everything in good fiction expresses action. Let your imagination run free until it finds the most dramatic possibility. The elements of the novel are:

Character   *Setting*
Action   *Tone of Voice*

(The nonfiction equivalents are *subject*, *natural shape*, *background*, and *tone of voice*.)

Character

Character is the most important element, and generates the others. In fiction and drama, there are three basic types of character, in reverse order of importance: (a) function characters, (b) minor or "tag" characters, and (c) major characters.

FUNCTION CHARACTERS

A function character is one who performs a single function in the story, without being involved in the motivational pattern of the major characters. The taxi driver who takes your main character from the airport into Manhattan is a function character as long as he merely drives the car: "On the way to Manhattan the taxi driver managed to scare the daylights out of Arnold with his mad swervings and constant honking."

The minute you give the driver a "tag" he becomes more than a function character: "On the way into the city, the taxi driver with the red hat managed . . ." The red hat is a flag alerting the reader to the importance of the taxi driver. If he appears only this once, at the end of your book or screenplay the reader will want to know what happened to the taxi driver, why was he important, and why did you tell us he's wearing a red hat. The function character opens the door, serves drinks on the plane, or cashes the main character's check. He has no name and no distinguishing characteristics other than the function he's performing at the time he appears in your story.

This is not a difficult concept. Don't make it difficult by trying to be inventive in the wrong places. Inventiveness is what you will end up editing out of your manuscript to allow your reader to tell the difference between the main character and all the others.

MINOR CHARACTERS

A minor character has a "tag" or neurosis or single defining attribute that distinguishes him and makes him memorable. Where a function character is forgettable, a minor character must be sharply defined and instantly recognizable. But his definition, in contrast to that of a major character, is relatively superficial. A minor character may have a motivation, but he doesn't have a mission in life. He has, instead, a memorable neurosis or what Hollywood calls a "tag."

You establish the minor character quickly, so you can move along. If it takes too long to establish him, the reader immediately suspects he's a major character. My favorite example of the "tag" is the meeting that must have been held at the Disney studios once upon a time. Walt has been impatiently awaiting his twenty-one writers, who've spent months developing the major character for his new film and are now taking their time on the minor characters. He assembles the writers to hurry them along.

"How's it going?"

The writers' spokesman smiles. "We're making progress," he says. "We've divided ourselves into committees."

Walt shakes his head. "And?"

The woman in charge of Committee One speaks up. "Well, we think we've almost got ours," she says. She sees the boss nodding for her to continue. "He's very, very intelligent and sober. When the others don't understand something, they always look to him. He knows all the answers, because he's learned and authoritative. He's kind of like a doctor and we're toying with the idea . . ."

Walt scribbles one word on his 3″ × 5″ card: "Doc."

Committee Two reports that they've named their character Trimalchio and made him quite different from Committee One's character. "He's dumb, constantly making silly remarks, falling all over himself."

Walt scribbles "Dopey."

And so on. No one will remember Grimalchio and Trimalchio—but no one can forget Doc and Dopey, Grumpy and Happy, any more than we forget Santa's reindeer or the Three Bears. The essence of the minor character is an unforgettable tag.

When the writer can't remember which character is which, the story is in trouble. A character who isn't instantly memorable should be thrown out. Who wants a book of forgettable characters?

Here's a more familiar example of how you handle minor characters. Your hero's sister is meant to be greedy, to contrast with him. In one scene, we see her bed—covered with forty-three stuffed animals (greed by way of description); in another scene, at the dinner table, she reaches across and spears six french fries from her brother's plate (greed in action); another time, she and her mom are on the way downtown. "Let's buy you a new dress," Mom says. "Can I have two?" the sister asks (greed in dialogue). Or suppose she's standing in front of the mirror, wishing she were richer so she could wear a satin gown (greed in thought). You don't use the word "greed," of course; that would be telegraphing your message. But by the time we've met your character twice, we're suspecting she's greedy; by the third meeting, we know she is, and we're proud of ourselves for understanding her character.

You've successfully programmed us. The mechanism has worked.

MAJOR CHARACTERS

A major character has a mission in life, based on a major ambition or motivation, and expressed through a simple combination of the *major* human emotions. Two emotions in combination, but not more than two, can shape the motivation for a major character. Keep in mind that the character is a construction, a mechanism, and not a human being. Human beings entertain numerous emotions, often simultaneously. The result if often madness, rarely art. Art comes from decision, the willful focusing of emotion to put pressure on action.

Another useful set of terms for character, borrowed from drama, is "protagonist" / "antagonist." Both protagonist and antagonist are major characters. The protagonist is the hero, the one who dominates most of the action. The antagonist is the opponent, the one who acts against the protagonist. The antagonist doesn't even need to be a character. Sometimes the protagonist is pitted against the elements, as in *King Solomon's Mines*, or against himself, as in *Hamlet*.

The major character's mechanism consists of *motivation*, *mission*, *obstacles*, and *change*. As we examine them one by one, we move naturally from character into action.

Let's start with *motivation*. Something makes your character tick—love, hate, greed, despair, anxiety—one of the major emotions. Or a combination of the two. Greed and love would be interesting and a more dramatic combination than greed and hate because they provide internal tension as well as dramatic potential. You should avoid more complicated combinations until you've written several novels.

Your story gets started when the character is given a *mission*, or decides to undertake one. Motivated by their love for comfort in tension with their courage, the hobbits' story in Tolkien's *Lord of the Rings* begins when it's clear that the Ring of Power must be returned. Their mission is to return it. In another story, a private eye throws in the towel in the opening scene, and announces he's following his head this time instead of his instincts, and giving up the profession. Then in walks Rachel Ward to suggest that the secret of her identity may be connected with his. He falls in love with her at first glance—but she might be his sister. His mission is clear: to find out who her parents are and what her relationship is to him. Now the story can begin.

Screenwriting theorists agree that the dramatic plot contains two major turning points or "plot points," each related to the hero's motivation.

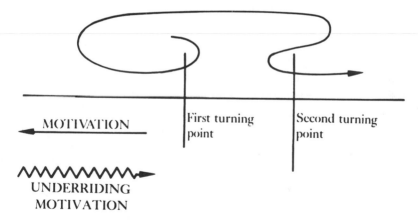

MOTIVATION

First turning point

Second turning point

UNDERRIDING MOTIVATION

In the private eye's story, at the first turning point, his primary motivation (to stop detective work) is *reversed* by *his* decision to aid Rachel Ward, a decision that activates his characteristic motivation to investigate anything that needs investigating. The decision sends him off into the Serengeti of obstacles until he reaches that second turning point, the decision or action that determines the final course of his story.

Action occurs when the major character, your hero, for example, meets *obstacles* to his mission. His motivation guarantees that he'll face the obstacles. His character, and the mythic pattern behind your story, will determine whether he overcomes the obstacles or is defeated by them. Moreover the obstacles must fit his character and his mission; a flying saucer on the battlefield cannot be presented as yet another challenge to Alexander the Great (unless your story is a comedy).

Like all else, obstacles must be divided into beginning, middle, and end. Otherwise the results can be ludicrous. Your job is to find enough obstacles to make your story last as long as it needs to last, then to put them in their natural order. Natural order includes their rhythmic relationship to one another and to the momentum of the story. When it comes to obstacles, timing is what separates the ingenious writer from the inept. For example, at the end of the film *King Solomon's Mines*, as Deborah Kerr and Stewart Granger walk into the sunset, we can't have her slapping at a mosquito. They've faced snakes, quicksand, leopards, hungry cannibals, and the worst of love and guilt and desperation. If mosquitoes are to be in your story, they should be among the first obstacles (along with the heat and less dramatic obstacles).

The card system is particularly helpful with this step, allowing you to arrange and rearrange the obstacles like different-sized blocks until you discover the most dramatic progression (the one that keeps your audience involved). The one exception to the conventional progression of small, medium-sized, and large obstacles could occur at the beginning of the story where you set a large obstacle against your character in order to involve him immediately in a dramatic situation and, at the same time, hook your reader into imaginative involvement.

When your hero overcomes the last and greatest obstacle, the action line is nearly concluded. Many writers simply stop at that point; others wind down the story in a few paragraphs or pages. The difference is measured in emotional impact on the reader: One method shares the writer's conclusive viewpoint with the reader, bringing the story's vision into focus; the other leaves the audience to reach its own conclusion.

Regardless of how exciting your action line is, unless your main character undergoes a significant *change* from first to last he fails the test of great drama. Since the time of Cervantes's *Don Quixote*, the reader of novels expects psychological development, or at least outward change. If the character is the same at the end as he is at the outset, he's perceived as superficial—and his effect on the reader will be superficial.

This mechanism is perhaps the most difficult for new writers. The following scheme will help you make sure that your character is developing:

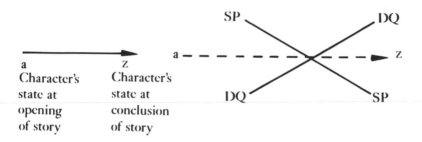

a   z
Character's   Character's
state at   state at
opening   conclusion
of story   of story

On the left, the straight time line indicates the character moving from start to finish of a story (or even of a scene). Actually drawing the line forces you to conceptualize "a" and "z." What state is your hero in when the story begins? Is "z" quite different from "a"? On the right, the drawing indicates two major characters interacting as the time line (a→z) progresses. To take the Don Quixote example, at position "a" Sancho Panza is a realist, while Don Quixote is an idealist. By the time the story ends, they've changed places. Sancho Panza now believes what he used to doubt, Don Quixote's doubt has replaced his fantasy, and now Sancho Panza becomes a source of strength to his master. Structure is a matter of deciding at what point on the time line the intersection of the two charac-

PSYCHOLOGICAL DEVELOPMENT
OF THE MAJOR CHARACTER

External Influences

Sue's job

Sexual encounters
   with men———→pseudo attack | ——————————————————————→

Daniel———————————————→ | meets Sue ——————————————→

Mother?   (Mother's influence not | — — — — — — — — — — —
   yet decided)

Father   hunting accident————→meets Daniel → hunting again→

Internal Influences

Conscious — — — — — — — — fear of men because of pseudo attack

Unconscious — — — — — — — — fear of her father ——————————→

Sue's Age

9   10   11   12   13   14   15   16   17   18

"The Backstory" |Your narrative of Sue's story
   Story begins

---

ters' developments occurs. In *Don Quixote*, it occurs about halfway through Book II.

   In any novel, each major character must be fully defined
in relationship to every other major character. If you're dealing with three or more, the graph can become extremely complicated, the mechanism in danger of faltering. For this
reason, it makes sense to stick with one or two major characters for your first books.

   The chart above may be helpful in tracking the course of
your major character's development in relationship to events
(or action line).

Your major character is Sue Randolph. Her story moves from the age of 14 to 18, but you need to know what happened to her before 14 that causes her to act as she does in the present. Events are charted against her reaction to events, the latter both conscious and unconscious.

For example, when Sue was a small girl her father took her hunting and taught her his outdoor skills. But when she was nine, her father was seriously injured in a hunting accident. Her conscious response at the time was sorrow, her unconscious response was guilt (because she happened to be with him).

The story begins when Sue is attacked at the age of fourteen by a bully at the high school and, at a crucial instant, saves herself with her old hunting skills. Conscious response: anger and elation. Unconscious: aversion to men, as the guilt becomes fear. We're beginning to understand the complexity of Sue's motivation (a mixture of love-hate) and her mission (to find a man like her father who can protect her and also win her admiration and loyalty—and who won't betray her). But after the attack, as her action line begins, she's just about giving up on men. When Daniel comes onto the scene, we can see what he's up against. He's going to have to be careful if he hopes to attract her attention. In this story, his relationship with Sue gains ground when he plays chess with her invalid father and virtually ignores her.

Seeing it on a chart like this allows you to be objective about the character. I use "it" rather than "her" in order to reemphasize the mechanical nature of fiction. If you know this much about your main character as you plan your novel, you don't need to know more. More will only make your job more difficult. Less is better. The chart helps with the overall structure of action: As events bunch up we know we're at the crux of the story.

As you construct scenes for Sue's story—father meets Daniel, Daniel asks father if he can marry Sue, Daniel and Sue go hunting, and so on—strike a different tone for each scene, based on the particular combination of events inside

Sue's head and external events. Consistency in characterization comes from dealing with a clearly constructed character
(whose motivation and mission are understood). Variety and
drama come from the combination of your character's internal
components with external events. Sue, in the actual story,
moves from insecurity and fear of men to security and love
of Daniel.

Action

Action isn't plot. Action is recognizing and embracing your
story's mythic pattern or natural shape. The wooden concept
of plot can get in the way of this discovery because it appeals
more to the Continent than to the islands, more to reasoning
than to intuition. Is your story happy or tragic? If it's happy,
the hero begins unhappy and moves toward happiness. If it's
tragic, he begins happy and ends unhappy. The action lines
that take a middle course veer into the chartless seas of intel-
lectualism. I'm not recommending against such voyages, but
I am suggesting that they're generally more productive toward
the end of your career than at the beginning.

If "plotting" has helped you through the first draft, when
it comes to revision throw away your plot as Lillian Hellman
recommends and just "tell the story." Allow its organic shape
to emerge from the awkwardness of your draft. That shape is
what I've been referring to as "story" or "action." It's not
invented, but discovered. In the play *Seven against Thebes*, the
duel between Polynices and Eteocles must come last among
the seven duels, or the story makes no sense. In the film *Urban
Cowboy*, the bucking contest must conclude with the hero
against the villain, or the action line fails to move the audience
dramatically. Just imagine what would happen if the major
match in *Rocky* came in the first few minutes of the film and
you'll understand the meaning of "natural pattern."

The history of Sue Randolph begins before your story
about her begins. Don't be confused by this. Story is what the
reader reads, in the order you allow it to be read. Everything

else (called "backstory") serves story, preceding it or putting it in context. A story has a Beginning, a Middle, and an End, each of which must be dramatic in different ways. The Beginning is a dramatic hook that involves the reader. The Middle is dramatic in a stepped fashion to maintain suspense, presenting the obstacles in ascending difficulty. The End is dramatic in a conclusive way, leaving the reader with a clear feeling. When the White King answered White Rabbit, "You begin at the Beginning, go straight through to the End and then Stop," he was referring to the story, not to the writer's process of making the story. It makes no difference whether you begin writing at the story's beginning, at its middle, or at its end. How you put it together is what makes the difference.

Drama begins when something riveting is going on. Now you can understand why there's no contradiction in William Goldman's advice that you "start as far into a scene as possible" in order to maintain the audience's dramatic involvement. He's using two terminologies simultaneously, as Aristotle was when he said that Homer's greatness was that he began "in the middle of things." Aristotle meant that the story-beginning of *The Iliad* was in the middle of the history of Achilles' quarrel with Agamemnon. Goldman means that opening a scene in the middle of an argument makes for better story involvement than does beginning with a gradual buildup. Gradual buildups are for history, or for real life, or for logic or chronologic. They explain why life can be boring, while drama should not be.

The beginning and end of your story are relatively simple when it comes to dealing with them dramatically. The middle is what causes most problems. But don't forget you can divide the middle, too—into beginning, middle, and end—as often as the division is necessary to create the rhythmic energy of dramatic writing. These middle divisions lead to "cycles of action." In the following diagram, obstacles are given numeric status, the greater the number the more serious the obstacle. Note how the middle itself is divided for variety and rhythm, yet without breaking the rules of progress discussed above:

Beginning	Middle	End
(dramatic hook)		(dramatic conclusion)
4	1-2-3 / 2-3-3 / 3-3-4 / 4-2-3-4 etc.	5→

Obviously this is only one of many configurations. Paramount uses the structure of *The Bad News Bears* as its model of a successful story:

1. A rotten team suddenly improves.
2. They fall apart again.
3. They start a long, hard climb back.
4. They prevail.

Which pattern works best in your story is your responsibility, your major creative decision that will take your readers or viewers with you across the Serengeti or leave them stranded. You work with your cards until you find the most effective pattern for the middle. After each proposed configuration, ask yourself, "How will the reader respond if I tell the story in this order?" Then ask, "Do I want him to respond that way?"

Sometimes, once you've gotten the pattern down, you'll need transitions between beginning, middle, and end. Most of the time you'll discover that transitions aren't necessary. If the story elements are clear enough, the reader will make the transitions with more imaginative energy than you can with words. Just as the nonfiction writer gets out of the way of the natural shape of his subject, the fiction writer gets himself out of the way of the story and lets it "tell itself."

Recognizing the pattern of your story or action line is no great trick. For one thing, there aren't that many mythic patterns (one scholar calculated there are only 36). The romantic pattern is perhaps the most familiar:

a. Girl and boy meet.
b. Girl and boy interact.

    c. Girl and boy combine or separate (depending on whether you're after the happy or the tragic ending).

But the heroic pattern is also familiar. It's the old quest pattern:

    a. Hero enters the unknown.
    b. Hero struggles with what lies there and finds something of value.
    c. Hero returns with it to the community.

This pattern is as old as the epic of Gilgamesh and as contemporary as *Forrest Gump*.

    Great writers don't invent stories; they retell them, just as *Apocalypse Now* retells Joseph Conrad's *Heart of Darkness*. It's the development that distinguishes one creative work from another, and makes them worth our attention.

    Finally, the two kinds of action are *action* proper and *dialogue*. Action occurs when people *do* things, everything from rappelling down a mountainside to gesturing with an eyebrow. *Dialogue* is active talk, not *conversation*. Read the dialogue in Ernest Hemingway's "Hills Like White Elephants" or James Joyce's "Ivy Day in the Committee Room" to understand this point. Good dialogue advances the story line ("I would do anything for you." "Would you please please please please please please please stop talking?"). Conversation moves us nowhere ("Hi, Joe. How are you?"). Good dialogue is action.

Setting

When you're choosing the setting of your story, follow the same fictional rule that dictates the choice of the most dramatic possibility. When you decide where to set your story, choose the locale that will enhance the tension of your story line, adding its own kind of pressure. A love story in the jungle will be quite different in its dramatic forces from one conducted on the Harvard campus. Beyond that rule, setting is dictated largely by character.

Before you do exhaustive research into the setting of your story, set up your first road map in your imagination. Even if you haven't been to Haiti, imagine yourself there as you think about the shape of your story. Imagine what people in Haiti feel and think. When you check your facts during assembly, you'll be surprised to discover how accurate your imagination was in most respects.

Tone of Voice

One thing now remains for the fiction writer: to decide upon tone of voice. The tone of voice has to do with your relationship to your audience, your view of your own narrative position with respect to the reader. Will you speak like an aunt at the Thanksgiving dinner table, or like a priest from the pulpit? Or like a government bureaucrat trying to confuse taxpayers into ignoring how the government has swindled them? Any of these is possible, but a decision is necessary before you can comfortably begin and, without intimidation, move the first draft right along.

Once you've made the decision about voice, try it out for a few pages. If it feels right, you'll be on your way into the story without being aware of voice. If it doesn't feel right, you'll know that you're struggling. Stop after five pages and reconsider the tone of voice. Try it another way. (This includes the decision of whether to write in the first or third person; the latter will probably work best for your first novels because it assists you in seeing your characters objectively, as fictional mechanisms rather than as extensions of yourself.) Once you're on track, one more thing: Tell your story as though you were trying to keep people awake.

Page One

The first page is crucial in dramatic writing. Normally it should introduce the protagonist and the setting, and reveal an imminent decision or confrontation that will change the protagonist's behavior. My favorite examples include the first pages of Jerzy Kosinski's *Cockpit*, Herman Melville's *Moby Dick*, Frank Herbert's *Dune*, and Stephen King's *The Shining*. On the first page, the protagonist is in jeopardy—in the *middle* of the jeopardy, not the beginning. After that decision is made or that particular confrontation is faced, something new happens to obstruct change or foreshadow another confrontation.

That's an abstract, mechanical formula, of course. The writer must flesh it out until it's no longer abstract, though it will still be mechanical. The effect of the mechanism is to hook the reader into wanting to read more.

A sympathetic protagonist isn't necessarily likable (Kosinski's *Cockpit* and Shakespeare's *Richard III* have very unlikable protagonists). But any major character has to be interesting, involving. We have to care, and the writer's job is to give us a reason for caring about this person's problems. If the character is not sympathetic, when outside events come in to obstruct, we won't care about what the hero decides to do or not do.

Scenes

Like drama, fiction is best constructed in scenes. If you use the card method for constructing your novel, many of your cards will naturally be scenes, the basic units of dramatic fiction. A scene is a tripartite structure, presenting:

> Who is where
> What's going on? (or What's the problem?)
> What happens to solve or not solve the problem

There can also be a linkage or foreshadowing:

> What could happen next?

This last question is your hook to the next scene. It's often unnecessary to be explicit. In fact, the more dramatically you present the scene and its resolution or lack of resolution, the less necessary is the hook. The scene itself serves as a hook. In revision, we often discover that the transitions can be removed if the writing is good enough. William Goldman's writing and Steven Spielberg's directing are dramatic examples of what can be done without transitions.

Once you've dealt with these questions you're done with your scene. It may be 500 words or 5,000 words (different writers prefer scenes of different lengths), but the unit is complete and it's time to move on to the next unit. The scenes stand on their own and speak for themselves, as they move the story forward. If you read your favorite novelist with an eye to the structure of scenes, you'll see how much easier the whole thing is than you thought. It's doing too much that ruins first novels, not too little.

Index Cards and Patterns of Dramatic Action

The index cards, as we've seen, are useful organizational crutches. In the fiction (as well as nonfiction) agenda, they help you organize your time. When used structurally, they can help you organize the patterns of action in your screenplay or novel. There are as many ways to use the cards structurally as there are differences among writers. But many writers have found it helpful to divide the cards into sets based on *character interaction*. Color coding the cards will make patterns even clearer.

For example, you have a screenplay with a college romance—let's say the main character's name is Mark and his romantic relationship is with Jennifer, who becomes his fiancée. The secondary character or third main character is named Harvey, Mark's college roommate. Call the scenes in which Mark, the hero and main character, appears alone "A" scenes. All the "A" cards are meant to help you establish Mark's character when he appears alone. All the cards in which Jennifer and Mark appear together can be called "B" cards and are meant to establish and develop their relationship. All the cards in which Mark and Harvey appear together are "C" cards; the cards in which Harvey and Jennifer appear, "D" cards; "E" cards when Jennifer appears alone and "F" cards when Harvey appears alone. Since I'm going to refer to these card sets throughout this section, let me set them in a color-coded table for your reference:

Card	Color-Coded Character or Relationship	Color Code
A	Mark	Red
B	Mark and Jennifer	Pink
C	Mark and Harvey	Orange
D	Jennifer and Harvey	Yellow
E	Jennifer	Green
F	Harvey	Blue

This may sound complicated but it simplifies things tremendously. You can now go through your cards and make sure, at every stage in the writing process, that each relationship is developing properly. As I suggested in chapter 4, you'll know something's wrong in the organizational process if you only have one or two B cards and you have ten each of A, C, and D cards. We said the B relationship was between Mark and Jennifer. There are five times as many D scenes, the interactions between Harvey and Jennifer. Since there are fewer B cards in your final tally, Mark and Jennifer's eventual engagement is going to appear less important than the relationship between Harvey and Jennifer. This seems pretty obvious, but it is a detail that writers frequently overlook because they don't organize their cards effectively.

By making the decision to give the cards different set names, you've allowed yourself to ensure that the proportion of scenes for each action data is the correct proportion, the proportion you envisioned for your story's natural shape. There should be more A scenes with Mark alone, since Mark is the hero and main character, than E scenes with Jennifer alone or F scenes with Harvey alone. There might not be any scenes with Harvey alone and maybe one E scene with Jennifer alone.

To establish Harvey's character you might want just one F card. But you don't necessarily need one. You might be able to establish Harvey's character in a scene between Harvey and Mark (a C card). It depends on how important a character you want to make Harvey. If he's a secondary character, the chances of him having his own scene are very small. So you shouldn't have six F cards, unless you want to rethink your story. Maybe you want Harvey to be a major character after all. And maybe you should keep the larger stack of D cards depicting Harvey and Jennifer, and make Jennifer's engagement to Mark the result of her inner conflict. Mark could be her second choice—second to Harvey. But such a change would also make Mark a secondary character and Jennifer or Harvey the main character. Harvey and Jennifer's relationship could become the central romance of the story. So what appears to be one simple change here could change the entire character of your book or screenplay. If you don't want to make drastic changes, then you'd better get rid of those F cards and most of the D cards.

To get rid of the extra F cards, ask yourself how you can do the same things with Harvey in a scene in which Harvey is in the company of Jennifer or Mark. And you check that out by comparing it to the existing C and D cards (Harvey's scenes with Mark or Jennifer) and converting the F card to a C card or D card. If you can't see any way of doing that, then erase the card.

What you're doing first with the card sets is developing the proper proportions of your action, its rhythmic patterns. What you do next is develop the proper dramatic logic of your story.

Novelists and screenwriters mustn't forget that their audience or readers don't care at all about the chronology of the story. They care only about the dramatic logic of the story. The dramatic logic of the story is nothing more than the structure of beginning, middle, and end. The beginning is the hook, the end is the satisfying closure, and the middle is rhythmically arranged to consistently involve the audience, without once losing their attention or once letting the action lag, unless the lag is for purposes of rhythm and suspense. In the middle, the most difficult part of writing because it's the part where you really have to think of creative solutions, your problem is how to make this story both long enough and dramatic enough. If it's a film, you'll have to make the story last two hours. If it's a novel, 250–300 pages. If the story slows down, you lose the audience. So the story's got to be moving forward all the time.

You arrange the set cards (A,B,C,D,E,F) in a way that constantly gives the reader something stimulating or new. You are free to arrange those cards in any way you like, as long as it's dramatic. You don't have to arrange the cards chronologically. You might assume that when a character is 12 years old at the beginning of a story and 16 at the end, the scenes where the character was 13 would come before the scenes where the character was 15. Though logical, that arrangement is not necessarily dramatic. The audience doesn't care about chronology and won't be confused if you jump around in time as long as the dramatic progress of the story constantly moves forward.

Let's go back to our example, which is a screenplay about love on a college campus, with Mark and Jennifer as the principal characters. As long as the love between them is making progress toward the happy conclusion we want for this story, it doesn't matter in what order we show their appearances together (Jennifer's appearances apart, Mark's appearances apart, or Harvey's appearances with Jennifer or Mark). You can even show the conclusion of the story at the beginning, as in *Looking for Mr. Goodbar*. In Judith Rossner's novel, the opening scene *is* the closing scene. *Looking for Mr. Goodbar* opens with the horrible murder of the heroine. Following this grisly opening scene, the reader becomes engrossed by the rhythmic patterns that unravel in the middle of the story. The writers— of both the screenplay and the book—hold our full attention at every moment and move forward so that by the end of the story we have forgotten what's going to happen. And when the murder is reenacted before our eyes—in the very same words that we read at the beginning of the book—we are *surprised* because the rhythm has always held our attention in the present and made us forget where we're going.

So there's an example where you can put a card—let's say an A card (the heroine alone)—out of chronological order to begin the dramatic rhythm at the end. Then you take all the other A cards in the story. The first A card was when she came to New York and looked for a job. Then there were A cards about how she got more and more deeply into social work and then more and more deeply into sexual needs and self-destructive habits. The last A card in the pile was the murder she brought upon herself. In a logical or chronological situation, you wouldn't put the last A card first. But Judith Rossner put that scene first because she told herself, "I bet I could do this. Let me see if I can get the audience into this kind of mode."

Hooking your readers or audience with your closure is an exception rather than a rule, but you can see that the rules are flexible. The important rule is that you must maintain the constant forward motion of the rhythmic pattern.

To go back to our earlier example, let's say we're going to work on the dramatic logic of our B cards—the cards in which Jennifer interacts with Mark. You should have a whole pile of B cards. How do you decide which card to use first? Let's say you've already established what the opening scene of the story is, because the opening scene must be the most dramatic possible scene you can give the readers or audience, a scene that will hook them into your story. Your closure is the scene that will leave them with the clear vision of the end of your story, whether it's to make the audience feel good or whether it's a tragic vision that purges their emotions. You've already decided those two points. Then how do you decide in the middle where to put a given B card (an interaction between Mark and Jennifer)? How do you decide on the "rhythmic" order of the B cards? Let's call the B cards—to go inside this one category for an example—B1, B2, B3, B4, and so on, according to their chronology. In scene B1, Mark and Jennifer meet for the first time. In B2, Mark and Jennifer hold hands for the first time. In B3, Mark and Jennifer kiss for the first time. And so on to B52, in which Mark and Jennifer walk off into the sunset together. B52 is very close to the end of our story, if not *the* end of our story. But that's only the *chronological* end of the B cards.

How do you decide what B card to put first? The nondramatic writer would say, "Obviously the one where they meet would be the one you put first." But that's not what the drama needs. The drama demands a hint about the shape of the impending relationship between Mark and Jennifer. The sooner that hint occurs, the more satisfied the audience is because the audience likes to predict the outcome of the story and the shape of the pattern. The sooner the writer enables the audience to predict, the sooner the writer has involved the audience's imagination. The writer's aim is to engage the audience's imagination so that the audience feels it is creating the story. It works the same way for a novel or a movie. So you don't want to have that scene in which Mark and Jennifer meet early in your story if all that happens in it is that Mark and Jennifer meet. That decision doesn't add anything to your beginning. Remember the question you should constantly ask yourself after every scene: What did I establish in the audience's mind in that scene? What did I want to establish? And did I establish it?

So what you want, as you consider cards B1 through B52, is the first scene in which the shape of their relationship is predictable, even if the prediction is very slight. In fact, the slighter it is, the better, because the more sophisticated the writer can be in planting clues, the more power the audience has. The audience will pick up the slightest clue, the most subtle implantation. Many writers don't have enough trust in their audiences, so they overclue—they overplant—and the audience says, "Ugh, I can see this coming!" Overplant only when you want to fool the audience. This is a rhythmic pattern favored by Alfred Hitchcock, or William Goldman, or Woody Allen. So you plant, very subtly, let's say in B7, that this is going to be a happy relationship. But B7 also includes in it the beginning of a lot of problems. Yet there's this one sign in B7. Maybe it's just a glance between them in which you know they love each other. Let your audience root for that love, even though Mark and Jennifer are about to go into what looks like something that's going to tear them apart. Put B7 first among the B scenes in your drama.

So what's happened is: Let's say we've had an A scene in which we've established Mark alone. Then a C scene in which we put Mark and Harvey together so that we know Mark's general problem—he's a hero without a girlfriend. Then we think about what B scene we should put in first. Our normal reaction would be to put in B1, because that's where Mark and Jennifer meet. But I'm recommending putting in scene B7, in which their relationship can be predicted—because B7 is more dramatic at this point in the pattern than is B1. With B7, you're establishing *hope* on the part of the audience. You're using the psychology of the audience to determine the order of each subset. The determining factor is: What does the audience want to see first?

Let's take B7 further. We're putting it first, with its hints both of hope and of complications. The writer knows that Mark and Jennifer are going to fall apart only so they can get back together. The audience doesn't know this yet. But the audience hopes that will happen because B7 suggests that it might. The audience's curiosity is now rising. So you end B7 just when the audience has gotten this hope. And you go to another scene—an A scene, a C scene, a D scene, an E scene, an F scene. By the time you've moved all those action patterns forward, it will be time for another B scene.

Which B scene do we use second? And where do we use B1 since we've decided not to use their first meeting as the audience's first clue about Mark and Jennifer's relationship? All that happens at B1 is that they meet. No matter how interesting that is, it's still less dramatic than B7 because B1 didn't have that element of hope. They might not even like each other when they first meet. It might have been simply a casual introduction. So why use B1 at all? The audience has been hoping through the last six non-B scenes that this is the relationship for Mark. They already know from the scenes we put in before B7 that Mark needs a relationship. So now they're hoping that Jennifer has the same need. If the audience is to see that hope fulfilled, they'll want to know a little more about how Mark and Jennifer's relationship got so complicated in the first place, because it's obvious from B7 that that wasn't the first time they met. And one of the things they'll wonder about is how Mark and Jennifer met. So the audience's curiosity—a dramatic demand—will provide a place for scene B1. Effective structuring is responding to the dramatic demands that you have incited in the audience.

The audience likes being hooked into watching or reading a good story. But they're still *curious* about the chronology. So we can put B1 in to show the audience how our two characters met and to satisfy the audience's curiosity on that score. But B1 doesn't have to be the *next* B scene. We can put in any other scene that plays the audience's emotions the way we want them played. The author's decision of how to play the audience's emotions is the key to structuring drama and fiction.

So depending on how you want to play the audience, you might want to put in a mild scene like B1. Or you might not. You might put a more dramatic scene than B7 next, such as B13, whatever B13 is. We put B13 in there because we want to play the audience a different way. If we do B13 next, we raise the audience's hope and curiosity even more. We can still put in B1 later. Sometime later we will need a lull to counterpoint the ongoing action with another action pattern, such as A or C. When we need the lull, we put in B1. The audience will understand instantly that we put it in to satisfy their curiosity—and to give them a little rest from the intensity of the preceding B scene. They'll understand that we did it to whet their curiosity for the next scene, which will be an A scene, a C scene, a D scene, an E scene, or an F scene.

To summarize, by dividing the action line or cards into subsets A, B, C, and so on, and by numbering each subset chronologically, you allow yourself to organize the action dramatically. Dramatic order is far more important than the chronology. But the author must have a firm grasp of the chronology before deciding to scramble the chronology for dramatic effect.

An excellent example of chronology subordinated to dramatic order is the film and book *Birdy*. The story goes back and forth in time between the main character's insanity—or alleged insanity—after he has been involved in the Vietnam War. Beginning with the end of the chronology, it moves to scenes in the war, to his childhood from the age of about twelve to the age of about nineteen, and to his childhood friendship. There are three sets of scenes there, with subsets that include scenes of the character individually and scenes of his best friend individually, and, of course, scenes of their friendship. And the chronology of those three sets is scrambled, both in the novel and the movie.

If we considered only chronology in the book or movie *Birdy*—and the movie follows the book pretty closely—we would be puzzled if not confused. First we'd see this guy in what looks like a mental institution, but nobody even tells us that. And he's crouching on the corner of his bed. What's going on? Then we're seeing him years and years before, with a stolen pocketknife, and meeting a kid who turns out to be his best friend—we don't know that at the time either. He's meeting a kid who gives him back the knife after he offers to give it back to the kid. Then we see the war scene. Then another scene in the institution. And then still another scene where the two kids are dressed up in pigeon suits. These chronological shifts continue throughout.

If we were looking for chronology, we would be baffled by the story. The truth is that even a four-year-old—the one who happened to be sitting on my lap during the movie—was

HYPOTHETICAL DRAMATIC PATTERN

B13	Jennifer tells Mark she never wants to see him again
A4	Mark drives his car into a tree
C4	Harvey visits Mark in the hospital
D9	Harvey fails to convince Jennifer that Mark still loves her
C10	Mark pries Harvey's conversation with Jennifer from a reluctant Harvey.
A5	Mark, alone, thinks about Jennifer and himself.
B1	Mark and Jennifer meet.
C5	Mark calls Harvey and tells him not to bother him about Jennifer anymore.
A9	Mark, alone, thinks about Jennifer and himself.
B3	Mark and Jennifer kiss for the first time.
B10	Mark and Jennifer make love for the first time. Mark realizes what Jennifer means to him, and resolves to rekindle the romance that got off on the wrong foot.
A7	Etc. . . .

not puzzled for one moment. The progress of the movie takes that chronology and rearranges it in dramatic order. The opening scene captures our full attention and all the scenes move the story forward so that something always happens. The highs and the lows are rhythmically arranged. And there is an incredible ending, a satisfying closure to the story (especially in the movie). All of it satisfyingly subordinates chronological order to dramatic order.

Yet the writers of the screenplay and the author of the book made sure that no part of the chronology was missing in any of the subsets of the action. By rearranging the chronology in dramatic order, the reader's or audience's imagination is always engaged in unscrambling the chronology. When the audience is thinking about the chronology at the same time the drama is unfolding, you have a collaboration, an imaginative tension, between audience and writer that makes for the most successful kind of fiction and drama.

SIX

Publishing in Time

WHEN Karl Marx was living in London, he received this letter from his Leipzig publisher: "Dear Herr Doctor: You are already ten months behind time with the manuscript of *Das Kapital*, which you have agreed to write for us. If we do not receive the manuscript within six months, we shall be obliged to commission another author to do this work."

In the world of publishing there are many anecdotes about the tempestuous relationship between writers and publishers. Some are amusing and charming, but others deal with heartache and misunderstandings, confusion and delays, painfully slow response and no response at all. To publish in today's market, a writer is up against "Catch 22"—you must have published already, or you must realize it's going to take you a long time to get published. But that's not an unnatural situation; most things that are worthwhile take a long time at the beginning.

Recognize this fact of life at the outset and decide that your first publication will take time, energy, stamps, and ego-bolstering—and, most of all, the admission that publishing and writing are two separate activities. You cannot let your writer's ego be affected by the publishing process, which, by nature, entails repeated rejection. Of course, that's easier said than done, but doing gets easier with practice. You need to develop a special part of your mind and your routine to deal with publishing and professionalism. If you can learn to keep your publishing activities separate from the writing activities we've already discussed, you'll develop a suitable callous on the left side of your brain, one that's strong enough to protect the right side so it can continue its creating.

Time and energy are necessary, not only for the actual transforming of thoughts into words, but also to familiarize yourself with the procedures and etiquette of manuscript submission. Principles of time-and-self-management are essential. You need to organize yourself for publishing as you have for writing. If you can do this, you'll increase your chances of being taken seriously (as a professional) by the editors to whom you submit your work.

The Writer's Habitat, Materials, and Filing Techniques

You must have complete control over the surroundings in which you write daily. After all, your work space is the heart of your professional career. When two writers become friends, they inspect each other's work space to see what improvements they can make in their own. My ideal workroom would be set up as follows:

Desk 1 is my organizing and work desk. The top of it is large enough to leave free working space but also to contain frequent reference books, "In" boxes for my regular correspondence with publishers, and a six-slot file, all labeled to make routine sorting automatic. On the two-drawer file to the left of Desk 1, I have my telephones (turned off or transferred during prime writing time), a radio for classical music, and an electric pencil sharpener.

My computer word processor is perpendicular to the file cabinet and can be reached by swiveling my chair (which rolls easily on a floor-protecting plastic sheet). To the left of that is the printer, within reach, and the rest of Desk 2 is taken up with just-printed material and the compact edition of the *Unabridged Oxford English Dictionary*.

The television is placed where it's not too tempting. I have to stop working to watch it, or set up Desk 4 (a card table usually tucked to the right of Desk 1) if I'm watching it for work.

Then Desk 3: holding less frequently used reference books, but otherwise kept free for projects that need to remain out between work sessions.

Shelf 1 contains my published writing, Shelf 2 scrapbooks and *The Encyclopedia Britannica*. Shelves 3 and 4 contain frequently consulted books and records, and on Shelves 5 and 6 there are dictionaries and various literary encyclopedias as well as notebooks containing projects temporarily on hold.

I've reduced my files to two four-drawer cabinets, and as they become full I thin them instead of adding to them. File 1 contains correspondence relating to my writing projects being marketed, and three drawers of general correspondence. File 2 holds drawers of research and ideas.

The room has plenty of pacing area, a comfortable armchair with reading lamp, and my grandfather's rocking chair. A map of the world along one wall provides ready reference.

Note that my situation represents an already published writer. It takes you a while to obtain separate writing space and everything that's in it. Until you get to that point, your work space may look like this:

A word processor, or typewriter, on a corner table will do for starters. Cinder block shelves can provide adequate space for all the reference essentials. Here the word processor is the centerpiece of one side of the work space, while the rest is devoted to research materials. Keep a space for regularly used supplies—for paper, erasers or other correction materials—on one side of the word processor. A dictionary and any other references (except a thesaurus) should be kept near notebooks (or a tape recorder, or both) and 5" × 7" cards. Another area of shelves should be reserved for correspondence to publishers. The basic rule here is—design your work space for the tasks to come.

Only you can arrange your work space. Ideally it should be impregnable to the assaults of others' demands. You can't let anyone else arrange it because the arranging is part of your artistry, part of your style. Your goal is to have "a world within the reach of your fingers" surrounding the place of creation.

People are often unaware of the unconscious choices they make about work space. Conscious knowledge of your preferences allows you to control your productivity. Years ago I realized that I'm much more productive when my desk is facing a wall rather than the middle of a room. I remembered that my childhood desk faced a wall, and it was cozy and a good place to work. I immediately adapted my desks to the way I feel best when working.

You need to give yourself the best possible conditions in which to create. Try to cut down on distractions or frustrations. One of the best ways to do this is to have your writing and research materials, manuscripts, and marketing data near at hand and organized. That way, you won't spend hours looking for an idea jotted on a yellow card or a letter from a certain editor. All North American Monarch butterflies winter in a twenty-acre plot north of Mexico City. The butterflies understand the relationship between habitat and productivity.

The choice of the materials you use should be precisely related to your personal style. If you write best with green ink, don't just chuckle about it, bring in an endless vat of green ink. If you compose best on narrow-lined paper, or with a carbon ribbon, make sure you're always supplied with these. Nothing is more sacred to a craftsman than his equipment, and no one can tell you which are best for you. The best are those you feel most comfortable with, the ones that will make you productive once you've applied good time-management techniques to their use.

Many writers feel the need for physical continuity during the first draft. Eugene O'Neill favored a ledger for the drafts of *Strange Interlude*. In ancient times, scrolls were used, the ultimate in continuity. Word processors bring us to another plateau of continuity and flexibility. In choosing your materials you need to find out exactly what makes you comfortable. But remember that knowing why particular materials make you comfortable isn't nearly as important as the discovery *that* they do.

A good filing system can mean the difference between effective use of creative time and inefficiency, between productive insanity and destructive chaos. Devise a filing system that is suited to the way your mind works, and to the type of writing you do. Good files are an essential part of a wholesome habitat.

There are two filing basics:

1. an upright steel filing cabinet with sliding drawers to accommodate 9″ × 12″ manila file folders;
2. and a metal card-index holder which can be placed on the desk for instant reference.

Divide the filing cabinet into the following sections:

- *Works in progress.* Keep one folder for each piece of writing or story in progress. File all ideas, clippings, or thoughts that occur to you. Go through the folder periodically and reorganize the contents until gestation is completed. This is the formative stage that precedes the card system described in chapter 4. Acquire the habit of noting the source of all ideas. It's much easier to record such information as you go along than to reconstruct it later.
- *Ideas for possible future writings.* Since the creative mind moves from idea to idea, and from project to project, the writer must be prepared to catch all the thoughts which tumble from the islands. While concentrating on one project, the mind often suggests an idea for a totally unrelated project. The folder system is a practical way of collecting such ideas on cards because it embodies the "freedom" of the mind itself. As ideas crystallize, jot

them on separate cards or pieces of paper and drop them into the appropriate folder. Projects will eventually cross-breed, one leading to another, even though they may be in different media and designed for different audiences. This type of organization utilizes the writer's creative energies in a way that's natural to their development.

• *Finished manuscripts.* In a designated drawer, file a Xerox copy of the finished work, note the date and place sent for each submission, date received back, rejection letter, and further note (if any). Each manuscript's folder includes pretyped labels for the next submission, and no time will be lost in sending it out again. This method also keeps your motivation intact. Typing up a new label right after receiving a rejection is depressing and can paralyze you into not submitting.

• *Retired manuscripts.* This is a section for unpublished manuscripts that have been submitted and are, for the moment, "retired." In Hollywood this section is known as the writer's "trunk." We also call it your "library."

• *Accepted manuscripts.* Here you store manuscripts that have been accepted and are awaiting publication.

• *Published manuscripts.* Your archives or "dead" file. Many writers throw these away.

Divide your desk-top card file into the following sections:

• *Magazines* you like (and / or magazines likely to buy your type of writing), including name of editor, address, and phone number for queries. Read *Publishers Weekly* regularly, and update your cards when you see that editors have changed positions.

• *Publishing houses* most likely to accept your type of writing together with appropriate editor (for books).

• *Manuscripts ready for submission.* Keep a card for each, listing title, where and when sent, date returned, where to send next, and so on. As leads occur to you for a partic-

ular project, jot them down on the card; when the project returns, you've done your marketing in advance.
- *Manuscripts sold.* Keep track of how much money you received for each manuscript and on what terms. You may exaggerate payments and advances (in either direction) to your friends, but *you* at least should know accurately how much you've been paid for your writing.

As your career advances, you might change from the card file to a drawer in which you file correspondence with particular publishers, agents, and editors. Since editors do change jobs frequently, it's a good idea to duplicate their correspondence with you and file it both under their names and under the publishers for whom they work.

Another file might contain all correspondence dealing with a single book or project.

The Network and the Author-Editor-Publisher-Audience Circle

Yes, there is a network, and yes there is a "blacklist" (the blacklist is also known as "memory"). It's much harder to publish your first work than it is to publish your second; the second is also very hard, but after that it gets progressively easier. Your career will snowball, as careers do in every business and in every professional field. The beginning of any relationship, because of the principles of First Time, is always the most difficult.

Since the industry relies as much on connections as on talent and ideas, begin developing your own network of contacts. Allocate a time period each working day to advance your publishing career (time aside from writing time, but only a fraction of writing time—e.g., if you spend two hours per day writing, allocate 15 minutes to doing something about your publishing career: That 15 minutes per day, over 200 working days in a year, becomes 50 hours per year!). Start a file of the most influential people you know, and, from time to time, send your published work with a note. Making these people aware of you is the first step, and it needn't be tied directly to a formal submission. Common sense might also dictate asking advice, on occasion, from a member or members of your network about what distinguishes manuscripts that are accepted by publishers from the unacceptable—without asking them to publish your work. It's relatively easy for an editor to help a writer with advice; few editors, once you've made initial contact, fail to respond to such a request posed reasonably and courteously. Not a demand—a polite request.

Two secrets about the network ought to cheer you considerably:

1. It's more difficult to get out of it than it is to get in in the first place. Publishers and editors are still asking J. D. Salinger for manuscripts, decades after his last book and announcement that he's no longer writing. They don't believe him. The network won't let go.

2. The line between being in the network and being outside is not really like that heavy, dark tar line running down the middle of a hot summer highway. Believe it or not, the publishing industry is actively looking for writers of promise. The William Morris Agency sends computer form letters to anonymous professors in English departments, asking them to recommend promising students. If William Morris does this, gaining access to the world of publishing isn't impossible. Of course, there's a way to go between the contact and having the manuscript accepted. If you know someone in the publishing world, you already have a bridge to the network. It's up to you to cross the bridge, professionally and with determination.

The circle on page 135 describes the continuing relationship among the four principals involved in publishing. Notice that the two closest to the audience are the author and the publisher. Publishers who aren't close to the audience aren't publishers for long. When they talk about what their audiences like or want or need, they deserve the author's attention.

The author-publisher relationship is more intimate and

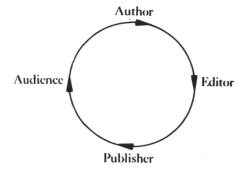

personal than most business relationships because the product involved is the writer's self-expression. Most problems in the relationship stem directly from this characteristic. Resentment is the most common problem. Writers can write what they want, but the publisher must put out a book that will sell. The choice to publish any work means taking a public, financial risk. Publishers have to be businessmen, gamblers, and people of culture—and the best publishers combine the successful qualities of all. Because of the risk publishers take, writers owe them at least the sincere attempt to understand their viewpoint. Just as writers resent publishers who don't see the value of their work, publishers resent writers who don't appreciate their problems, even though they may respect the same writers for standing behind their beliefs. The publisher is also acting on belief, and deserves recognition from the writer for that.

Some writers are so eager to have their work in print that they consent to any revision or rewriting of their material. Others would prefer to remain unpublished rather than allow the publisher to alter their manuscripts. Professional and long-lasting relationships dictate that the writer consider a position somewhere between these extremes.

Obviously publishers and writers are interdependent; one can't exist without the other. The best relationship is one of mutual respect, and the best way to build that relationship is through professionalism and communication on both sides.

The editor acts as an intermediary between the writer and the publisher, between creativity and its markets. The editor's function is to put a marketable product into circulation by intervening between the writer and the publisher.

Editors are either in-house or free-lance; both kinds help the writer by giving professional and impartial assistance to the manuscript, all the while respecting the vision the writer is or is not conveying. An editor tells the writer what might not be acceptable to publishers or the writer's audience, or when to pursue an idea with more vigor. An editor tells a writer when to stop writing and points out, if the writer is too close to the subject matter, what the manuscript is "really about." He or she tells the writer what to cut, and, if necessary, shows how to cut the manuscript. An editor can also give the writer help with the mechanics of writing, from spelling to syntax; and points out awkward sentence structure, phrasing, or organization of ideas. And an editor can help the writer with the proper physical format.

Good editors are frank and objective; they support first, criticize second, mingling praise with constructive criticism because they care about writers. If you're lucky enough to find an editor who is both honest with you and gentle, you're very lucky indeed. Don't submit your work unless you've prepared yourself to listen to what an editor says. Only the novice regards every written word as sacred. Professional writers know that the revisionary process is an integral part of writing, and welcome help with it. When the editor criticizes, even though it hurts, let the hurt work itself out on a racquetball court or by jogging or in a weightroom until you've learned through practice to overcome it. Anger is the least productive response to honest criticism.

As mentioned earlier, you can't use family, friends, or lovers (except in extraordinary relationships) as editors. You don't really want these people to be completely honest with you, and they certainly don't want to be. When you give them something to read, you want them to support you. "Please tell me how much you like this"—not "Tell me what you think."

In-house editors serve both the writer and the publisher. Their functions may range from acceptance and rejection to manuscript editing and creative development. For the publisher, the editor's duties include design, marketing, and production of the accepted manuscript. Once a project is deemed worthwhile, the editor's responsibility is to make it ready for the public.

Free-lance editors generally work with writers before the manuscript goes to a publishing house, bringing it to the point of readiness for submission. To find a free-lance editor, consult *Literary Market Place (LMP)*, make a choice, and write to that person. Explain your project and ask the fee for dealing with it. Most free-lancers will want to read the manuscript and give an initial report of what needs to be done before financial arrangements are undertaken. The general range of reasonable fees is published each year in *The Writer's Market*, but fees vary greatly from city to city. Keep in mind that editorial work on manuscripts of a technical nature costs more.

Marketing Your Work: Resumés, Market Study, Queries, and Manuscripts

You'll save yourself headaches and heartaches when submitting materials for publication if you present them—and yourself—professionally and authoritatively. If you have formed an image of yourself as a writer with great potential, you need to communicate that image to the publisher.

It's a good idea to put pertinent information about yourself in your query letter. But many agents and editors prefer a brief resumé listing your background, education, and previous publications. A sample is on the following page. The editor with information about you at a glance approaches the manuscript with a more positive mindset. Subtlety, not blatancy, is the key: Less is more.

Before submitting your manuscript, research your market thoroughly by consulting *The Writer's Market, Writer's Guide to Publishing in the West, Literary Market Place (LMP)*, and

Carmen Cramer
545 Estrada de los Abogados
Glendale, California 91205

Education:

California Institute of the Arts	1994
University of California, Santa Cruz	
BA in Literature/Creative Writing	1992
Instituto Internacional, Madrid, Spain	1990
University of Southern California	1987

Work Experience:

The Rangefinder Publishing Co.	Editorial Director
Photo Lab Management Magazine	7/94 to present
Santa Monica, California	Contributing Editor
	10/92 to 7/94
	Staff Writer
	11/89 to 10/92

The Guide to Bay Area Book Publishers	Associate Editor
San Francisco, California	9/88 to 10/89
	Dance Reviewer
	8/87 to 9/88

Publications:

"Untimely Headaches: Managing Your Time," Feature-length article, *Photo Lab Management*, September 1994.

"Shooting Stars," Feature-length article, *The Rangefinder*, December 1993.
"Supervisor's Notebook," Three-part article, *Photo Lab Management*, 1992:
    "Communication Techniques: Overview"
    "Communication: What's It All About?"
    "Communication Techniques: Problem Solving"

"Baryshnikov's Footnotes," two-part feature, *The San Francisco Ballet Magazine*, 1989.

other industry directories. You may also wish to browse in bookstores to see who publishes your kind of book. Of the most appropriate publishers for your particular work, select the ones you find most attractive (wouldn't you really rather be published by the most prestigious publishing house that prints your kind of book?), and make a list of them in order of priority.

Write down the name and address of the editor most likely to be right for your work, and submit directly to that person. Never address an article or manuscript simply to "The Editor." The telephone can be useful in marketing. Call a publishing house and ask for the name of the editor who would be right for your work. Then send the piece directly to that editor.

Don't forget that publishers are interested only in your public voice. The publisher doesn't want to know about your secret relationship with your gerbils, and how that relationship might deteriorate if your work is rejected. Your letters to editors should be businesslike and direct, with no unnecessary references to your private life.

> Your address
> Phone number
> Date

Kay Russell
Editor
Smothers Books (Address)

Dear Ms. Russell:

Enclosed for your consideration is an outline, character synopsis, and sample pages from my Gothic romance, *Passion's Strong Heart*. The story shows how Martha Aguillard, a Cajun rock singer, gives up a life of glamour when she finds the man who makes her dreams come true. The setting is New Orleans, where I spent six years as military attaché to the French consul.

I look forward to hearing your decision. Thank you for your consideration.

Sincerely,

The editor who becomes interested in your public voice and establishes a professional relationship with you might, of course, become interested in your private language and life. But the gerbils come later. First, show publishers what you can say to their audience. "Don't tell them what they don't need or want to know" is a principle of business. Don't mention that this is your first novel.

Once you've made contact with an editor you have another possible bridge to the industry—a member of your personal network. Keep in touch with that editor. Since editors change positions and companies frequently, it's a good idea to check periodically with *Publishers Weekly* and *The Writer* for information about these changes. Use these resources to update your card file.

Book fairs and conventions are a good place to meet editors. They attend conventions precisely for that purpose, giving writers the opportunity to make queries and submit proposals. Both parties also have a chance to size each other up.

Go through all your proposed projects and, without discarding any, rearrange them in order of marketing potential. Then send out the most marketable projects first. If you're successful, the other ones will find their place in due time. In making decisions about a project's marketability, follow the book or book review sections of the largest newspaper in your area to keep abreast of trends and response. Subscribe to *The New York Times Book Review*. Read the trade publications. Leaf through a variety of magazines to see what kinds of articles are used in each. There's no excuse for sending an article to a publisher who'd never use your kind of article—yet something like 90 percent of all submissions are exactly of that nature. Think of the advantage you have if you've done your "homework."

Based on what you know and can learn of a publisher's reputation, send your piece to the best place first. The rule here is never allow yourself to think that your work isn't good enough for a major publisher—if it isn't good enough for one publishing house, how can it be good enough for any? But don't depend solely on the large commercial publishers. They're the toughest to break into. You can build your self-confidence and your credits by submitting to the smaller publishers, including local newspapers, and the publishers and magazines listed in Len Fulton's *The International Directory of Little Magazines and Small Presses.*

The Publish-It-Yourself Handbook by Bill Henderson recounts the experiences of famous writers like Edgar Allan Poe, Stephen Crane, Upton Sinclair, Zane Grey, James Joyce, Carl Sandburg, and Ezra Pound, who were published initially by small presses—or who published their own works—because the major publishers weren't initially interested in them. Small presses today are practically the only market for poetry and short stories by unpublished writers.

There is a marketing method that puts the advantage on your side, allowing you to determine interest in your project without waiting through the prolonged consideration period that follows submission of the entire manuscript. The query letter developed as a result of the writer's frustration at not being able to make multiple submissions and at having to wait sometimes as long as a year for an answer from a publisher.

Queries are useful for marketing novels, nonfiction books, or articles for magazines. They aren't generally used for short stories or poems or other short pieces.

You may send out a query when your project is completed, when it is still in progress, and when it is only in the early stages of conception and planning. In each case, the nature of the query and the query process are somewhat different. For the sake of illustration, we'll assume that the query is being sent out while the piece is in progress.

Before you write your query, make sure you've thought carefully about your own psychology and how it might be affected by the query process. Not surprisingly, writers react quite differently to responses to their queries. Here is the spectrum of possibilities for a query about a project you have not yet completed:

- You send out 20 queries and receive 12 positive responses: You are delighted, quickly complete the project, and submit it to your first choice among the responders.
- You send out 20 queries and receive 12 positive responses: Depending on your vulnerability, you are horrified and immediately cease all work on the project (at least 50 percent of writers react this way).
- You send out 20 queries and receive 12 positive responses: You are puzzled by the apparent contradictions and waste six months trying to find out if you're encouraged or discouraged by it (or trying to figure out something else about the response).
- You send out 20 queries and receive 4 positive responses: You are delighted, and so on.
- You send out 20 queries and receive 4 positive responses: You are horrified, and so on.
- You send out 20 queries and receive 4 positive responses: You are confused, and so on.

I leave it to you to imagine the remaining possibilities. But if you don't stop to figure out how you're likely to respond to a given scenario, you're ill-advised to query at all. The query is your tool, and should not turn on its maker; yet I've seen many projects derailed by premature marketing, or queries sent out before the sender decided how he or she might respond to the responses.

At AEI we refer to a "pilot" or "initial" query, a one-page summary of the work aimed to hook the editor to ask for more. Although this falls under the category of a "query letter," in our opinion this summary need not be accompanied by a letter at all—simply send the page itself (with your return address at the top or bottom), without personalizing it for the editor's sake. Your envelope, of course, will carry the name of the editor you think would be most interested. You might put some boxes at the bottom of your page:

☐ Yes—send outline and sample chapters.
☐ Send complete manuscript.
☐ Sorry, not for us.

If there is real interest, the publisher will probably jot a hand-written comment, so leave a little space for one. This initial query expedites copying and mass mailing.

The rule in writing the query letter is "less is better." The one-page approach is typical of all successful management, from advertising to investments. The clearer an idea, the more likely it can be stated briefly, and the greater the chance of arousing the editor's curiosity. Think of the query as a piece of prime-time advertising to the best possible audience: the editor who has the power to publish your work.

The editor's question in reading the query is, "Can we sell this?"—and the more your query does to answer that question positively, the better chance you have of eliciting interest. Aside from the Sentence—your brief description of the manuscript and its theme—the most important section of every query concerns the possible readership.

The approach to the audience can be general or specific, depending on the nature of your manuscript or article. If you make a good case for audience, the editor need only verify your case. If you don't, the editor must try to make the case for you, and your chances of getting the publisher's attention are thereby lessened.

The general approach to audience means identifying your readership in terms of conventional editorial and publishing. People need love. People fear death. People who read *Sunset* magazine like articles about activities that require sunny days. Depending on your project, a number of assumptions might identify an audience: "Anyone who has ever wondered what goes on behind the scenes in the world of contemporary music will find this insider's report unforgettable." (Be sure to tell the editor what gives you the stance of an insider.) In this query for a nonfiction book about the great composers, conductors, and performers of twentieth-century music, the general audience approach appeals to reader curiosity and the desire to live vicariously. That audience is interested in knowing what the great artists are like as real people. They want to know how the music world works—what makes it tick—the same way Arthur Hailey's fiction readers want information about airports, hotels, and hospitals. Your query reminds the editor that such an audience exists.

The specific approach to audience is based on data that can be verified by the publisher's marketing department. For example, let's say you've written a guide to organizing a church choir—on the face of it, perhaps not an exciting possibility for the publisher. In your query, however, you provide the editor of a publishing company that specializes in religious books with three pieces of data: (1) No such guide now exists, (2) 226,800 church choirs exist in the U.S. alone, and (3) they can all be reached through the *Church Choir Newsletter*, which sells a full-page ad for $25 a month. Now you've presented financially impressive data about a specific audience. Of course, the situation varies from project to project. But you can apply similar data to your project.

Competition in the marketplace, handled skillfully in the query, can be a plus, whether or not competition exists. If there is a great deal of competition for your project, you turn that into a plus by pointing out the success of other books of this kind, mentioning title, author, publisher, dates of publication, and sales if you know them. You'll need to show how your book takes a different approach that will make it stand out from the competition. In other words, you always begin a sales situation by turning negatives into positives. If no competition exists, you turn that situation into a plus by emphasizing the need for this kind of book or article. Be specific about the need; otherwise you elicit the cynical response that the book doesn't exist because nobody wants it.

Should you mention the length of the work and whether or not the work is completed? Though some editors prefer that you do, there's no need to state those matters unless you find a way to state them positively. The keynote of the query, with regard to length and format, is flexibility; many editors like to take a hand in shaping a piece of writing for their specific audiences.

For query letters about a volume of poetry there are exceptional guidelines. Summaries don't help editors to understand the marketability of your poetry. They prefer to know your track record, the number of your poems in collection, where you've studied, whether you've won any awards or fellowships, and the workshops you've attended.

Once your query is written, refer to the list of possible markets for this project compiled earlier, including the names of the editors most likely to be interested. To find editors for nonfiction books, look at some recently published books that are similar to your project, and examine the acknowledgments page, where the author may have mentioned the editor's name, along with a few words of thanks. Address envelopes for all the publishers you're considering, enclose the query and a self-addressed stamped envelope (so you'll receive responses from the No's as well as the Yes's), and mail them out on the same day. Then make up a chart like the one below:

Name of Project: *The Gods of Music*

Query sent to	on	Response Rec'd
Norton	2/3/94	
Simon & Schuster	"	
Random House	"	
Viking	"	
Doubleday	"	
Crown	"	
etc.		

As the chart demonstrates, your next step is to wait for the majority of responses. Three weeks is a good waiting time; by then, you'll have received the bulk of the Yes's and Maybe's.

When your waiting deadline has arrived, put the responses in order of your own preference. In addition to the prestige of the publishing house, you should be alert to the element of sincerity in the publisher's response. Then send the manuscript, article, or samples to your first choice with a letter something like this:

Your address
Phone number
Date

Ms. Karla Olson
W. W. Norton & Company
(Address)

Dear Ms. Olson:

Thank you for your positive response to my query regarding the novel, *Too Far from The Occident.* I'm happy to say that I received a similar response from other publishers—Simon & Schuster, Houghton Mifflin, Delacorte, and Doubleday. Based on your response and on my study of your latest catalogue, I'm making my first submission to Norton.

I appreciate your consideration.

Sincerely,

While waiting for responses to your query letter, you should be preparing polished manuscript samples for submission. Since articles involve less time in writing or planning, wait until you've received a Yes response before writing the article. For nonfiction manuscripts, you'll need to send sample chapters, whole books if complete. For fiction, send the first 50 pages. Most fiction editors will ask for more if impressed by the first 50 pages. This may startle writers who think plot is most important, but fiction editors look at the voice in which the story is told and the movement of the action. If the first 50 pages don't grab them, it's unlikely that the rest will.

Prepare three or four submission packets at a time. Expect many rejections, plan on them in advance so they won't take you off guard. Each packet should contain your cover letter, outline of the project, your credits, and your self-addressed stamped envelope (SASE) along with the envelope prepared to go out to the publisher. When a piece comes back, slip it into the next packet before you even look at the reject slip. Don't miss taking advantage of time's work for you: If you have to become depressed over each rejection, at least become depressed after you've mailed out the piece again.

What the editor sees when opening your envelope (if it's an article) or box (if it's a book) undeniably forms a first impression. As the editor begins reading, the impression continues—for good or bad. It's not surprising that the University of Chicago's *Manual of Style* states that a professionally prepared manuscript has a much better chance of being given a serious reading. If your manuscript is sloppy, that sends a subliminal message (which, in the case of most editors, isn't subliminal at all) about you.

Editors frequently return manuscripts unread simply because they can see at a glance that it would take too much time and work to get it into publishable shape. Many are returned unread because they are obviously the product of someone who hasn't even bothered to find out what professional manuscripts look like. All the information you need for proper manuscript preparation can be found in *The Writer's Market* or *The Chicago Manual of Style*. The more your manuscript looks like a finished product the easier the editor's envisioning process. The editor's job, after all, is to ask: "Can I see this article or book in print?" The answer to this question will be easier if the mechanics of your work are virtually letter-perfect.

The only acceptable color for paper is white, just as the only acceptable ink is black. The paper should be 8½″ × 11″. Don't exercise originality when it comes to these basics: They are the traditional medium for professional communication. Paper should be opaque bond paper, of any brand or weight with the exception of two unprofessional types: onion skin (which you can see through, and which is too flimsy for processing) and any erasable bond (the chemical surface of which is impossible to process, because it neither takes nor receives ink in a permanent way—not to mention what it does to the hands of the editor who reads it). Manuscripts may be sent either loose in boxes or bound.

Double-space your text and leave generous margins. Use a legible printing ribbon and use a letter-quality printer if you're using a word processor. If you're using a word processor, don't justify the right margin. Do not use an italic or cursive typewriter for manuscripts.

Proofread your manuscript carefully. Consult a dictionary if you haven't been diligent through the revision process. Look at the obvious things, such as page-by-page headers and page numbers and chapter headings. Make sure the text pages are consecutive. *The Chicago Manual of Style* tells exactly how to correct mistakes on your manuscript with professional proofreading marks. A few errors so marked per page indicate your knowledge of the industry's usage; more than one or two demonstrates laziness or lack of pride.

The screenplay has a form of its own, and it's best to study a professional screenplay and follow its format. Books by Syd Field and Ben Brady (see bibliography) give samples of screenplay pages as well as excellent introductions to writing drama. The feature or television film screenplay runs from 100 to 120 pages in length, and is bound in a paper or cardboard cover.

Unlike other works, the screenplay should always be protected by registration with the Writers' Guild of America. The registration number appears on the title page of the screenplay.

When you send the manuscript to the publisher, enclose your printed credits, if you have them, and a brief cover letter referring to your earlier correspondence to and from them;

enclose return postage and specify how you would like the manuscript returned; enclose a return postcard to let you know the manuscript arrived safely; and enclose a self-addressed return envelope in the case of shorter pieces (in the case of book manuscripts, the postage is sufficient).

Since undeclared multiple submissions are considered unethical in the industry, send your work to only one publisher at a time. Nowadays it's generally acceptable to submit Xeroxes; but, if a relationship doesn't already exist between you and the editor to whom you're submitting, state that your Xeroxed submission is "not submitted elsewhere" to show that you're not engaging in multiple submission. If a piece is accepted, the original may be requested by the publisher.

If you haven't heard from the publisher after the normal two months for consideration, phone or write asking politely about the status of your manuscript. If a publisher keeps your manuscript beyond all reasonable expectation—say, for example, four months—without responding to your inquiries, simply write a letter to say that you're withdrawing the manuscript from consideration, and submit it to another publisher.

All these activities, of course, are ones you accomplish during your regular, disciplined "publishing time," that fraction of your writing time devoted to pursuing the publishing side of your career.

Rejection

If you can't stand—or can't learn to stand—the idea that your work may be rejected, you should give up the dream of writing. Becoming professional means learning to deal with rejection with dignity and determination. Besides, rejection slips aren't so bad. Over the years, as I've listened to writers complain about them, I've come to realize that we surely prefer them to at least one alternative:

A dark Lincoln limousine pulls up in front of your house in the morning. Your hair is still in curlers as a woman in a severe tweed suit walks up the driveway with a leather attaché case under her arm. "Hello, Jan Matthews," she says, handing you an envelope. "My name is Ashburton Mary Calhoun, senior editor of Pachyderm Books. I wanted to return your manuscript in person to tell you we thought it was awful." She tips her hat. "Have a nice day."

The reject slip is the industry's alternative to blatant callousness; it's not worth brooding over. Brood over a personal visit from Calhoun, but until that happens keep up your momentum.

Fear of rejection is inevitable for writers, since writing involves an extension of the self. The ability to keep moving forward despite rejection distinguishes professionals from amateurs. Rejections can even become a badge of success. All successful writers have amassed a hill of them. The goal is to control the rejection slips rather than be controlled by them. Some people do this by burning them; others do it by using them to paper the bathroom wall. A famous composer is said to have written this letter: "I am sitting in the smallest room in my house. Your criticism is in front of me. Soon it will be behind me."

When an article or manuscript is returned to your mailbox, you already have your "linkage." Before even looking at the rejection notice, take the manuscript out of the return envelope and slip it into the addressed envelope for the next submission. Put that in the mail and only then, if you must, read your rejection slip. Record it on a submission list so that you don't resubmit the same version of a manuscript to an uninterested publisher a second time. Some publishers send a rejection letter first class mail and return the manuscript separately by fourth class to lessen the blow. Above all, don't let your response to the rejection delay getting the manuscript in circulation again. It's not going to get published if it sits around the house.

Rejection slips vary widely. A careful study of them can lead to building bridges with editors. A personal signature can mean more than a completely printed form. But the general rule among editors and publishers (who read countless manuscripts) is not to say more than their time allows. An editor is usually not interested in being addressed personally by a writer unless the editor has included specific comments about how to improve your manuscript with the response. One way of addressing the editor—building the bridge—is to write back asking why your piece was rejected, including a copy of the editor's letter when you do so. Most editors, if you read their rejection letters correctly and query them courteously, will take the time to answer such a question.

Many editors will distinguish between their rejection letters as follows:

1. Lowest level—a printed form—generally sent if the writer hasn't addressed a particular editor.
2. A note with a personal signature—it may still "sound" like a form letter. Polite but no particulars.
3. A note as above, but with particular details about rejection, brief suggestions about needed revisions, and an invitation to see further work.

When they have any interest in your work, they will say so, as in a #3 response. If they send you a #2 response, you may conclude that they found too many things wrong with the concept or execution of your story or manuscript to allow them time to respond in more detail.

The less work needed to make a manuscript publishable, the better the response from a publisher. If you have received less than a #3 response from an editor or publisher, it's improbable that asking an editor why your manuscript was rejected will build a bridge to the publishing industry for your personal network. If the editor didn't find it practical to analyze the shortcomings of your manuscript in the first place, you'll only put her on the spot by asking her a second time. Editors don't want to be hurtful, and the kind of letter they have to formulate to avoid deepening a writer's rejection wound is also too time consuming. One publisher relates:

"I recently had a three page single-spaced letter from a writer reviewing the history of another writer's lack of success in publishing a book and, by implication, trying to get back at me for rejecting it. Did I understand genius and the writer's frustration? The writer also wanted to take me to lunch to discuss the book in detail—it was some 800 pages."

Any personal correspondence from an editor is worth a follow-up on your part. But be cautious about how you interpret their language, and don't be discouraged!

Publishers and editors suggest the following guidelines for interpreting and responding to their comments:

1. Consider any editorial suggestions seriously, though you may feel bruised at first. Upon consideration, do they make sense? How could you rectify what's wrong? Get your islands working again.
2. Has the editor misunderstood what you're attempting to say? How could you make it clearer?
3. If so, only if clarification (and suggestions for change) might change editorial opinion, write an explanatory letter. But don't do so as a means of self-justification against the establishment.

Some editors may use the phrase "We can't use it right now" merely to soften the letdown. Editors are often grieved when writers leap on any gentle phrase as encouragement. Before saying no, editors usually try to find something positive to say, even "We can't use it *right now*," and many writers take the words as literal truth. However, some editors may mean the phrase literally, so if an editor writes, "We can't use it right now," write back and ask, "When can you use it?" If it's not clear what the editor means, it's the editor's fault. If you receive encouragement from an editor, ask "If I changed the ending would you be interested in seeing it again?" If you plan to resubmit your revised manuscript to an editor, query first with a copy of the original rejection letter. Then be sure to note that the manuscript is a revision of a previously submitted one.

It's not uncommon for a writer to have 36 rejections and then be accepted—or 50 rejections in the U.S., and finally be published in England. Be patient. Suspense novelist Elmore Leonard's *The Big Bounce* was rejected 84 times before it was sold as a Gold Medal Original, with Warner Brothers making the film. Larry Kasdan's first script sold after 64 submissions. Make a chart of submissions and fill in the blanks without thinking about it. Note any constructive feedback and suggested revisions. Modify your submission list if the comments or lack of response in an area you thought might be most marketable for your work indicate the contrary. Unless a half-dozen editors make the same criticism of your work, plan to send it out at least 30 times before you begin major revisions that require withdrawing it from your active file. Frank Herbert's *Dune* was rejected by some 20 publishers.

Agents, Literary Managers, Contracts, Self-Publishing, and Legal Issues

The first step in finding an agent is to write something that will interest the agent. The writing must be good or the subject important before any agent will represent you. But, basically, you find an agent exactly as you find a publisher:

1. Write a one-page query, making clear what your book is about in one or two sentences. Be professional.
2. Write a five- to ten-page synopsis, outlining your book chapter by chapter or event by event. Some editors don't like synopses with novels, but almost every agent and many editors will request one.
3. Book titles should be clear and immediately intriguing but generally not based on catchy phrases or puns. A book may go through several title changes before its final title is established.

4. If you have significant publishing credits, cover your publishing background in your letter. (If you don't, your letter should be brief.) Whatever you do, don't emphasize your lack of track record.

5. Send the query, synopsis, and letter with the first chapter of your book to an agent by name. A list of agents can be found in *An Insider's Guide to Editors, Publishers, and Literary Agents* as well as in *LMP (Literary Market Place)*.

6. You can send your presentation (query, synopsis, and letter) to as many agents as you like. Agents will understand that this is only a query that doesn't obligate either of you. Mail ten to fifteen presentations at a time, as you can afford it.

7. Plan several mailings in advance in order to avoid rejection syndrome. If an agent expresses interest, call the agent and ask how this particular agent can help you.

"What's a good agent?" is a difficult question to answer. Agents work strictly on commission and are, as a result, mainly interested in highly commercial "properties." Agents often help new writers, but most deal only with writers they regard as solid commercial prospects or extraordinary literary talents. Most agents nowadays ask writers to query before sending the manuscript. This doesn't mean they won't read your work; it means they don't want to read subject matter that doesn't fit in with their own marketing. Since they work on speculation and commission, they have to deal with several (or many) writers at a time, and are more inclined to devote their energies to promoting a potential best-seller. They're usually interested in working with an author who produces continuously. Someone who writes two short stories a year may not be worth taking on. Agents may urge new writers to handle their own submissions of short stories. And agents may or may not help you sell articles.

Some reputable agents now charge reading fees, deductible from future commission. Agents receive a commission on everything they sell, ranging from 10 to 15 percent, and will nearly always negotiate a contract that will more than justify their commission.

A literary manager performs the same marketing functions as an agent, but also serves as a producer when your book is filmed.

Other tips about agents or managers:

- Where the agent or manager lives is not important. How often the agent goes to New York, and how many New York publishers the agent deals with, *are* important. It's difficult to be an effective agent without regular personal contact with New York publishers.
- Independent agents may be more open to new clients than large agencies, and may work harder for them.
- Don't be afraid to ask an agent for credentials and track record. The best criteria for choosing an agent are the agent's previous sales. If an agent won't send you a list of clients, don't deal with that agent.
- Your work is automatically copyrighted under the law of 1979, so you shouldn't worry too much about your work's security unless your work is of obvious high financial value (for example, a book that reveals the culprit in last year's most famous crime, or a book that shows you a valid way to make a million overnight). In general, if you're worried about a particular agent or publisher, you shouldn't approach that person or company in the first place.
- If an agent asks for a written contract, check with an attorney before you sign it.
- Agents are always happy to see material with film or television potential. If your material has possible adaptation for television or film, emphasize that in your query.

If you decide to let an agent represent you, it's a good idea to trust your agent with the marketing for six months. Then ask how it's going. An agent's knowledge of market can be invaluable. But keep in mind that if you have a good book, getting an agent won't be difficult and you won't need an agent to work miracles.

Many new writers are published for the first time through their own marketing efforts, not through an agent's. Finding someone who believes in your work as much as you do—enough to go out there and sell it—is rare indeed.

Many writers swear by their agents.

Many swear only at them.

Few agree about them.

If you don't feel the need for someone to stand between you and the publisher, you don't need an agent or manager. If you decide to use an attorney, make sure the attorney has had direct experience with publishing contracts. A literary attorney can negotiate the contract for you as well as an agent.

One way of getting an agent is to make the sale yourself, then call the agent to represent you in the contract negotiation. Few agents will turn down this opportunity, and you've automatically become "represented." Agents or literary managers are especially useful for working out package deals which include screenplays, TV scripts, and foreign rights. Large publishers often prefer to deal through agents (though many deal directly with the authors), and some publishers will deal only through agents. *The Writer's Market* (see bibliography) offers extended discussion of agents and rights.

Finally, one day, you'll receive a letter of acceptance from a publisher who wants to contract for your book. What do you do now? First, you celebrate. You deserve it! And it's better to celebrate now before you go any further. The next step, if the publisher has included a contract, is *not* to sign the contract and return it.

The next step is to read the contract carefully, make notes about your questions, and call the publisher to ask your questions. If the answers don't satisfy you, consult your attorney (if you have an agent, the offer will have been made to the agent). Don't be afraid to negotiate. Remember that the contract you receive is "boilerplate," meaning that nearly all writers dealing with that particular publisher receive the same contract. The publisher probably expects certain modifications. How much modifying you can do is a product of the situation and your skill—or your attorney's or agent's skill—in negotiating. But never fear that you'll lose a contract because you ask questions or engage in negotiation. If the publisher is interested enough in your work to send a contract, it's negotiable to some degree and the publisher will tell you clearly when you reach the point after which there can be no more negotiation.

Unfortunately, most writers do panic when they receive a first contract, a reaction that goes far to account for writers' paranoia about publishers. The contract spells out the rights and responsibilities of both parties—and if the one you receive doesn't, make sure that it does before you sign it. Generally the publisher obtains rights to the manuscript by agreeing to pay the writer royalties on each copy printed or sold in the edition he's responsible for producing. But variations are infinite. Here I'll spell out some general guidelines and suggest that, where common sense and careful reading fail, you consult an attorney or free-lance consultant who specializes in the field.

Generally the publisher assumes the responsibility for editing the book, designing and printing it, and distributing and accounting for it. Note that advertising isn't included in the list. Most books published in this country receive little or no advertising, and if that concerns you, the time to raise the question is before signing the contract.

The contract should state how and when the book will appear, and what recourse the author has if the book doesn't appear within the stipulated time. The usual arrangement for royalties is a sliding scale whereby royalties increase as copies sold increase. A typical royalty clause might read as follows:

ARTICLE—. Author's Royalties. The Publisher agrees to pay the Author or the Author's duly authorized representatives, after publishing the said work as set forth in ARTICLE—, the following royalties and other payments subject to the terms and conditions herein stated, which royalties and other payments will be accepted by the Author as full compensation for any and all rights, grants, and undertakings provided in this contract:

a. A royalty on all copies of the regular edition sold by the Publisher, less returns (and subject to the exceptions hereinafter named) as follows:

10% of the publisher's invoice list price on the first 5000 copies sold; 12½% on the next 5000 copies sold; and 15% on all copies sold thereafter.

In addition, the contract generally stipulates the author's deadline for submission of the completed manuscript, and often ties advance compensation to that deadline. Keep in mind that if an advance is given upon signing the contract, the deadline becomes somewhat less intimidating to the author. Most advances are in two or three parts; generally publishers tie the payment of advances to delivery of the manuscript. Partial advances are tied to the writer's progress in completing the manuscript. In general, the writer should receive at least one-third of the advance upon signing the contract, less up front if the existing submitted material is skimpy (an outline or a few sample chapters).

The contract should stipulate exactly what rights the publisher is purchasing and what financial provisions are made for compensating the author for each of those rights— from hardbound book, to paperbound book, first and second serialization, abridgment, anthologies, book-club sales, electronic rights, foreign rights, television, and motion-picture rights. Some contracts give the publisher an option on a future book by an author. Before signing, make sure the option stipulates a favorable time period for consideration of a new project, to make sure the publisher doesn't hold up the project indefinitely. The more you're published, the less you will want any kind of option deal on a future book until that book is under way and ready for its own specific contract.

Self-publishing and vanity publishing are different from other forms of publishing and are not to be confused with them. Vanity publishing is a pitfall to be avoided; self-publishing is an honorable tradition and testimony that writers believe enough in their own work to publish it themselves. Edward Fitzgerald's *Rubaiyat*, Thomas Paine's *Common Sense*, William Blake's poems and drawings, *Bartlett's Quotations*, D. H. Lawrence's *Lady Chatterley's Lover*, Mark Twain's *Huckleberry Finn*, and *Robert's Rules of Order* were all originally self-published; self-published writers also include Mary Baker Eddy, Percy Bysshe Shelley, Lord Byron, Edgar Allan Poe, Zane Grey, and Carl Sandburg. Bill Henderson's *The Publish-It-Yourself Handbook*, listed in the bibliography, is an excellent guide to self-publishing.

The best warning I know of against vanity presses is their own advertising and contracts. A vanity press is a subsidy press that operates unethically, though legally, by charging you two to three times more to print your book than you'd pay if you printed it yourself. Vanity presses operate by phoning or advertising for hopeful authors and promising to treat them better than commercial publishers treat them. Although they refer to themselves as "publishers," if you keep in mind that publishing means to "make public," they are not publishers but printers. Where they fall short is in distribution and marketing. Bookstores normally don't stock vanity-press books, nor do major book-review columns review them. If you succumb to vanity publishing, you have allowed your own vanity to take advantage of you.

Don't worry too much about "legalities," both in writing

and in publishing. Most of the time, for most writers, legal matters play a very small role in their lives and careers. With that preliminary, here are some things to keep in mind.

"Permissions" is the legal term for the act of getting permission from the copyright holder to include, in either whole or excerpted form, previously copyrighted material within your own work. Permissions can be expensive and troublesome, so if your work is heavily dependent on them—as anthologies are, for example—be prepared to deal with their cost and complications. It's a good marketing idea to find out in advance if and where permissions can be obtained because that's one of the first questions the publisher to whom you submit your work will want answered. The publisher will also want to know how much they cost, although publishers tend more and more to have the writer bear the cost of permissions (partly to discourage writers from overusing them). Quoted materials from people interviewed always require written permission.

When requesting permission from a copyright holder (usually a publisher), send that person or, in the publisher's case, the "Permissions Department" a letter similar to the following:

> Your return address
> Date

Dear Ms. McCormick:

I'm requesting permission, North American rights, to use an excerpt from Molly Bloom's soliloquy in James Joyce's *Ulysses* in my own nonfiction study entitled *Praise of Love*. A copy of the excerpt, and the title and copyright page of the book from which it was Xeroxed, is enclosed. I'm also enclosing a copy of the material as it occurs within my own typescript.

Sincerely yours,

If you don't send the copies and an indication of the way the material will be used, you'll be asked to do so by return mail. If you do, you'll generally receive a "form contract" with boxes checked, giving you permission:

1. free;
2. for a flat fee, as stipulated, though you can sometimes negotiate; or
3. for a percentage of your royalties as stipulated here (you can and should negotiate).

Once the negotiations are concluded and both parties have signed the permissions agreement (which isn't always a formal negotiation), the copyright holder will send you what's called the "permissions" or "credit line," to be printed in every copy of your work, generally, though not always, on the copyright page. The credit line must always be printed exactly as the copyright holder stipulates.

The laws today are both ambiguous and changing when . it comes to such matters as libel and defamation of character. In general, it's a good idea to proceed cautiously by following good research principles and making absolutely sure that, for every item of information you include in your nonfiction book and for every character or event in your novel, you can trace your source with precision. This will enable you or your publisher at any point in the process to ascertain the exact legal status of all questionable items. But in either case, the writer's best protection is preparation.

It's no longer true that lawsuits are directed only against publishers. Nowadays they're directed against anyone and everyone who might possibly provide money to the party suing. A libel suit must still prove malicious intent, so it isn't as great a risk as most unpublished writers think it is. The general rule here is accuracy and truthfulness. Public figures are in the public domain, but that doesn't mean you can say anything you want about them. You can say anything that's true and anything that's not damaging. But the rule is to be careful when you approach damaging statements, doubly cautious in ascertaining the accuracy of your sources.

You've got all you need to begin. Now it's up to you to harness time for your dreamwork. When married to your Managing Editor, Time will prove the most inspiring, most invigorating, and most enduring Muse you can imagine. Taking only one step a day for your publishing career adds up to roughly 200 steps a year—with weekends off. Sooner or later, the industry will admit you and you'll be part of the network that finds it harder to let go than to welcome. Until that moment of welcome arrives, your alliance for success will be your unswerving *belief* in your career, and the determination to make your dream of publishing come true.

SEVEN

Myth and Story

Writers need to connect with their dreams, that gateway to the unconscious where creativity is born in the mix between inherited myths and individual perspective. At the same time, the more writers learn about myth, the more they'll understand their writers' minds. Films, like novels, often go astray because writers lose sight of the "mythic deep structure," outlined as "the hero's story" in chapter 5 (p. 113). It can be liberating for the writer to recognize that as words are to story, so story is to myth. Story is the source of words, yet the words you use are in a sense arbitrary; you could tell the same story with a different set of words. Myth, not words, gives shape to story.

Therefore, agonizing endlessly over your choice of words isn't necessary. A good storyteller has words at his or her disposal because the storyteller's clear vision of the story's mythic shape unlocks what Beowulf called "the word-hoard." If the story is clear, the words will come. "Perhaps the secret to talking," writes Walker Percy in *The Second Coming*, "is having something to say."

A story, clarified, will cause the words needed for its telling. In the same fashion, myth is the source of story. The same myth causes—inspires and shapes—countless stories. Films like *Gone with the Wind* and *The Prince of Tides* may even "improve" on the story told by the successful novels they were "based on." When this happens it's because the filmmakers recognized the mythic shape beneath the novel and brought it into the sharper focus demanded by the dramatic form.

Examining the myth beneath your story ("mythic story analysis") will help you clarify your story. In the film *Indecent Proposal*, the story went astray because the "mythic deep structure" was lost sight of in the glow of the star system. Underlying the story is the Mephistopheles myth—Faust's "pact with the devil." In this myth, the hero longs for something he can't have (knowledge, power, money, sex); the devil comes to offer it to him in exchange for his soul. He accepts the bargain, and enjoys what he longed for until he realizes the enjoyment is hollow. The devil then comes to claim the bargainer's soul. In the final act, Faust either is redeemed and given a second chance (as in *Damn Yankees* and *The Devil and Daniel Webster*) or is taken, howling, down to hell (as in Goethe's *Faust*). Note that in either version the important catalyst is the antagonist's (the devil's) *consistency*. Faust may change his mind, and wish the deal undone; but the devil sticks to his guns.

In *Indecent Proposal* the Hollywood star system plays havoc with the story's mythic pedigree. As Robert Redford's persona (the dapper, wealthy John Gage) makes its impact on the emerging story, we end up finding Gage more engaging than his victims, Diana (Demi Moore) and David (Woody Harrelson). As the story proceeds, because Redford can't be "the bad guy," Gage becomes less and less satanic and more and more like the tragically romantic Jay Gatsby. The effectiveness of the process by which story is generated from myth depends upon the storyteller's ability to pinpoint, clarify, and transform our emotions by aligning the characters' motivations properly to evoke them. Halfway through *Indecent Proposal* we lose all patience with the histrionic David and the temperamental Diana. Instead we find ourselves rooting for Gage, the devil in this myth, to get what he wants; by the end of the film, the dramatic focus is on Gage's romantic sacrifice, which, by default, establishes him as the true hero of the story.

In American culture, our most private feelings about money are said to be as difficult for us to talk about openly and honestly as our feelings about sex. It was a brilliant choice on the part of the filmmakers (Adrian Lyne directed the film) to evoke the Faust myth in a time of recession, pinpointing sex and money as elements in an equation that stirs our unconscious anxieties and expectations. The brilliant choice of mythic material explains the film's healthy box office. People were willing to pay to deal with this myth. In troubled economic times, we couldn't resist a film that promised to explore the relationship between integrity and instant affluence (compare *The Fountainhead*). With lottery mania sweeping the nation, audiences were enthralled by the scene of David and Diana making love on the money they've won in Las Vegas.

But audiences left the film confused, disappointed, and feeling cheated. What we expected was one variation or other of the myth: *Devil tempts man and woman by promising to end their vulnerability. They accept the pact, and are destroyed by their own greed.* This version of the myth becomes a *cautionary tale,* allowing us to continue working hard at honest pursuits rather than sacrificing our integrity for "the quick buck." Or: *The devil tempts, etc. They accept, but when their joy turns to ashes in the devil's spell, the heroes find a way to break the spell and live happily ever after.* Here the myth allows us to feel the power of *redemption,* that life does offer second chances. Once we've escaped the devil, we'll know better than to sin again (one of my clients, a real estate woman, has a sign on her desk that says, "Please give me one more big commission and I promise not to piss it away.")

As it is, *Indecent Proposal's* "mythic deep structure" reads something like this: *Devil tempts man and woman by promising to end their vulnerability. They accept the pact, try to make their dreams come true with the money, realize the devil has prevented them from doing it, get confused; the heroine confronts the devil, who does lovely things for her; she finds herself falling for him; leaves her heroic com-*

panion in the lurch; he, meanwhile, isn't even enjoying their sudden affluence; she and the devil become "an item"; the hero makes a grandiose gesture with the entire windfall; the devil figures the hero is a good guy; the devil makes a romantic sacrifice that sends the heroine back to the hero; hero and heroine try to figure out what happened; and the devil, in a halo of nobility, rides alone into the sunset. This may work for the star, but it doesn't for the audience.

One of the simplest ways of checking your "mythic structure" is to ask yourself which ancient hero's quest your story most closely resembles. If it's a story of apparently endless obstacles testing the hero's endurance, your myth may be the myth of Hercules, the hero known for his "labors." Find a dictionary of mythology, like Pierre Grimal's *The Dictionary of Classical Mythology*, *The Oxford Classical Dictionary*, or *Funk & Wagnall's Standard Dictionary of Folklore, Mythology, and Legend*, and look up Hercules (Greek: Herakles). The shorter the entry, the better, because what you're looking for is a simplified overview. The shorter entry will give you the essentials in fewer words. The essentials tend to be, as Aristotle taught, *formal;* you'll discover in the dictionary entry the underlying structure of the myth. Seeing that structure clearly will allow you either to follow it in your retelling of the story or to depart from it knowingly in a clear-cut variation where you choose to revise the ancient myth. People have been revising myths, bringing them "closer to the heart's desire," from the beginning of storytelling. Since myth moves us primarily through the unconscious, it will shape your story one way or the other. You simply have more "creative control" if you know where you're starting from.

All stories seem essentially to be variations of the primal quest myth. That myth gives shape not only to entire stories; but also, each scene in a story can be clarified by recognizing that the following questions are applicable on both the microlevel of scene and the macro-level of plot:

Who's the hero?
What is the hero's problem?
What does the hero do about it?

The quest may be internal or external, psychological or military; the hero may be reluctant or audacious, inspired or possessed. He will almost always have an ally, who may or may not turn out to be a friend but is at least a confidant (allowing the hero's self-expression to be overheard by the audience around the mythic campfire).

Mining Your Dreams

Joseph Campbell summarized the relationship between dream and myth in this elegant formula: "Myth is public dream; dream is private myth." The mysterious residence of the mythic material which informs the stories your islands urge you to tell is the unconscious, collective or personal. It makes sense that access to the unconscious is useful to the writer. To study the relationship between dream and the arts, I co-founded (with Marsha Kinder, then my colleague at Occidental College) *Dreamworks*, an interdisciplinary journal devoted to dream, myth, and art. When we conceived the idea for the journal, we wrote letters to those we considered leading lights in all the arts; we were amazed at the strength of response we received to our inquiry about how much dreams influenced art. Our advisory board included such literary luminaries as John Cage, John Fowles, Ursula Le Guin, Denise Levertov, and W. S. Merwin. Contributors included Ingmar Bergman, Robert Bly, William S. Burroughs, Richard Condon, Federico Fellini, Paul Mazursky, Joyce Carol Oates, Alain Robbe-Grillet, Hubert Selby, Robert Penn Warren, Peter Weir, and Orson Welles—all testifying in various degrees to the process of dreamwork as one by which the door to the islands is more easily opened sleeping than awake. The funniest response was from Stephen King:

> I don't have many dreams or nightmares. If I dream I usually don't remember them. The only dream I have that recurs is one about being in a large old house—a very eerie, spooky place. I am on the third floor and there's a door across the room that communicates with the attic. I have been told that there is a mad woman in the attic but no one can find her

because the place is so full of junk and old furniture that's been stored away. It's very hot and I've got my shirt off and I'm typing. I know that if I don't stop typing the noise will disturb her and she'll come get me but I'm compelled to go on. So I'm typing and all of a sudden the door pops open and it's much worse than I can imagine—it's like the door leads to this crazy part of the house. And this woman comes out and she's got all this white, frazzled hair and her face is very crazy and she's got this big butcher knife which she's going to kill me with—at which point I wake up and spend the rest of the night clutching my wife.

Does that count?

Columbia Studios executive Stefanie Allain wrote: "The dream is an internal poem, written during the hours of sleep, unaffected by forced, artistic intent. I was born in New Orleans, where people have a superstitious respect for their dreams. I learned to regard my dreams as a guide to a hidden source of knowledge."

Nikos Kazantzakis's Zorba (in the novel *Zorba the Greek*) put it this way: "What a strange machine a man is. . . . You fill him with bread, wine, fish, radishes, and out of him come sighs, laughter, and dreams. Like a factory." The human brain is indeed an image factory that never stops processing images: receiving them from out there, storing them, recombining them, remembering them sometimes, forgetting them often, creating them, sending them back out again in a perpetual-motion Ferris wheel. Being in touch with the unconscious factory floor can keep a writer centered.

But the writer's use of dreams is quite different from the patient's in therapy. Writers want to use dreams not as the basis for analysis and interpretation but as the raw material for their waking work. Science fiction writer A. E. Van Vogt reported that he contrived an alarm-clock / tape-recording device that awakened him throughout the night and automatically recorded his ramblings upon awakening. He claimed that he found story solutions by this method of eavesdropping on his unconscious.

In my consulting practice, especially with novelists, I encourage writers to gain access to the unconscious through a method of "dream incubation" that is as old as the ancient civilizations of the Egyptians and the Greeks (who erected temples for the purpose; troubled devotees would bring their problems to the goddesses of sleep and dream and would spend the night in the temple awaiting a revelation from the unconscious). Gayle Delaney is one of a number of practitioners who employ this method in psychological therapy—see her *Living Your Dreams* in the bibliography.

Here's how it works. You've run into an impasse in your story. You don't know why you can't get to the next scene with your character, Valerie. Your Managing Editor sets up an assumption before you go to sleep: Valerie has a secret she's not revealed to me yet. The secret is in the islands. Your Managing Editor *incubates* a dream, sending a telegram to the islands and asking for a response: *What is Valerie's secret?* Trusting in your process, you will continue to fall asleep focused on this question until your dream provides an answer. Keep in mind that the answer may not be in the language of your Continent of Reason. Dream language is likely to be island language, metaphor instead of logic. One novelist client receives entire scenes vividly spelled out when she follows this process. Others receive only glimpses of the barrier that's been holding them back. But the longer this practice is followed, and the more confidence you have in it, the more fruitful it becomes.

The incubation works even when you're not actually asleep. Ursula Le Guin follows a practice she refers to as "guided reverie," where she sits under a tree, visualizes a being in the fictional world she's creating, and follows that being around until it reveals more and more about the surroundings in which it lives and the problems and feelings it experiences in those surroundings. I often suggest that clients go for a walk with one of their characters, first garbing themselves in the dress of the period in which they're writing. As one client walked along the beach in Santa Barbara, the character she was with suddenly revealed a truth she'd hitherto concealed. At that point, three dolphins jumped out of the water—and my client rushed to the nearest phone booth to call me. I can't guarantee the method will always produce dolphins, but it has an uncanny effectiveness. One student was told to take his character to dinner at his favorite restaurant—which he actually did—and to ask the character why she'd been lying to him and how was he supposed to tell her story unless she told him the truth? He reported back to the workshop that she confessed to him, at the restaurant, after a few drinks, that she was cheating on her husband. So the next night he returned to the restaurant with the husband, and found out *he* was cheating on his wife. For the third night, he wanted to ask them *both* to dinner, and make them confess to each other. I wouldn't let him, pointing out that this would probably ruin his story.

All these scenarios, as you can see, will cause your Continent great distress unless your Managing Editor points out that "no harm is done" by being "artistic" within the time previously negotiated from the ordinary clock.

Everyone dreams. Some people say they don't dream, but that's been proved clinically untrue. Some people remember their dreams, some people don't. But remembering your dreams is a learned behavior. In classes on "Literature and Dream" I've found that nearly everyone will begin remembering dreams as quickly as after one night and as slowly as after ten days of persistence (if you're out of practice remembering your dreams, it takes a while to convince your islands that you really want to hear from them and let your Continent know that it's okay for their voices to rise to consciousness).

As an advance plan for recording your dreams, follow these steps:

1. *Prepare your recording devices so they're close at hand when you wake up:* a large, blank pad (lines, after all, are devices of the Continent's urge for control), and a reliable writing instrument—a felt-tip pen is better than a pencil, which could

break, or an ink pen, which could run out of ink, etc.

2. *Make sure that you're not going to be awakened artificially.* The jangle of an alarm clock is sure to dispel the most vivid dream. If you've conditioned yourself to being awakened every day to this jangle, it's likely that you don't often remember dreams. If you must use the alarm clock, set it to a classical music station. Preferably practice the dream recording process at a time in your life when you can awaken naturally after the amount of sleep your body truly desires.

3. *Before going to bed, tell yourself you're going to remember your dream.* This is the Managing Editor setting up the ground rules for the Continent and islands. Then go through the incubation process of formulating what you'd like your dream to tell you: "I need to know what the turning point of my second act is going to be." Because, as Carl Sagan points out in *The Dragons of Eden*, we react more strongly to auditory stimuli than to any other, it helps to say this "incubation phrase" out loud.

4. *Upon awakening, "set" the dream in your mind.* Before moving your body (some people think dreams are stored in the synapses of the nervous system, which is rearranged at each movement), or even opening your eyes (which brings in new stimuli), try to find an image from your dream: "a red dress." Once the red dress is found, bring it into focus: "It has a V-neck, and she's wearing a pearl choker." Dreams seem to "come out backwards," tail-first. You remember the end, then the step before the end, and, when you get good at it, all the way back to the beginning. Re-viewing the red dress leads to re-viewing the pearls leads to re-viewing the face of the woman wearing the dress leads to re-viewing the room in which she's putting on the dress—to the reason why she's putting it on, to the preceding encounter with her twin brother, to the horses they ride in on, and so on. You've pulled the horses up by the tail of the red dress. Don't forget that it's important to "see" this image sequence before you start writing, or it is likely to either dissipate as you reach for your pen

or be altered by the transcribing process itself. Once the images or image sequences are clear—

5. *Reach for your pen and pad.* If you can, do this without turning on the light or leaving the bed or moving more than absolutely necessary.

6. *Record the images as quickly as you can.* What we're after here is "automatic writing," where the images flow from your pen without pauses for the Continent's usual insistence on mundane things like punctuation, spelling accuracy, or logical consistency. If the dream revealed a woman in a red / black dress, don't stop to figure out if the dress was red or black. If the woman was Mary / Andrea, don't choose: Write both. The beauty of the islands is that they don't insist on such choices. When you get a glimpse at how they're "thinking" (to them, Mary and Andrea are the same person) you've truly gotten in touch with associations and connections that only your mythic unconscious is capable of making for you.

7. *Record how you feel about the dream.* When you've written down as much as you can remember, finish by recording how the dream made you feel. Was it a nightmare? Are you filled with joy? Puzzled? The exact same images can terrify you one day, elate you another. You can't later judge the psychological or creative value of the content without knowing what's called your "affect" regarding it.

8. *Date the dream, and record any immediate parallels you can see to your creative work.* If the dream doesn't seem to have answered your incubation question directly and clearly, give it a few days. Look back on it. Compare it to other dreams that responded to the same question. Sooner or later, I guarantee you, you'll begin to see patterns that will be both fascinating and useful. Anaïs Nin said: "What the psychoanalysts stress, the relation between dreams and our conscious acts, is what poets already know. The poets walk the bridge with ease, from conscious to unconscious, physical reality to psychological reality."

Dealing with "the Doorknob"

Since receiving Stephen King's letter I developed a method for my clients for working with the unconscious that I call "dealing with the doorknob." The doorknob in question is the one that opens the door to the attic behind which the dragon of your own unconscious lurks. Sometimes a book would come to me for editing that had all the earmarks of success. The characters were well-constructed, the descriptions of setting filled with pungency and drama, the writing style crystal clear and compelling. But something was missing. After years of looking for that missing something on the surface, I discovered that what was missing in cases like this wasn't on the surface at all. The manuscript, in fact, was *all* surface because the writer had carefully (whether consciously or unconsciously) avoided turning that doorknob and entering into the unknown, possibly painful, world where ancient dragons lie. He or she had not "dealt with the doorknob," going inside to the heart so that what came out, in the writing, mattered to us deeply because we could see in it the heroism of the writing itself.

The writer's job, after all, is itself a hero's quest. You hear the call of inspiration. You answer it. With great trepidation, self-doubt, questioning, you go into the unknown of your own past, your own unconscious, your own deepest fears and anxieties. There you face those dragons, risk being mauled by them as perhaps you once were in your formative years. At best you slay them, at worst return to tell us how you received the wounds we can now see. The writer is shaman and sorcerer, willing to go into realms forbidden to those residing always in the safety of the Continent.

The heroism begins when you put your hand on the doorknob. Remember, as you do, that the person holding the doorknob from the outside is a different person from the terrified child who long ago might have turned it closed on the other side. Aside from being an adult, the person whose hand is on the doorknob is a *writer*. But it's a writer with a protective Managing Editor, who will make sure that no harm is done to that heroic part of you willing to turn the doorknob and walk back through the door that leads to forgotten or repressed pain. The first time you dare to touch the doorknob, you don't have to open it. You may merely keep your hand on the doorknob as long as you comfortably can bear it. Then, when you're ready to turn the knob, you don't have to open the door entirely. You open it a crack at a time, until you believe in your own control—your own ability to stop this process at will (an ability the child did not have).

Why are we doing this? Because the pain is the truth at the heart of your story; and this time you can have the pain serve your creative purposes instead of serving the pain as you may have done once. The writer who revisits the demons inside the door will not see them as your demons, but as demons that affected you long ago, affected the you that was you then and is no longer you now. Writing, in this sense, gives us control over our old demons. But we must meet them face-to-face behind the doorknob.

EIGHT

Breaking into Show Business

Show business is like three-dimensional chess: Whether you're a seasoned pro or a novice, each move you make changes the entire pattern of the playing board. All your plans must be reevaluated after each step forward, backward, or sideways. This chapter offers insights I've gained in my second career as a writer-producer—about time, about dramatic writing, and about breaking in.

Script-processing programs like Scriptor and Movie Master have made the writer's typing job far less taxing. Where changing a character's gender once might have entailed retyping an entire script, a process requiring many hours, a word-processing script program now makes it possible to make such a change in minutes. Computers also make a script that is not in the accepted professional format inexcusable.

FAX machines and modems make feedback from script consultants, agents, and producers wonderfully convenient. These mechanical Muse's assistants have also taken away the excuse for not revising, revising, revising. If you plan to become a "force in the industry" and aren't yet "on line," I heartily suggest that as the first investment in your new career. If your reaction is to say, I'll do it when I make my first big sale, I suggest you reexamine your commitment to a writing career. A real estate agent doesn't wait to get a license until after the first sale is made. Your writing equipment *is* your license.

Screenwriting Revisited

What follows, from my experience as a writer-producer, are amendments or additions to the principles discussed in chapter 5, "The Elements of Fiction and Drama."

More on Character

Real people are complicated; characters should not be. Characters may be complex (meaning having more than one dimension), but if they're complicated (meaning having a plethora of contradictory motivations) we end up saying, "He's not a good character." A good character is a *structure*, a *mechanism*. Even the greatest major characters are relatively simple: Falstaff, with his love of life that knows no boundaries of class and his longing for companionship with the boy who will be king; Don Quixote, with his unflagging idealism overbalanced by his lack of common sense; or even Hamlet, who's simply torn between his living mother and the ghost of his father.

I now find it's useful to distinguish between "minor" characters (as discussed on pp. 102–103) and "supporting" characters. A minor character is identified by a single characteristic, which reveals itself each time the character appears: The little girl is greedy; the priest is always humming to himself because he lives in a dreamworld; the sheriff is angry. But the sheriff, if he's a minor character, is as angry at the end of the film as he is at the beginning. Anger is his single and sufficient tag.

A supporting character is less important than a "major" character, but more important than a "minor." Like a minor character, the supporting character has a tag or neurosis by which he's made memorable to the audience: He limps. But his tag should derive from a singular motivation; he limps because inside he's wounded by hate. The jilted lover is out for revenge. Whoopi Goldberg's character in *Ghost* is a con artist. But unlike the minor character, the supporting character develops from "a" to "z," from the beginning of the script to the end. By the end of the film, the jilted lover has learned that the price of revenge is too high; she moves from her "a" of seeking revenge to her "z" of letting it go. Whoopi has learned that she really *is* a medium. Note that it takes no more than three beats (a beat is a unit of action in which the story moves forward) to depict the supporting character's development. "A," "m," and "z" are often enough; you don't have to spell out every station of the character's progress along the way. The audience will fill in "b" to "l," and "n" through "y"; that's precisely what gets them *involved*.

Where a major character's conflicted motivation goes through changes, or what is known as the "character arc," an imaginary curve joining "a" to "z" (as discussed on p. 107), the supporting character experiences a one-dimensional change based on his or her single "motivation"—expressed in that character's action, thought, dialogue, and description. A greedy character learns that greed may not be the best policy; a loving character learns to hate. Where a jealous minor character remains jealous at the end of the story, a jealous supporting character learns to forgive. The supporting character often commands the subplot (which either mirrors or contrasts with the main plot to bring it into sharper focus) in such a way that his or her one-dimensional change provides perspective on the major character's multidimensional change—without competing with the major character. Ben Kingsley's character in *Searching for Bobby Fischer*, reflecting the changes in his pupil, moves from being focused entirely on winning to understanding the relationship between competition and being human. The main action line of this film, commanded by the boy, is enhanced by the counterpoint provided by the three supporting characters: his father (Joe Mantegna), his Washington Square opponent (Larry Fishburne), and his master teacher (Ben Kingsley). Each of the supporting characters changes as the boy changes. But where the boy changes on more than one level, their change is one-dimensional.

Screenwriter and novelist clients have found the following charts helpful in focusing characters:

CHECKLIST FOR **MAJOR** CHARACTER:

Character Name: _____

TAG (physical or behavioral
characteristic): _____

MOTIVATION: (inner conflict)	+	−
MISSION in life		
in story		
OBSTACLES:		
CHANGE:	"a"	"z"
	"h"	"p"

CHECKLIST FOR **SUPPORTING** CHARACTER:

Character Name: _____

TAG: _____

MOTIVATION (single): _____

CHANGE: FROM "a" _____ TO "z" _____

CHECKLIST FOR **MINOR** CHARACTER:

Character Name: _____

TAG: _____

As we move from major to minor character, we keep simplifying by deleting elements. Here are the same charts filled out
by way of examples:

CHECKLIST FOR **MAJOR** CHARACTER:

Character Name: Allen Bono

TAG: always dresses formally

MOTIVATION: (inner conflict)	+ to be the best he can	−he doesn't trust himself & is afraid of everything
MISSION in life	to trust himself & stop being afraid	
in story	to get back to life again	
OBSTACLES:	he's dead & in the hands of the "higher authorities"	he doesn't know how to get from death to life
	his wife doesn't believe he's in touch with her at first	his wife realizes he's worth a million dollars to her dead
	his law firm is glad he's gone so they can stop pursuing the case he was on	
	Gwen West is making his wife consider dropping the case	
CHANGE:	"a" he doesn't trust himself	"z" he's gained his confidence
	"h" he's married someone he trusts	"p" when his wife stops believing in him he's forced to rely on himself.

CHECKLIST FOR **SUPPORTING** CHARACTER:

Character Name: <u>Gwen West</u>

TAG: <u>she's terminally chic</u>

MOTIVATION (single): <u>money at all costs</u>

CHANGE: FROM "a" <u>she's fooling the world</u>

TO "z" <u>she's found out</u>

CHECKLIST FOR **MINOR** CHARACTER:

Character Name: <u>Norman Adashek</u>

TAG: <u>he hates women</u>

Through-lines

Television's concept of the "through-line" is extremely useful to the writer trying to shape a screenplay. Whereas a character arc is based on the character's progress from "a" to "z," a through-line is based on the *audience's* psychology. A through-line answers the question, "What will keep the audience watching for the entire two hours of the film? What will bring them back from the commercial? What, if this is a miniseries, will bring them back night after night?" The answer to the question is the through-line of the story. In the miniseries *The Thornbirds* it was, "Will she sleep with the priest or not?" In the miniseries *Lace*, "Which of the women is her mother?" In many stories, it's a simple "Whodunit?" But most novels, though successful as books, won't work as miniseries, usually because their through-lines aren't clear enough, or compelling enough, or simple enough to persuade the impatient television watcher not to switch channels.

Channel-switching, along with the Lucas-Spielberg revolution of extremely short motion picture cuts, has added immensely to the demand for constant conflict and drama. Imagine your audience as holding up that channel selector like the Statue of Liberty's torch. For all writers' complaints, most people, including you, have so many entertainment choices that they expect to be entertained every minute! After you have written each scene, you must ask yourself these questions:

- Where's the conflict?
- How does the scene move the story forward? What does each character in the scene want?
- Is the scene necessary?
- Why will the audience continue watching?

And don't forget that "leveling" question you don't want to hear *anyone* asking: *"So what?"* If someone reacts with that question to a scene you've written, don't be defensive; rethink the scene.

Description and exposition must ride piggyback on scenes that move the action forward. Though Merchant-Ivory continue putting beautiful films together, the American box office and television have all too little patience for a movie that dwells on scenes of mere descriptive beauty. In the opening shots of *Much Ado About Nothing*, British director Kenneth Branagh shows how both objectives can be accomplished simultaneously. Against the dynamic, intensely dramatic backdrop of the arriving horsemen, he intercuts shots of Leonato's palace in Messina and the milieu of Beatrice—which is about to be turned upside down by Benedick's arrival. It's not enough to show pretty pictures. Pictures must have purpose in the action line. After the second fly-fishing sequence in *A River Runs Through It* we become impatient, wondering why are we watching these guys fishing?

Transitions and Linkages between Scenes

Most of the time, transitions between scenes aren't necessary. A transition is the piece missing when a story moves from "a" directly to "c." In "a," the character parks the car. In "c," the character is already on the porch ringing the doorbell. The transition, "b," would be the character walking across the lawn. When the audience "fills in" the transition, it becomes involved in the action. When every transition is spelled out, a kind of bad writing referred to as "painting by the numbers," the audience feels patronized and uninvolved. Not to mention bored. When you remove logical transitions, you open your script to the audience's imagination—making the audience smart. When you spell out all the transitions, step by step, you put the audience to sleep.

A "scene linkage" is a kind of transition, with the specific purpose of setting up the audience's expectations for the scene to follow. The character, Alexandrea, rings the doorbell. Suddenly, from the character's POV (point of view), the door opens. But before the audience can see what's behind the door, the POV switches to that of the door itself (the screenplay, at this point, might read, "CLOSE ON—ALEXANDREA'S FACE"). Alexandrea's dialogue: "Oh, my GOD!" And we "cut to" the next scene. The line of dialogue is the "scene linkage," which sets up our expectations. We don't see what she saw, but from her reaction we know it's something awful.

Whenever possible, replace your Continent's desire to create a logical transition between scenes with a dramatic scene linkage instead—what film and TV people call the "cliffhanger" (from the classic scene that ends with our hero dangling from a fraying rope on the face of a cliff). The most dramatic scenes end with energy propelling you into the next scene, leaving you in suspense, leaving the characters in jeopardy. The word "cut" is not an accidental one in cinematic grammar. It comes from the pair of scissors cutting out the undramatic transitions; as television executive Norton Wright puts it, "Art is life with the dull spots removed." The editor moves the film back to a point of dramatic linkage, makes his cut, then reveals the next scene: Alexandrea's body, in a dead faint, on the porch—the front door closed.

The "Backbone" of Action

The *three-act* structure of a feature film is as old as drama, no doubt because it's intrinsically natural (*every* thought and action, when it's reported dramatically, has a beginning, a middle, and an end). The *seven-act* structure of a TV movie has evolved as network television's version of the natural three acts, the further subdivisions reflecting the commercial breaks: The first commercial comes after the first twenty minutes (Act 1), and the remaining six commercial breaks after each of the remaining six twelve-minute segments. In effect, the natural "Act 2" has been subdivided into five parts to serve the commercial breaks while at the same time guaranteeing a rhythmic rise and fall to the action line, punctuated by cliffhangers at the end of each act, that will keep the audience tuned in after each commercial.

It's generally accepted by script analysts and writing instructors in both television and film that the "skeletal structure" of a good script consists of six general steps, linked by "turning points," and spread appropriately across the three acts of a feature film or the seven acts of a TV movie. Beneath each step lies the "mythic deep structure" as the "hero's journey" carries the audience along with it:

Step 1. *Introduce the hero.* Who is he? How do we relate to him? Why is he fascinating? Give a glimpse of the "ghost" or "skeleton" in his closet. Your goal here is to involve us with your major character, the one with whom your audience is to identify. The story will be told from his or her viewpoint, so we must get that viewpoint focused at the outset (see the opening of *Tootsie* as an excellent example, where Dustin Hoffman's character goes from one audition to another, only to be told, "You're too old!" and he replies: "I can be younger"; "You're too young!"; "You're too short"—and finally, "We're looking for a woman!"). Show your hero in action, set the mood of the film. In this step, you're answering the question, "Who's the hero?"

Here are the questions a network story analyst would ask himself of this step:

- Is there a rooting interest in this story?
- Is the main character a hero? Does he make decisions? Instigate the action?
- Do you like the person our main character is helping?
- Does the hero have a reason to get involved?
- Is there any emotional commitment on the part of the main character?
- Is there a point of view here?
- Is our main character concerned with other people?

Step 2. *The hero's call.* He's faced with the "inciting incident" or crisis which calls him in a different direction from the one you've set him on in Step 1. He must respond, or avoid a response. He must embrace the mission or reject it. If he rejects it, obviously he'll reconsider—or there'd be no story. The hero's acceptance of the mission he's called to—reluctantly, valiantly, cautiously, or in any other way—concludes Act 1. In Step 2, you're answering the question, "What is the hero's problem?"

- Is this problem of interest to the audience?
- Is the situation desperate enough?

Step 3. Act 2 in a feature film and Acts 2, 3, 4, and 5 in a television film involve *the hero facing the obstacles* to his mission—a series of rhythmically rising and falling complications based upon his quest, moving the story forward into—

- Do these complications arise naturally from the hero's character and his problem?

Step 4. *The peak crisis* (the final turning point), at the end of Act 2 (feature) or Act 6 (TV), where all looks hopeless and the lead character seems about to be defeated by the repercussions of the initial crisis, but screws his courage to the max to bring about—

- Is the hero truly in jeopardy?
- Will the audience care about his jeopardy?

Step 5. *The climax* or conclusion to the hero's mission (feature Act 3, TV Act 7), in which she or he satisfactorily resolves the inciting crisis, and achieves—

- Has the hero remained in charge of the crisis? Or is it out of his hands?

Step 6. *The resolution:* a real change in the hero's circumstances, internal motivation, and prospects for the future. You've answered the question, "What does the hero do about his problem?" The accompanying illustration (Illustration A), courtesy of executive producer Norton Wright, graphically depicts these six steps—any one of which can include a "twist."

- Does the hero really change, or is his change superficial?
- Is the resolution positive?

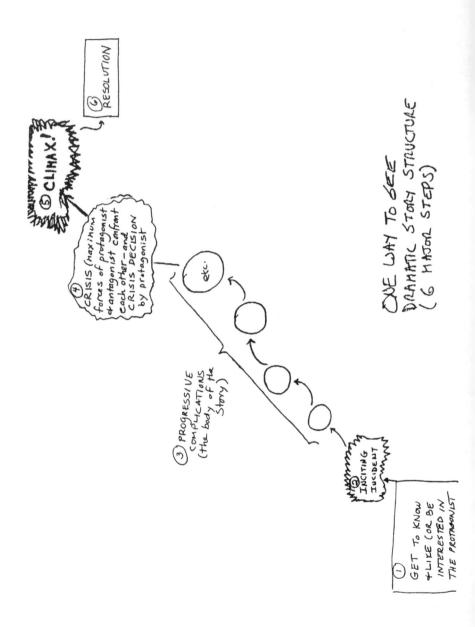

"Illustration A"

ACT I.		ACT II.	
1.		13.	
2.		14.	
3.		15.	
4.		16.	
5		17.	
6.		18.	(CLIFFHANGER)
7.		ACT III.	
8.		19.	
9.		20.	
10.		21.	
11.		22.	
		23.	
12.	(CLIFFHANGER)	24.	(BIGGEST CLIFFHANGER!)

(HOUR BREAK)

ACT IV		ACT VI	
25.		37.	
26.		38.	
27.		39.	
28.		40.	
29.		41.	
30.	(CLIFFHANGER)	42.	(CRISIS CLIFFHANGER)
ACT V		ACT VII	
31.		43.	
32.		44.	
33.		45.	
34.		46.	
35.		47.	
36.	(CLIFFHANGER)	48.	

THE END

"Illustration B"

"Illustration C"

"Illustration D"

What Is "the Twist"?

A *twist* (also known as a "reverse") is a sudden turn of events, or discovery, in the action line that throws the story into an unpredictable, more intense, more dramatic direction. A look at great novels and films will reveal that not all of them contain remarkable twists. Twists aren't necessary, or even expected, in a novel or script. But when they occur, and occur effectively by being derived from characters and action already established, they will earn you extra applause and recognition, as in, "What a great twist!"

The twist in the film *My Girl* occurs when the hero is stung to death by bees and the heroine, who's spent her life in a mortuary, must deal with death in an unavoidably personal way. The twist in William Goldman's *Magic* is revealed when the audience realizes the storyteller isn't who we've thought he was. In Steven Spielberg's *Jaws*, based on Peter Benchley's novel, the most dramatic twist lies in the characteristic vulnerability of the hero: He's afraid of the water. Imagine if Captain Ahab in *Moby Dick* or Santiago in Ernest Hemingway's *The Old Man and the Sea* were afraid of the water! Josephine Hart's *Damage* is constructed around a double twist: The hero falls in love with his son's fiancée; the son walks in on his father in bed with her—and subsequently falls to his death. Sophocles' *Oedipus the King* is one twist after another. In John Steinbeck's *Of Mice and Men*, just as the dream is within grasp, Lennie kills Curly's wife—and his best friend must make the hardest decision of his life. The twist in Part 2 of Cervantes' *Don Quixote* is that Don Quixote and Sancho Panza are reading about themselves in a book called *The Adventures of Don Quixote!* In the film *Silence of the Lambs*, the double twist occurs when, at the showdown in Act 3, the FBI raids the wrong house while the heroine, on a hunch, finds herself face-to-face with the killer. One of the most effective final twists occurs in the film *The Mechanic*, when the kid who's hired to kill the greatest killer comes home in triumph only to blow himself to bits when he turns on the ignition of his sports car. So the dead killer has the last laugh. The art of the twist is to make it surprising when it happens and inevitable when you look back on it. Twists often coincide with "turning points."

Illustrations B, C, and D are Norton Wright's actual worksheets that we use at AEI in working with writer clients or in preparing a story for one of our television buyers. Wright's charts provide you with an overview of the conventional seven-act structure of the network television film, as well as the individual scenes as they are spread out across the acts. Note that the seven-act structure is simply television's way of dividing and conquering the second and most challenging part of the universal three-part dramatic structure (beginning hook, middle development, and conclusive end). Shakespeare divided this second part into three; his plays have five acts. The made-for-television movie (MFT), its structure keyed to the need for commercial breaks, simply goes one step further. All dramatists can profit from examining the TV structure's mechanics because it is based on the absolute need to hold an audience in an environment of "channel surfing," where the ever-ready remote control threatens the movie's ratings.

Illustration B is the blank worksheet for constructing the teleplay, to be duplicated and kept in your file for use each time you work on a new story. Note that Act 1 is disproportionately long, with 12 scenes for a total time of 20–24 minutes, instead of the usual 6-scene act that lasts approximately 12 minutes (24 minutes for Act 1 + [12 minutes × the remaining 6 acts] = 96 minutes total running time). This structure has evolved on network television to ensure that the audience is fully involved before the first commercial break.

Note also that scenes 12, 18, 24, 30, 36, and 42 are what is known as "cliffhangers," shaped to bring the audience back after the commercial—with the "biggest cliffhanger" coming at the end of Act 3 (known in TV as "the hour break"), when the audience seriously evaluates its options of switching to another channel, and the "crisis cliffhanger" (as in Step 4, above) coming at the end of Act 6.

Illustration C shows what the charts look like (in the abstract) when you start to fill them out, the progressively thicker arrows meant to express the "rising action." Note that these charts, like all the advice in this book, are descriptive, not prescriptive. They're examples of how professionals prepare stories, and are obviously flexible. If the buyer likes the concept of a story, and its subject matter gets his attention, his next concern is making sure the story has sufficient "development"—that there is enough dramatic material to hold an audience through the seven acts. This worksheet is aimed at satisfying the structural needs of your buyer's Continent. If, during your pitch meeting, you can assure the buyer that your story has the required seven-act structure, you've created a positive lens through which he will read the pages you leave behind.

Illustration D is a comparison between feature films and television films, showing how the six steps of dramatic development are spread across the feature film's three acts and the MFT's seven acts. As mentioned, the difficulty of finding your way through the vast wasteland of Act 2 is conquered by the writer more easily when it's subdivided (into three middle acts by Shakespeare; into five middle acts by TV).

The Card System Revisited

The card system is the screenwriter's equivalent of the director's storyboard, providing an overview of the fictional world created in your story. The color coding described in chapter 5 (pp. 116*ff.*) may not be as useful for the screenwriter as the following system that has evolved from it:

Each character still gets his or her own color (Mark *red*, Jennifer *green*, Harvey *blue*, etc.). But instead of making scenes with "Mark and Jennifer" *pink*, make them half-red and half-green (i.e., start with the card color of the character whose scene it is, e.g., Mark's red; then cut a green card in half, and tape it to the right of Mark's red card—so the resulting

composite is red on the left, green on the right). This will
show at a glance that Mark and Jennifer are in the scene, and
from the overview you'll be able to determine where more
scenes involving both characters are naturally indicated.
Here's how a Mark / Jennifer scene card might read:

This schematic illustration is a television screenplay in progress, the Roman numerals showing the seven acts. Large "T's"
written on the right of the cards indicate "turning points," the
larger the T the larger the turning point. Cards with black
borders indicate nighttime scenes. Cards with one corner cut

indicate exterior scenes; "whole" cards indicate interiors. Arranged this way, the cards become a schematic visualization of the story's natural shape. It's an interesting illustration of how deep structure informs surface structure that the script fleshes out this "writer's storyboard" only to have the director, when he takes over the filmmaking process from the writer, proceed to "deconstruct" the script into his visual storyboard. Comparing the writer's card display to the director's storyboard would show the same family resemblance as that between chalkboard football plays drawn by the coach in the pre-game locker room and the "video chalkboard" overlaid on the now-completed play by television broadcasters. The video chalkboard retraces the play path that was, in effect, successfully programmed by the locker room chalkboard. The director's storyboard recapitulates the structure laid out by the writer before he fleshed out his script. Often weaknesses in the script are revealed at the moment the director tries to storyboard it visually. The writer is called back in to "fill in the blanks."

When it comes to writing screenplays and stage plays, you may find 3″ × 5″ cards more useful than 5″ × 7″ cards. Posted on a corkboard, and color-coded as described above, they provide you with a "bird's-eye" view that you can't achieve on the limited size of your computer screen. The cards, by the way, needn't be typed and needn't even be neat. Remember, they are tools that *you* control, not machines to control you. If they're beginning to govern your "flow" or in any way slow you down, ignore them; go with the flow. Use the cards when you stall, to get the flow started again.

All of this may sound mechanical, but remember it's only the result of my allowing the Continent to summarize and analyze the creative process. In reality, the process is more like trimming a Christmas tree. At each stage, you must stand back, squint a little, make sure you're on the right track, and sometimes undo what you've just done—before going on to the next stage. It's a give-and-take. Don't be intimidated by the apparent logic of the process; let your intuition decide what's useful, and discard the rest.

Revision

"How many revisions are normal?" The flip answer, of course, is, "As many as are necessary to sell the work." But it may be useful to know that novelists normally revise a manuscript at least two or three times before submitting it to agents or publishers; it then may undergo another one or two revisions before being published. Screenwriters may revise a screenplay—and *should* revise a screenplay—as many as twelve times along the way to production. Most "first drafts" have undergone six or seven rewrites before the producer, director, and even agent take them seriously. As much as these mechanics may assist you, the process by which *myth* becomes *story* is an evolution more than a mechanism.

When in doubt, follow this simple "cut or conflict" rule of thumb: If a scene of your novel or screenplay is not necessary to the ongoing action line, you must either cut that scene or add *conflict* to it. If the scene is absolutely necessary for "background," or to give the audience / reader a glimpse of the backstory, find a way of adding conflict to the scene. If the leading character, for example, is having a conversation with the country priest in the small town in Louisiana where she thinks her roots might be, make sure he's reluctant to give her the information she needs; make her work for it. If you can't find a way of adding conflict to the scene, then figure out what the essential background elements are that made you want to play that scene—and move them to another scene where there *is* conflict. Your priority must always be the needs of your story and its audience, not your fondness for this or that detail. Cut or conflict. A good script, like a good book, is a page-turner. Each page ends with an unresolved conflict. The reader can't wait to turn the page to find out how the hero "gets out of this one."

A Career in Show Business

The most invigorating thing about the writer's career in the entertainment industry is that it forces you at every turn to reexamine your own fortitude and stamina. Screenwriters have a given screenplay optioned four or five times before it gets a "green light" for production. Each time an option expires, they regroup and go out to sell the script again. The worst thing about a writer's situation in Hollywood is that no matter what you do or how good you are you can't control the random impact of personality and timing. And just plain bad luck. One day your project is set to get a "green light," the next morning the star decides he won't do this script unless he's also the director—and you lose another two years in development limbo.

What do you do about a situation beyond your control? You concentrate on the parts you *can* control, and turn to other projects. In the meantime, until you're earning a living from your writing, keep your "day job." Or arrange to work from your savings or retirement fund. Persistence, for writers in film and television, must become a lifestyle; it's the only program that makes sense. As television writer Cynthia Whitcomb advises, "Put no deadlines on your career." Telling yourself that you're going to persist "for another five years," then, if you haven't accomplished your goals, you'll move to that little farm in Louisiana, is self-sabotaging and self-fulfilling. (I know: I've actually gone down to look for the farm!) Saying you'll persist until one of your scripts becomes a film is, in the final analysis, the only sane philosophy because it takes you all the way to the last act: Either one of your scripts becomes a film, or you die happily persisting.

For a writer in Hollywood (a generic term for television and motion pictures, industries with global reach but geographically centered in Los Angeles and New York), persistence is well served by networking. Someone who's "in" obviously can help you get a foot in the door. That someone can be a producer, an actor or actress with "clout," a director, another writer, or an agent. If you know one of the first three, you simply find a way to pitch your story; if the response is positive, ask if you can send the screenplay. If your screenplay is outstanding, nothing is rarer; if your actress friend is interested, she'll know what to do with it. Think of it this way: You're doing her a favor! Good material is the foundation of great acting careers.

If you don't have close friends in the business, you'll want to find an agent. Though this is no easy task for the newcomer, it can be done. The guides listed in the reference section of the bibliography will help you. Generally speaking, you approach "literary agents" in entertainment the same way you approach publishers or literary agents in the book business. You can call them and try to pitch your story by phone. Or you can send a letter and a synopsis (this combination is also called a "query"), telling them who you are, what you've done, and what your story is. If they like the sound of your query and feel your story is commercial (meaning they can make money by selling it), they'll ask for the script. You can send out as many simultaneous queries as you like, and can receive a current listing of literary agents from the Writers Guild of America / West in Los Angeles. Don't put "copyright" on your submission, by the way; it marks you immediately as an amateur.

Another good way to meet an agent or a producer is to keep your eye out on the adult education classes at your local university. When a Hollywood insider comes to town, sign up for the course and introduce yourself during the break. Writers' conferences often include speakers from the film industry, who are more easily met when they're away from the chaos of L.A. or New York. All it takes is one good contact to get started—so don't be shy! People who succeed in entertainment must have chutzpah, and insiders recognize and respect it when they encounter it on the road. But don't forget that it's not your personality they're buying; it's your screenplay. An outstanding screenplay and a confident personality are the winning combination.

Don't submit your scripts or outlines directly to studios or networks. If you do, you'll receive a form letter, and the return of your unsolicited work unopened, along with a letter directing you to submit through an agent or an independent producer. It's also not unusual for an unsolicited submission to be returned with a "release" form and a letter asking you to resubmit your screenplay with the release signed. The release protects the motion picture company from any legal obligation to you should they be in development or production with a film similar to your idea.

Nuisance suits are common in this business of massive box office receipts, and the deeper its pockets, the less likely the company will read submissions from strangers. The idea you think is "original" may have been pitched to them a dozen times—and already be in development. Almost every month we receive "duplicate" submissions from writers who are convinced they have original ideas. Everyone seems to be drawing from the same external sources.

Though everything you write is copyrighted automatically under the laws of the United States and signatories to the Geneva copyright convention, professional screenwriters register their claim to material with the Writers Guild of America (offices in Los Angeles and New York). The registration process, which is always advisable, is available to members and nonmembers, for slightly different fees. Your screenplay or treatment (ideas and titles can't be copyrighted or registered!) is placed in an envelope and sealed with the date of registration on the outside. It goes into a file, available to be opened in the event that someone other than you produces a picture from your screenplay without your permission. In such events, which are extremely rare as the press coverage accorded to the rare instances suggests, your registration of the material simply proves that, on the date of registration, you were claiming it to be your own. That's the best you can do, other than employing common sense about who you deal with, to protect yourself. If you're paranoid about being "ripped off," and are afraid of sending anything you write out into the world, you shouldn't be writing professionally.

Small independent production companies are always looking for stories—fiction and nonfiction—for television and film. You can also approach us by sending us a query, or by calling (the directories in the bibliography list telephone numbers!). We react to inquiries, first, by considering the *kind* of story being pitched. In most cases, if we decline it's because the story doesn't appeal to us subjectively, or we don't think we can sell the story to the networks or find financing for it as a feature, or we've seen so many similar stories that another one will make our eyeballs fall out. If we pass, you shouldn't take it personally.

In those rare cases (we're eagerly seeking these) when you've submitted a story we'd love to know more about, we'll call or write asking you for the script or treatment (whatever you've told us you have in the letter). In the case of nonfiction, for which television is insatiable, all you need is access to someone's story rights. Let us know about it, and we'll tell you how to secure the rights from them as well as how to protect yourself. We often connect writers who have promising stories with their choice of reliable agents we've bought from previously, so that the new writer can be properly represented as he enters into a business arrangement with us.

Writing for television is entering into a hierarchy. It's extremely difficult to break in to this most lucrative of all writing careers, yet nearly as difficult to leave once you're in because it is indeed a close-knit world. You get in by writing a great "spec script" (meaning that you're speculating the time to write it, rather than being paid by a production company to write it). A spec script is your greatest asset, because you own it and no one can take it away from you without paying you to do so. The only asset stronger than a spec script in Hollywood is two spec scripts. While you're sending one around, don't let its marketing jeopardize your motivation. Work on your next script. By the time you've sold your first, if you've been industrious you may have written a half-dozen scripts—and it will be easier to sell them all. The first question you're asked in negotiations for optioning your script is, "What else do you have?" It's extremely counterproductive to be waiting to sell the first one before you work on the next.

The Pitch

In the story swap that is Hollywood, the two units of exchange are money and the pitch. Like a good auctioneer, the storyteller tells the story, in a pitch to potential buyers. Ideally the buyers react by saying, "That's a great story; let's buy it; let's develop it." The pitch is the live, oral delivery of a story's essence—and most of the time it's the pitch, more than the screenplay, that "gets their attention" and "gets you in the door." It's not enough to know how to write a screenplay; you must also develop your pitching skills, or at least make sure you're working closely with someone (agent, manager, co-writer, producer) who is a great pitchman.

The best writer isn't always the best pitchman, which may explain why so many mediocre writers have their films made. But a film, after all, is *not* a literary medium; it's a visual medium using words as one of many elements. Writers complain, "No one reads." But in the film business reading is indeed a sometimes necessary evil and a last resort. Why should filmmakers read? Reading is what you do only if you can't hear the story, or see the movie. A great story should be dramatized, acted out. Director Carlo Carlei *(Flight of the Innocent, Fluke)* says he rarely looks at the script once he begins filming the movie; he concentrates on what he's seeing through the eye of the camera. If films were written events, we'd be watching, in the darkened theater, a hand turn the pages on the screen.

Film is closer to the mythic source of story, to drama itself, than any other medium that involves words; and therefore a good pitch draws more from drama than from words. One of Hollywood's famous Louis B. Mayer legends has to do with the way he received pitches. He judged stories only when they were presented to him by a mime, who was allowed 90 seconds to give him the heart and soul of the story—without words. If his *ass* burned, he said, he developed the story into a script; if he felt nothing, it was a pass. People refer to the story as one more example of Hollywood's cultural philistinism, but I have a feeling Aristotle would have acknowledged the formal validity of, and approved of, Mayer's method, however odd that might seem to the Writers Guild. Mayer wasn't looking for wonderful words; he was looking for a compelling story, reaching beneath the surface to the mythic depths. The heart and soul of the story. What might *move* the audience.

If you haven't yet been able to focus your story into a moving statement that compels your audience to tears, you shouldn't be upset. Your story simply isn't ready to come out yet; its gestation is incomplete. Your goal is to produce an emotional reaction, Aristotle's *catharsis* of "pity and fear." Postpone the pitch meeting, and go back to the drawing board.

I'll never forget a television pitch I heard about. The pitch was made to the head of a major cable network, who'd agreed to meet with the prospective financers, the producers, and the novelist whose wonderful novel they'd optioned and wanted to develop into a film. The novelist had been selected by the group to deliver the pitch—who were correct, in retrospect, about recognizing his nervousness before the meeting as a bad omen. When the busy executive finally opened the meeting, the novelist began to read from his story notes. Minutes into this awkward pitch, the executive interrupted. "What the hell's going on here?"

"I'm just giving you the highlights of the story," the novelist explained.

"Didn't he write the story?" the president asked one of the financers, then turned back to the writer: "Why are you looking at notes? Get out of my office! If you can't remember your own story, how am *I* going to be able to sell it to an audience?!"

The meeting was over, and the producers learned to pitch the story themselves rather than let the novelist ruin their and his own chances with the next television executive. People in television and film take stories very seriously, but do not see them as literary events deserving of respect just because they are written. They see them as commercial possibilities of luring story-hungry audiences to watch at home during an hour filled with competing alternatives; or at a theater where tickets must be purchased with hard-earned cash. As far as they're concerned, a pitch from notes is already a sign of trouble.

Ever since hearing that story, I don't allow students in my workshops to tell me about their stories by looking at their notes. I ask them to trust their mind's ability to gestate the story fully, and wait until they can *tell* me and the class about the story before they pitch it. Trying to prepare them for the real world, I don't allow them crutches they won't be allowed on the Olympic slopes.

The person receiving your pitch is listening for the backbone of the story, and its emotional heart. If he's taking notes, he's noting the major turning points, highlights of character. He's listening for its dramatic structure: the hook that compels the audience into the story, the development that keeps them involved, the conclusion that satisfies. Whether you're pitching a story by telephone, in a formal meeting, or in a "chance" encounter at a restaurant, cocktail party, tennis court, workshop, or conference (Hollywood is famous for carefully arranged "chance" encounters), keep in mind some general principles about pitching stories:

No two pitches are alike, not even two pitches of the same story by the same person. The pitch is where the writer at his or her most intensely individual meets the industry at its most human. For all its millions of budget dollars, the film business is extremely personal. Open up and tell them what's so important about this story of yours. To do that effectively you have to see the movie in your mind's eye, envisioning the hero's story beneath the words you happen to use to portray it. Never forget that your purpose in the pitch, as it will later be in delivering the script, is to pass the fire of your vision onward in the relay race which is filmmaking. You are the initiator of the flame, and want to hand it off to the next keeper of the flame (the financer) who will hand it on to the next keeper (the director) who, if the hand-offs have occurred well, will find the ultimate keeper of the flame in an appreciative audience whose "word of mouth" will spread the fire like a conflagration! Your pitch is where it all begins. You must make sure they understand the shape, power, and personal importance of the flame.

Understand your audience. Before you make the pitch, ideally you'll research its recipient as much as possible. If you're pitching on the telephone or at a meeting, don't arrange the pitch until you know about the person you're pitching to. What are her likes and dislikes? What films has she been involved in making? What is she looking for? This market research is invaluable, if only to dissuade you from pitching to this particular person. A romance novelist trying to sell her book to a publisher who doesn't publish romances is wasting her time. A screenwriter trying to sell an action-packed, hard-edged, drug-smuggling story to Rob Reiner shouldn't be surprised if the pitch fails. If you encounter Mr. Reiner on the tennis courts and don't know who he is or what films he's done, introduce yourself as a writer and seek a meeting *later*, giving you a chance to do your homework.

The best pitches are done under pressure. The edge of nervousness you may feel is an asset, not a detriment. Performance anxiety, redefined as the positive force of elation, will help you do your best. If you're not "in the mood" to make a pitch, go anyway. Tap into the roots of your bad mood, turning the doorknob of fear or pain, and move forward. Louis Mayer locked the door when he was listening to pitches; it kept the pressure up. Rehearsals are a good idea, but they're not the same thing because the pressure's not the same. Scheduling a pitch meeting, by the way, is an excellent way to bring pressure automatically to bear on your pitch's gestation process. Knowing you have an appointment to perform helps clarify the feelings that originally gave rise to your story.

If possible, warm up your audience first. Because you've found out as much as you could, you will start by observing connections between the two of you: You're both from Kansas City, you both went to college back east. If your research bore no useful fruit, use the first few minutes of the pitch meeting to get to know your audience. Take a look around the office for things you can relate to. Get the other person talking about himself until you've achieved an exchange of interests. His job is to find writers and stories he likes. Relax as much as possible without losing your edge.

Never qualify your own pitch. An effective pitch is ruined in advance by qualifiers originating because of the writer's L.O.S.C. ("lack of self-confidence"). Don't apologize. Don't say things like, "Keep in mind this is just an idea at this stage," or, "It's only a first draft," or, "I'm flexible," or, "I've never sold anything before but I've come close," or, "If you don't buy this story, I'm going to sacrifice my firstborn on your assistant's desk." Your purpose is to pitch your story, not to provide a list of negatives that will mar objective reception of the story's potential.

Let the child come out to play. Audiences are composed of two kinds of people: children and critics (citizens of the islands of subjectivity vs. citizens of the Continent of Reason). Children with their eyes "glued to the screen," throwing themselves into the story, want to believe in the story and generously, hungrily, give it the benefit of the doubt. Critics remain alert at all times for the first flaw, the flaw that allows them to analyze and unravel the story's weaknesses. If you're going into your pitch meeting as a critic (by qualifying your pitch, for example), you're in trouble already. The quickest way to get someone to switch to "critic mode" is to reveal your *own* critic. Instead your visionary child should be addressing your pitch audience's visionary child. Tap into the same islands of enthusiasm the story came from in the first place.

Remember, or imagine, those urgent nights when you

wanted to borrow the family car because you had a "hot date." You psyched yourself up to talk to the keeper of the car, spinning a convincing story about why you absolutely had to have the car tonight. That psyched-up mood is a good starting place for a pitch—but it's not nearly as good as the mood you're in *after* the date when you've wrecked the family car, and now you know you really must give an outstanding pitch. "I'm all right, Dad. Don't worry. But they said I'm lucky I'm still alive. . . . Now, about the Mercury."

Sketch in just the broad strokes. Less is better. Your purpose is to tantalize the other person into getting involved with the script itself, or in one way or another move the project along. In trying to bring your audience into the mythic time and space from which your story came, don't worry about the words you use. Simply tell the story. Get your listeners there. Of course the story will come out differently every time it's pitched. A story in its oral shape is pure myth, always changing as it remains the same. The broad strokes are the key points that will allow you to re-pitch your story at the next level if you're successful at this one. Make it easy for your audience to visualize your story's beginning, middle, and end. Begin at the most dramatic point. Once you've got your listeners' attention, fill in middle and background as quickly as you can. This is a good time to pause for questions. You can reassess the close of your pitch while you gauge their understanding and receptivity. If you feel they're completely involved, rush to the ending! If they like the story at this point, they'll ask for more details to convince themselves that the story is whole and sufficiently delineated.

Focus on the main character. A story without a clear-cut hero is much harder to sell than one with a hero we're rooting for from the outset. Don't lose sight of your hero as you make your pitch. If your pitch is good, what will be remembered most is a great moment involving a hero it's easy to identify with: Rhett Butler saying, "Frankly, my dear, I don't give a damn!" Rocky running up the steps. Thelma and Louise (two strong heroes, in this case) holding hands as they drive off the cliff. Stella Dallas walking away in the rain after seeing her daughter married. The young boy (David Ladd, Jr.) running down the road calling "Shane!" If you make people care about your character's fate, they're involved.

Keep your pitch short. No pitch should last longer than 15 minutes. The best ones are often 5 minutes—let the audience ask for a longer version. I've seen a well-known screenwriter shot down at the studios because he couldn't pitch his story in fewer than 50 minutes. Words are not movies, and I wasn't surprised that development executives, juggling a hundred projects as they normally are, couldn't focus long enough to retain all the detail the writer insisted on delivering. After the first "pass," I told him I'd timed his pitch, 50 minutes. He didn't believe me. The next time we pitched the story, to a different studio, he took 55 minutes. The results were the same: a friendly, sleepy, but immediate pass. No one could convince the writer to shorten his pitch. After the third effort with the same results, I realized he wasn't seeing the story clearly. He was lost in his islands, making no accommodation for his audience's Continent. I bowed out of further meetings until this screenwriter went back to the drawing board.

Quit while you're ahead. If you see their eyes glaze over, you've gone on too long. When you've exceeded the attention span of the person you're pitching to, you're wasting your time and his. It's safe to assume that the person you're pitching to knows generally what he wants, or likes, or thinks he can sell. Once you've strayed beyond that area, he's likely to indicate disinterest and/or impatience. Read the signs. Don't continue beyond the "No." You know for sure that the pitch is over when the other person starts taking phone calls. And if you're unfortunate enough to be pitching to someone who's taking calls before you've even begun, you probably should ask to reschedule the meeting.

It's equally important to end your pitch when it's clear that your audience *is* interested. Too often, writers or pro-ducer partners threaten a sale by continuing to sell after the buyer has already said "Yes." Less is more. More can be too much.

Should you pitch only one story at a time? This is a difficult call for the new writer, who may not have more than one or two stories. But the general rule followed by professionals is to limit the pitch meeting to two or three stories at the most. You don't want to diffuse the buyer's focus, though it's always advisable to indicate that you have other stories. The right balance is achieved through practice.

A final word: Don't be discouraged if you receive a pass after you've given what you know was a good pitch. If you tell a good story, it will stay with the person you told it to even if it doesn't fit his present needs. You might get a phone call three months later: "Remember that story you told me about the bears? I have a friend at Universal who might be looking for something like that."

If you can't bring yourself to follow these "pitch" guidelines, or feel you are not a persuasive speaker, try to find someone who can pitch your stories for you: a writing partner, an agent, a manager, or a producer.

13 Rules for Breaking into "the Business"

From personal experience, including my mistakes, and the mistakes I see other writers make, I've compiled a "baker's dozen" rules for attracting success—and avoiding failure—in Hollywood:

1. *Visualize your future success.* You must see yourself receiving that Oscar or Emmy, or holding that first check and deciding what you will do with it. Then move forward a step at a time, keeping your visionary design in mind and regarding the obstacles in your path as "hurdles" rather than "impediments." Remember that it takes planning as well as endurance to become an "overnight sensation" in ten years or less. If you build your career for the slow track, keeping your

"day job" until your writing produces a comfortable income, your chances of moving faster are enhanced. That's what *festina lente* ("make haste slowly") means. Meanwhile, having a long-range goal will ensure your personal serenity. Without putting your career on deadline, you'll achieve more perspective when setbacks occur.

2. *Take full responsibility for your career.* If you do acquire an agent, don't sit back and expect your agent to take over. Keep in touch, giving your agent ideas and suggestions (tactfully, and without making a nuisance of yourself). If you read a newspaper article in the business section that says Paramount is starting a romance channel and is looking for new material, tell your agent about the article and give the name of the person in charge of acquiring new material at Paramount. Nothing activates an agent more than a client who is productive in his own behalf. Don't ever assume that anyone else will have your interests and only your interests at heart. That's not their job. It's *your* job.

3. *Know your market.* Knowledge equals power. Find out what buyers are looking for. Directories listed in the bibliography of this book will help you with this task, but until you have an agent or manager (whose full-time job is to know the markets) you're going to have to assess the market by watching television, watching films, reading books, and attending seminars, conferences, and workshops.

4. *Be willing to learn the hard way.* Carl Jung said, "Neurosis is always a substitute for genuine suffering." He meant that suffering is the door to achievement and progress, and that avoidance keeps that door closed. If you're looking for an easy life, "this ain't it." If you're a masochist, willing to achieve through suffering, the world of the entertainment writer may be for you. Difficulties abound; learning occurs through confronting them. Life is a matter of exchanging one set of problems for a more interesting set of problems. You can be certain that a career in entertainment will be endlessly challenging. The question you must ask yourself is, "Am I willing to be endlessly challenged?"

5. Don't be afraid to trust people. No matter how many times you're burned by dashed expectations or unprincipled people or just plain bad luck, you'll have to go back into the fire, if you want to reach your goal. Yes, it's true that Hollywood has a reputation of being cutthroat and shifty; and it's also true that the reputation is based largely on fact. But the industry is also filled with trustworthy, challenging, highly accomplished people. The goal is to find them, to learn from them, to work with them.

If you meet the wrong ones along the way, you'll be finding out whom to avoid. Be cautious, but not distrustful; wary, but not paranoid. Don't assume that *everyone* is out to get you. In this career, as in any business, you cannot expect to progress by equating the future with the past. By the same token, trust your instincts about people. If your first encounter is negative, why continue? The sooner you move away from people who don't seem responsible and trustworthy, the sooner you'll open yourself to discovering those who are. If you have a good first impression of someone, trust that person until he or she proves unworthy of your trust. On the opposite side of the table, nothing makes a deal harder to close than sensing that the writer is filled with suspicion and distrust.

6. Reject rejection. In the film business the word "rejection" is rarely used. You hear things like "our plate is too full," "we're passing right now," "this isn't right for us but the door is always open." Most projects that succeed have gone through the same door more than once. Every "No" is a bridge to that future "Yes." Assume that every "pass" means: "Let's talk— what else do you have?" One executive cheerfully admits that *Good Morning, Vietnam* was on his desk three times before it was accepted by another studio.

But before you chalk up another "No," remember that the party on the other side of the desk may have his own insecurities. Sometimes standing your ground and presenting further ammunition will reverse an opinion. "This isn't what the public is looking for right now," the executive says. "Have you read *The Popcorn Report?*" you ask. The executive shakes his head. "According to marketing guru Faith Popcorn," you say, "fantasy adventure is one of the ten most important trends for the late nineties." "That's interesting," says the executive. "Where can I get a copy of it?" "I'll send you one," you say. And a relationship has been established that may lead to reconsideration of your script. Don't be afraid to stick up for your vision.

I tell my clients, when we get a pass, "Congratulations! Another wrong person has freed your project to find its right home." Someone told me there's a great blackboard in the sky with all the "No's" you'll ever receive listed on it, along with the "Yes's." The problem is, you can't see this great blackboard in the sky. Therefore the only constructive way to progress is to march through that list of "No's" as quickly as possible.

7. *Honor thy contacts.* Agents, managers, studio executives, story editors, producers, producers' assistants, agents' assistants—any one of these people can help you if you use respect and commonsense diplomacy. If you've received business cards during a cocktail party, a friend's dinner party, or after a seminar or conference, you are certainly in a position to follow up with a call. You will receive, at least, a call back. It may not be within 24 hours (do you really think the head of Creative Artists Agency [CAA] can return all his calls within 24 hours, or even return all his calls himself?). But you'll discover that people do call back. Why? Because they never know whence the next great film concept comes. A development executive's job is to pursue every possible lead.

However, it's up to you to treat these precious contacts with care. Don't call until you have something specific that might be of interest. This means careful research: What is this person interested in or what has he or she previously produced (one of the best resources for this purpose, *The Hollywood Creative Directory*, which includes executives and their companies' film credits, is listed in the bibliography)? Prepare your pitch so that it can be delivered in a few minutes; this way you tempt the person you're calling into asking to see your screenplay and / or asking you to a meeting. If he wants to read the screenplay, you're over a big hurdle; don't set yourself back by saying to him, "How do I protect myself?" (You've *already* protected yourself by registering your material with the Writers Guild of America, and you'll type your registration number on the title page of the script.) Respect your contact's time. If you sense disinterest before 5 minutes have passed, back off.

In developing contacts, I've discovered that it's better to ask them for advice than help. You're appealing to your contact's humanity without asking someone else to take responsibility for your project. "I realize this script may not be right for you, but I'd really appreciate any direction you could give me." If the script turns out to be right for that person, you'll soon know.

Finally, don't overuse your contacts. No one likes to be pestered. Communicate when you have something concrete to talk about.

8. *Stay off everyone's "life-is-too-short" list.* This rule is the corollary of "Honor thy contacts." The people you're dealing with are doing their best to remain positive in a crazy, high-pressure business. When you cause them negative feelings, and try to force them into needlessly pressured situations, you're asking for trouble. It's true a squeaky wheel may get greased earlier, but learn to squeak without irritating! Too often inexperienced writers cast doubt into their own deals by communicating their lack of self-confidence to the buyers. Share your insecurities and fears with your psychologist, not with your best prospects. Use common sense. If you finally receive that longed-for invitation to an industry party at an important "insider's" home, don't "work" the party so forcefully you'll never get asked back. Take it easy, remembering both your own and others' dignity. If someone does you a favor, don't take it or that person for granted. Writers who've struggled to "break in" often feel the world owes them. It doesn't. These are just a few of the many negative attitudes that lead to finding yourself on someone's "too-short" list. One

that bothers me the most is having a writer beg me for the opportunity to do something in the industry; then, when I've given the writer the opportunity, I suddenly become the focus of the writer's resentment—for not being paid enough, for not being recognized as worthy of greater things, and so on.

This rule has an opposite side of the coin: With everything at stake and living on the edge, you yourself can't afford negativity, or bad karma. Therefore, when one of the people you've relied on for support in your writing career gets onto your own "LITS" list by giving you, directly or indirectly, negative reinforcement, you should take immediate steps to correct their behavior by making them aware of it and of its impact on you; or, failing that, to disentangle yourself from them. By the same token, if an agent or producer does something unprofessional or hurtful to you, don't expect her to change her behavior next time out. Add her to your "LITS" list, and move on to find the right people to work with.

9. *Think big.* Hollywood is a state of mind full of dreams that would be considered insane at a bankers' meeting. Everyone wants to discover the next *Rocky*, the next *Star Wars*, the next *Remains of the Day*—keeping their fingers crossed that they'll recognize it when they see it. Don't be afraid to "go for the gold ring." If you believe you've created the "next James Bond" character, make that clear. Putting such a vision into the minds of potential buyers or financers is the best possible way to create a lens through which your script will be read. Of course, the script must deliver your promise. If it's not at the stage where you believe it's *that good*, don't send it out and don't talk about it. Wait until you're truly convinced of its artistic and / or commercial quality—then start "the buzz" in earnest.

At the same time, remember the story of the "Little Red Hen." Be prepared to do everything yourself while you're waiting for support from the creative team you've enlisted. One of Hollywood's favorite stories is of determined filmmaker Robert Rodriguez, who wrote, produced, and directed an outstanding "portfolio film" on a shoestring. Rodriguez wrote, directed, and produced *El Mariachi* for a total cost of $7,000. He took it to the distribution office of ICM (International Creative Management) for help in finding a Spanish-language distributor. When ICM viewed the film, they were so excited by his talent that they sent copies of it on videocassette all over town. The film was "picked up" by Columbia Pictures for theatrical distribution, and Rodriguez was signed to a multi-film deal! His belief in himself paid off in a business built by daring dreamers.

Of course, not everyone is as talented as Rodriguez; nor does every writer aim to direct. But if that's your secret agenda, make it part of the image you hold of yourself and the image you project.

10. Don't forget to *take vacations* regularly, letting go of the quest for a weekend or a week or two. Just as the writing process itself must alternate between concentration and "abandonment," the career of the sane screenwriter requires frequent relief from the stress of writing and pitching. So intense is the environment of the entertainment business that a weekend away every three weeks may not be enough. You'll need to experiment with a pattern that works for you.

Of course, during a vacation, you abandon the quest, but not the project; the moment, but not the mission. Your frustration at finding so few people "there" at the end of the phone lines on Friday afternoons or Monday mornings will diminish substantially when you go away yourself (whether to Palm Springs, or simply to a weekend at a friend's house, depending on your budget). Keep your perspective. And of course you'll keep your "day job" until your new career allows you to make a choice.

11. *Avoid "future greed."* More deals fall apart because of "future greed" than from any other single cause. Here's what happens: After all that waiting, someone wants your project. You can hardly believe your ears. You look forward eagerly to the meeting. The meeting goes well, and you're told you'll hear from "business affairs."

Up to this point, your "friends" on the cocktail party circuit haven't been terribly interested in your script or your dream; supportive, perhaps, but not "interested." They understand the Hollywood "dance," and that the enthusiasm of development executives or agents dissipates in a Los Angeles second if their production bosses aren't interested. But when the phrase "business affairs" enters the picture, your friends and acquaintances suddenly become "advisers." They ask what you think the deal is going to be, then tell you to hold out for top dollar. "Stallone got two million for *Rocky*, and that was years ago!"

Whether they're right or not, they've done it: They've activated "future greed." Now you're thinking: After all these tough years, one deal can put me on easy street for the rest of my life. You decide to switch agents, or to play "hard to get"—the variations to the pattern are endless. But the net result is, too often, killing the deal. You've made the other party's "life-is-too-short" list.

Another "adviser" problem goes like this: A producer wants to option your screenplay, asks you who your agent is. You talk to your agent, who tells you that the terms being offered are reasonable, though she'll try to improve them. You go to a cocktail party, where you run into a friend who "knows someone at William Morris." He can't believe you're going to settle for the number your agent thinks is reasonable. Before you know it, you're speaking with a William Morris agent who tells you that you could get ten times as much as what's being offered. "Does that mean you'll represent me?" you ask. The agent says, "I'll certainly read your script and speak to the producer who's interested. You go back to the producer and tell him that William Morris is representing you." The producer asks who at William Morris should he call. You tell him. He calls. Two days later he gets a response from the agent you spoke with. He wants to know what the producer is offering. The producer tells him. He says he'll get back to the producer. He doesn't. First, he hasn't read the script yet (that could take two months); second, he's not that impressed with the offer and figures something better might come along.

The producer gets impatient, pushes you for an answer. You don't know what to do. On the one hand, you want this deal; on the other, you don't want to offend the "powerful agent" at William Morris (whose assistant tells you, "The script is being covered," to add to your confusion; "being covered" means a "reader" is preparing a synopsis and comments, called "coverage"). You begin to wish you had used your old agent, who's no longer speaking to you because you abandoned her at a crucial point. The deal becomes another exhibit in the museum of broken dreams.

The problem is that cocktail parties, where most casual advisers and inexperienced writers meet, aren't exactly the focal point of clear business thinking. If apples and oranges are going to be confused (are you really Stallone?), the cocktail party is a surefire *locus* of confusion. Of course you won't get the best deal of your life the first time someone wants to option your screenplay. The idea is to improve your terms each time. Experienced writers will tell you: Just get the deal. If your script is sold through your own efforts, it's easy to find an agent to negotiate the deal for you. Call the agent you'd love to work with, tell him you've just sold a script but need an agent to close the deal. You'll find that he's delighted to represent you. But make sure he understands how important this first deal is to you, and that his purpose is to make sure your deal goes through. (This may seem self-evident, but it's not; agents have been known to "switch deals," replacing an inexperienced writer's script with that of one of their own highly paid clients.) When the negotiated contract arrives, sign it. Don't sabotage your own first deal with delusions of grandeur. Repress future greed.

12. *Lighten up.* For an industry that traffics in humor, you'll be surprised how little of it is manifest on a daily basis. Everyone in show business is so intense. Very early in my career I'd asked a Paramount executive in New York to read an "off-the-wall" comedy because I thought it had potential (it was called *Motor Home from Hell*). He promised, since he thought he owed me a favor, to read it immediately. I didn't

hear from him for months. Finally I called him, from Los Angeles. "Henry, I'm calling you about *Motor Home from Hell*—"

"Oh, yes," he interrupted. "We've all read it. We think it's very strange. I mean, some of the humor was so off-the-wall we just couldn't get into it—"

"That's all right," I said. "Send it back. I sent my last two copies by accident over to Burt Reynolds' office. They love it, and Burt wants Ron Howard to direct."

"We love Burt," said Henry, without missing a beat. "And we can definitely see him doing this film. When we read part of it out loud at the meeting, people laughed out loud because it *is* outrageous. Now with Ron directing—"

"Henry," I said, starting to feel guilty. "I'm just kidding."

A dead silence stretched from coast to coast.

"Kidding," Henry finally said. "About what?"

"About Burt and Ron wanting to do it."

Henry didn't laugh. Until two years later, when he told me that was one of the funniest conversations he remembered.

Don't forget to add humor to your daily grind, spreading it liberally on your regular rounds from development office to agent's office to producer's lunch. Not only will you feel better, others will appreciate humor as well. Being at least good-humored is an essential part of the "being-fun-to-work-with" rule. No one, not even another grouch, appreciates a grouch!

13. *Celebrate each step along the rocky road.* Financially and emotionally, show business may be the most difficult business in the world. While you're waiting for financial rewards, give yourself psychological boosters. Don't say, "Yes, the deal is signed, but I'm not celebrating until the check is in the bank." Say instead, "The deal is signed. That's a major step forward. Let's celebrate." Success, as Thomas Carlyle said, is "continued progress toward a worthy goal." Here are the steps worth celebrating: Someone other than your lover thinks your script is great; an agent accepts you as a client; you sign with the

agent; a producer likes your script; the producer offers you an option; you sign the option agreement; you receive the option check; you do the rewrite; they like the rewrite; the movie is "green-lighted"; pre-production begins; principal photography begins (meaning that you will now receive your full payment); you receive payment; the check clears, etc.

If you're looking, you'll find as many opportunities for celebration as for cynicism and despair. Your project was passed on at your first network pitch meeting? Celebrate: You got that first meeting. Sooner or later, if you stay in the game, you're going to score.

NINE

Recapturing Creativity

No doubt you were highly motivated when you began your struggle to establish a writing career. The joy of challenge, the exhilaration of creativity, lured you into going for your dream. But now you've struggled for so long that you may not be feeling that same joy. You may not be feeling it at all. What once seemed so promising now seems like folly at best, madness at worst. What's happened? You've allowed the struggle to overpower the hope and positive energy you began with. You've forgotten the natural cycle of the creative process, from concentration to abandonment. Keep in mind that motivation leads to work; which, when not punctuated with appropriate rest periods, leads naturally to exhaustion; which leads to frustration; then to depression; then, ideally, to reassessment and renewal. If you're pursuing a "creative" career, the process of keeping yourself motivated, like the challenge, is endless.

So what do you do when you're not feeling motivated?

First you try Re-motivation Rule 1: *Keep moving forward despite your moods.* You cannot allow achievement to depend upon mood. If you always have to be in a good mood in order to accomplish your work, then it's probably time to consult a therapist. You haven't grown up. Grown-ups have to get the job done no matter what mood they're in. Imagine a firefighter throwing down the hose because he's no longer in the mood, or a Super Bowl game dependent on the quarterbacks' moods, or an Olympic gold medal contender announcing she's not in the mood to skate in the finals. Edmund Burke said: "Never despair; but if you do, work on in despair."

If Rule 1 fails because the meeting with your agent went badly, or because you stared at your blank computer screen for the entire weekend, you can apply Rule 2: *When things get tough, take a vacation.* But do so in a carefully limited way. "I need three days off." At the end of three days, you're likely to feel much better. If not, try a few more days off: "I need another week away from this project." Never decide to abandon your project when you're tired. Things *always* look worse when you're tired. Remember that you're taking a vacation *only* from your work, *not* from your commitment to the work.

The moment you're officially on vacation, allow Rule 3 to percolate in your mind: *The difficulty you are experiencing is normal—and necessary.* Writing is the highest expression of human creative potential. So how could it be easy? If it was easy, everybody would be doing it (instead of just talking about doing it). Sometimes writers have a hard time with the stress simply because they haven't recognized their stress is necessary. It's not simply par for the course; it *is* the course. I once spoke on a panel with the late Louis L'Amour. He had just published his 93rd novel, and said to the audience that night: "I feel I'm finally beginning to master my craft." Afterward, one writer told me she was quite discouraged by L'Amour's statement. "Discouraged?" I said. "You should be elated! What that tells you is that no matter how long you live or how many books or scripts you write, you'll *always* feel challenged by this endlessly challenged craft." What better way to live than with the assurance that your work will provide you with endless discipline and demands for excellence. Doesn't it make more sense to congratulate yourself for having the courage to write than to berate yourself because you haven't already "succeeded"? If you're making progress, you're succeeding. Now you understand what St. Catherine of Siena meant when she said, "All the way to heaven is heaven."

Rule 4: *Don't doubt yourself.* Identify the negative influences that have caused your resolve to falter. Maybe a well-meaning relative made a remark about how painful it is to see you wasting your life pursuing a dream of being a writer. Maybe the doubting Thomas is your own dark angel—in the form of your Continent of Reason saying to forget about a writing career. Either way, it's time to get your Managing Editor back on the job. He may have to renegotiate the amount of time you're putting into your writing, enough to make your Continent more comfortable. He may have to point out that what people say can't affect you unless you allow it to. One way or the other, it's time to "talk to yourself," asking the three parts of your mind, "What's going on in there?"

Lack of self-confidence is for all of us the greatest enemy. No matter how successful you become, you'll see—it *never* goes away. But the successful person has managed to move forward *despite* his or her lack of self-confidence. Self-confidence increases when you continue to act (in this case, write) with no regard for your insecurities.

Rule 5: *Face your fear, and make it your ally.* According to popular anthropological accounts of the Malaysian Senoi tribe, a child dreaming of being chased by a monster would be told that the monster was, instead, his friend and that he should turn to face the monster the next time he's chased in his dream. We all know by heart that crises, when confronted directly, provide opportunity as well as danger. The first step is to acknowledge and face the fear, remembering David Viscott's observation (from his book *Risking*): "If you have no anxiety, the risk you face is probably not worthy of you. Only risks you have outgrown don't frighten you."

When a client or student tells me he's filled with anxiety, I assure him that not only is it a good—and normal—sign that he's afraid, but that he should try to be *more afraid*. The writing flourishes when you face your fear, owning it as yours. If you dare to turn the doorknob behind which the pain lurks, your fear can become a positive force. The hero's fear becomes a powerful ally, making his entire being alert and engaged.

Resolve to *Associate with positive people, and stop associating with negative people* (Rule 6). Nothing is more helpful than a positive support group, and nothing more damaging than constant negative reinforcement from "friends" and family. Make whatever adjustments are necessary to reduce or eliminate your contact with the naysayers. The positive people in your life are the hero's allies, who've encouraged you to pursue your dream no matter what, and are your true "saints," inspiring you to go on living to the utmost of your ability. The philosopher-poet Johann Wolfgang von Goethe said, "If you treat people the way they are, you make them worse. If you treat them the way they ought to be, you make them capable of becoming what they ought to be." The positive people are those who treat you the way you have imagined yourself to be, at your best.

This leads us to Rule 7: *Take responsibility*. When one of my artist clients told me, "I never get personally involved in my own affairs," I realized how often creative people try to remain detached from their own commitment—a defense mechanism with all-too-limited effectiveness. I call it "magic thinking": "If I'm real good, work hard, be patient, the world will honor me eventually. And I've been good, worked hard, so now I'm waiting for the world to honor me." The world hardly ever works this way. Most successful people have struggled long and hard, and endured through multiple failures before achieving their success.

Taking responsibility means following Rule 8: *Take charge of your own thinking*. You *can* control your own mind better than you may believe right now. Not all the time, but, as you practice, more and more of the time. When you think, "I am succeeding at being my best self," you *are* succeeding. Motivational experts agree that you must *see* your success, be able to envision it internally, before you can *experience* it in your actual outer life. It helps to remember that you can't fail at being you; you're the only one, in fact, who can do that—which means that *everything* you do is important, even being depressed!

It also helps to remember Rule 9: *Let go of the wrong kind of control.* You can do only what you can do, and then you have to let fate take over. Control what *you can do;* don't try to control the rest. Even the most successful people can't control everything—so why are you upset about things you can't control? The things you *can* control include work you can do in the next hour, or today, and calls and letters that will help you market your work.

Rule 10: *Try to figure out what you really want—and start living as though you already have it.* Function follows form. If you commit yourself to the *form* of your optimal lifestyle, it will follow in *function;* but function follows only when your commitment is truly in place. Important to your re-motivation agenda is reaffirming your commitment to writing. I call this fine-tuning. Your career will profit from fine-tuning at every stage. Be careful what you wish for, though, or you're likely to get it. A screenwriting client called to tell me that she'd gotten her wish: She'd been hired onto the staff of a successful series! But she'd forgotten to wish for a successful, "intelligent" series. Now she was paying for her oversight with 10-hour-a-day tedium.

Once you've gotten past fear, and returned to action, concentrating on the details of your work, conclude your re-motivation vacation with Rule 11: *Congratulate yourself, and celebrate!* "Let's drink a toast to folly and to dreams," writes Paul-Loup Sulitzer (in his novel *The Green King*), "because they are . . . the only reasonable things." Recognize your courage. After all, you've freely decided to take this *unsafe* road; you will never be choked with the tears of regret shed by those who lament "the road not taken." The creative path, as we know by heart, is the difficult path, the path of anxiety and despair and failure, as well as of challenge and elation and triumph. You deserve self-respect for the courage of your commitment (even when it doesn't feel like courage to you at all). You can't control receiving respect from others; you *can* control receiving it from yourself.

When all else fails, there's Rule 12: *Try just "coasting" for a few days.* Focus on the present rather than on the future. "If worse comes to worst," an actress friend told me once, "I'm happy now." It's hard for creative people, who probably work alone without regular validation from the world, to keep from living in the future. It's hard not to do this. But you *can* give yourself the gift of the present, when the present is actually satisfactory on most levels required for life: enough to eat, a place to live, friends and family. Don't deprive yourself of life's simple pleasures. Meditation helps. Exercise helps—especially long walks to new places. Vacations help. These breaks in routine, by taking you "out of your yourself" temporarily, bring you into contact with the present, allowing you simply to *be here now.* Most of the time, when this happens, you're able to regain your perspective.

Here's a final rule that applies to everything I've advised in *A Writer's Time: Ignore all rules that don't prove useful.* There is no right or wrong way to be creative. Ultimately each writer finds his or her own way. All the suggestions in this book are merely that: suggestions. Use what you like, discard the rest. My observations about the creative process are meant to serve as props and jump-starts along the way. They aren't prescriptions, but descriptions of approaches that have worked for me or other writers. Following every suggestion religiously will not, in itself, make you a successful writer. This book is merely your ally. *You* are the hero: Continuing to follow your own vision is the only sure road to your success.

TEN

Inspiration

Here's a serenidipitous collection of insights into the writer's life I've collected over the years.

Writing

This is the true joy in life, the being used for a purpose recognized by yourself as a mighty one; the being thoroughly worn out before you are thrown on the scrap heap; the being a force of Nature instead of a feverish selfish little clod of ailments and grievances complaining that the world will not devote itself to making you happy.

—*George Bernard Shaw*

I write to find out what I'm writing, and once I get the sense of that, the hard work begins. It's like driving a car at night, when you can't see beyond the headlights but somehow you get through the night.

–*E. L. Doctorow*

What makes a story tick? The time bomb that's set to explode on the next page.

—Gordon R. Dickson

THE FIRST STEP

The young poet Evmenis
complained one day to Theocritos:

"I've been writing for two years now
and I've composed only one idyll.
It's my single completed work.
I see, sadly, that the ladder
of Poetry is tall, extremely tall;
and from this first step I'm standing on now
I'll never climb any higher."
Theocritos retorted: "Words like that
are improper, blasphemous.
Just to be on the first step
should make you happy and proud.
To have reached this point is no small achievement:
what you've done already is a wonderful thing.
Even this first step
is a long way above the ordinary world.
To stand on this step
you must be in your own right
a member of the city of ideas.
And it's a hard, unusual thing
to be enrolled as a citizen of that city.
Its councils are full of Legislators
no charlatan can fool.
To have reached this point is no small achievement:
what you've done already is a wonderful thing."

—C. V. Cavafy

You always copy. Everybody copies, whether they admit it or not. There is no such thing as not copying. There are so few original ideas in the world that you don't have to worry about them. Creativity is selective copying.

—*Philip Johnson*

Imagination is more important than knowledge.

—*Albert Einstein*

Perhaps the secret of talking is to have something to say.

—*Walker Percy*

If one advances confidently in the direction of his dreams, and endeavors to live the life which he has imagined, he will meet with a success unexpected in common hours.

—*Henry David Thoreau*

I would rather be a meteor, every atom of
me in magnificent glow
than a sleepy and permanent planet.
The proper function of man is to live, not to exist.

I shall not waste my days in trying to
prolong them.
I shall use my time.

—*Jack London*

Iron rusts from disuse, stagnant water loses its purity and in cold weather becomes frozen: even so does inaction sap the vigor of the mind.

—*Leonardo da Vinci*

The most original authors are not so because they advance what is new, but because they put what they have to say as if it had never been said before.

—*Johann Wolfgang von Goethe*

Once the late Sinclair Lewis arrived in Harvard, drunk as usual (alcoholism is our main occupational disease), to talk about writing. "Hands up, all those who want to be writers!"

he yelled. Everyone's hand went up. "Then why the hell aren't you at home writing?" he asked, and staggered off the platform.

—*John Braine*

When you are not practicing, remember, someone somewhere is practicing, and when you will meet him, he will win.

—*Ed Macauley*

Beauty and elevation flash from the currents set up by intense speculation. Beauty is not the aim of the writer. His aim must be truth. But beauty and elevation shine out of him while he is on the quest. His mind is on the problem; and as he unravels it, and displays it, he communicates his own spirit, as it were incidentally, as it were unwittingly, and this is the part that goes out from him and does his work in the world.

—*John Jay Chapman*

I've never had [writer's block]—I'm not sure what it is. The only solution is to write and write and write. When I talk to students or others who've been blocked, I often find it was just an absence of thought—they didn't know what to write about. If you know what it is you care about, it's easy to write. Those who can't write probably shouldn't.

—*Tim O'Brien*

At forty I'm beginning to learn the mechanism of my own brain—how to get the greatest amount of pleasure and work out of it. The secret is I think always so to contrive that work is pleasant.

—*Virginia Woolf*

Saul Bellow, when asked how he felt about winning the Nobel Prize, said: "I don't know. I haven't written about it yet."

"How do you make sense out of the irrational?"

Carlos Fuentes: "You don't make sense, you make art—which is even better."

If you write a novel as I do, you start with only a line—for example, the fragment of a dream. You don't really know exactly what is going to happen. The writing is going to develop as you work and the pattern will emerge. At the end of the night, when you finish dreaming, you know that your dream has a meaning, but you haven't found it when you begin. My writing goes the same way. Its not premeditated, but it comes out as though it were, because as soon as I interpret the meaning, a pattern can be seen.

—Anaïs Nin

A book, according to Littré, is a gathering together of several sheaves of manuscript of imprinted pages. This definition does not satisfy me. I should define a book as a work of sorcery from which escape of all sorts of images to trouble the spirit and change the heart. I should say still further: a book is a little magic apparatus which transports us to the heart of images from the past among supernatural shades.

—Anatole France

Action is eloquence.

—William Shakespeare

A poem may be an unfolding of an emotion which is at first partly implicit. It may begin merely as a vague lump in the throat, and out of that tension the images of a poem may be used for purposes of passing from the implicit to the explicit. The poem itself might be the quiver of the transition from belief to realization.

—Robert Frost

I perceived that, to describe these impressions, to write that essential book, the only true book, a great writer does not need to invent it, in the current sense of the term, since it already exists in each of us, but merely to translate it. The duty and task of a writer are those of a translator.

—*Marcel Proust*

WRITER TO SOURCE

Go back
to the primary shapes
and simple color,
retrace the path
of innocence
to early stirrings,
where the first spark flares,
first tears and terror,
and small toes experience dew,
back where
knowledge aware unthinking
knows only its response.
Move forward from there.

—*May Harding*

Human consciousness is in perpetual pursuit of a language and a style. To assume consciousness is at once to assume form. Even at levels far below the zone of definition and clarity, measures, and relationships exist. The chief characteristic of the mind is to be constantly describing itself.

—*Henri Focillon*

Yes, there is something of labor in the creative process: but it consists in . . . the focusing of attention upon what is given, and not in the "struggle for expression." That is where the basic misunderstanding lies.

—*Denise Levertov*

Too often I wait for the sentence to finish taking shape in my mind before setting it down. It is better to seize it by the end that first offers itself, head or foot, though not knowing the rest, then pull: the rest will follow along.

—André Gide

Writer's block is only a failure of the ego.

—Norman Mailer

Editing and Publishing

An editor must engage himself to that most difficult of human problems—making up his mind.

—Fredson Bowers

The most important tool of the theoretical physicist is his wastebasket.

—Albert Einstein

You become a good writer as you become a good joiner: by planing down your sentences.

—Anatole France

As soon as any art is pursued with a view to money, then farewell, in ninety-nine cases out of a hundred, all hope of genuine good work.

—Samuel Butler

No man but a blockhead ever wrote except for money.

—Samuel Johnson

Time

The very first thing I do before I start to choreograph is to figure out how many hours I have before the première. I compare that number with the number of minutes it takes to perform the music. Then I know how many hours I have to choreograph so many minutes. It is very well known in the choreography world that only Balanchine can choreograph one minute of ballet in one hour.

—*Peter Martins*

But, as Bokonon tells us, "Any man can call time out, but no man can say how long the time out will be."

—*Kurt Vonnegut*

Today belongs to few and tomorrow to no one.

—*W. S. Merwin*

"When I die, everything'll die. The whole Zorbatic world will go to the bottom!"

—*Nikos Kazantsakis*,
Zorba the Greek

The future remains uncertain and so it should, for it is the canvas upon which we paint our desires.

—*Frank Herbert*

I'm amazed at how many people have emotional difficulties. I have none. If you keep busy, you have no time for them.

—*Ansel Adams*

"Don't waste your time on trifles," he said. "You are dealing with that immensity out there."

—*Carlos Castaneda*

God created time so everything wouldn't happen at once.

—*Jack Smith*

Hope is a memory of the future.

—*Gabriel Marcel*

What's the use of worrying? You're gone today and here tomorrow.

—Groucho Marx

Heroism, the Caucasian mountaineers say, is endurance for one moment more.

—George Kennan

You may forget but
Let me tell you
this: someone in
some future time
will think of us.
—Sappho

To me every hour of the light and dark is a miracle. Every cubic inch of space is a miracle.

—Walt Whitman

Men die because they cannot join the beginning to the end.

—Alcmeon of Croton

To live is to be separated from what we were in order to approach what we are going to be in the mysterious future.

—Octavio Paz

. . . the present does not exist, and since the past and future do not exist either time does not exist.

—Jorge Louis Borges

The future / Splits the present with the echo of my voice.
—W. S. Merwin

A people—and for that matter, also a man—is to be valued only according to its ability to impress on its experience the stamp of eternity: for it is thus . . . desecularized; thus it reveals its unconscious inner conviction of the relativity of time and of the true . . . metaphysical signfiicance of life.

—*Friedrich Nietzsche*

I have learned that complaints are useless, that nothing avails but patience, in the things we cannot change.

—*Petrarch*

Remember that the future is neither ours nor wholly not ours, so that we may neither count on it as sure nor abandon hope of it as certain not to be.

—*Epicurus*

Things exist only in the time they are moving from is to was.

—*J. Hillis Miller*

The future is what you dream.

—*Morris West*

We don't get older with the years, just newer—newer because mirror to the original, which we truly are, but which we need time, devotion, and detachment to discover.

—*Emily Dickinson*

This is the way things are within. If anyone counts upon one day ahead or even more, he does not think. For there can be no tomorrow until we have safely passed the day that is with us still.

—*Sophocles*

Everyone thinks about the parts of his life, no one thinks of the whole.

—*Seneca*

Ronald Knox, English cleric and translator of the Bible, when asked on his deathbed if he would like to hear a passage from his own New Testament, answered faintly: "No," he said, then lapsed into unconsciousness—and then just audibly added: "Awfully jolly of you to suggest, thought."

It is easy to sit with folded hands on the shore and criticize the skill of the navigator.

—*Petrarch*

Further Inspiration

I cannot hold my tongue, nor my pen. As long as I live, I must write.

—*George Bernard Shaw*, at 91

There is a vitality, a life force, an energy, a quickening that is translated through you into action. And because there is only one of you in all time, this expression is unique and if you block it, it will never exist through any other medium, and be lost. The world will not have it. It is not your business to determine how good it is, nor how valuable, nor how it compares with other expressions. It is your business to keep the channel open. You do not even have to believe in yourself or your work. You have to keep open and aware directly to the urges that actuate you. Keep the channel open.

—*Martha Graham*, letter to Agnes de Mille

If I'd had more time, I'd have written a shorter letter.

—*Mark Twain*

If you're reading through and stop, something is wrong. Cut it. If something bothers you, then it's bad. Cut it. . . . Purify. Refine. Make it precise. . . . First cut all the wisdom, then cut all the adjectives. Have no compassion, pity or sympathy when it comes to cutting.

—*Paddy Chayevsky*

Art is life with the dull spots removed.

—*Norton Wright*

If there is a fear of falling, the only safety consists in deliberately jumping.

—Carl Jung

For an artist, the thing is not dreaming, or talking, but work.

—Auguste Rodin

An artist, a man, a failure . . . proceed.

—e. e. cummings

If you're not talkin' to yourself, you talkin' to the wrong people.

—Cajun proverb

If all the grammarians in the world were placed end to end, it would be a good thing.

—Oscar Wilde

Art is the result not of calm and tranquillity, however much the artist may, on occasion, experience calm in the act of writing. It springs from tension and passion, from a state of disequilibrium in the artist's being.

—Leon Edel

People want to know why I do this, why I write such gross stuff. I like to tell them that I have the heart of a small boy—and I keep it in a jar on my desk.

—Stephen King

Success is the progressive realization of a worthy goal.

—Thomas Carlyle

I know I was writing stories when I was five. I don't know what I did before that. Just loafed, I suppose.

—P. G. Wodehouse

No man ever will unfold the capacities of his own intellect who does not at least checker his life with solitude.
—*Thomas De Quincey*

It is not the critic who counts, not the man who points out how the strong man stumbled, or where the doer of deeds could have done them better. The credit belongs to the man who is actually in the arena; whose face is marred by dust and sweat and blood; who strives valiantly; who errs and comes short again and again; who knows the great enthusiasms; the great devotions; and spends himself in a worthy cause; who, at the best, knows in the end the triumph of high achievement; and who, at the worst, if he fails, at least fails while daring greatly, so that his place shall never be with those cold and timid souls who know neither victory nor defeat.
—*Theodore Roosevelt*

Imagination: Being able to think of things that haven't appeared on TV yet.
—*Henry Beard*

Getting my distance, a prerequisite of my understanding of human events, is the way I begin work. Just as, of course, it was an initial step when, in my first journalism job, I stumbled into making pictures with a camera. Frame, proportion, perspective, the values of light and shade, all are determined by the distance of the observing eye.
—*Eudora Welty*

Writing is like Prostitution. First you do it for the love of it, then you do it for a few friends, and finally you do it for money.
—*Molière* (Jean-Baptiste Poquelin)

I read part of it all the way through.
—*Samuel Goldwyn*

I know the path: it is straight and narrow. It is like the edge of a sword. I rejoice to walk on it. I weep when I slip. God's word is: He who strives never perishes. I have implicit faith in that promise. Though, therefore, from my weakness I fail a thousand times, I will not lose faith.

—*Mahatma Gandhi*

Make them laugh, make them cry, make them wait.

—*Charles Dickens*

My feeling is that the concept of creativeness and the concept of the healthy, self-actualizing, fully human person seem to be coming closer and closer together and may perhaps turn out to be the same thing.

—*Abraham Maslow*

Think of it this way: You are on a road that leads only to success. If you keep moving forward on this road you will eventually get there. Certainly, there will be obstacles—call them failures. But you climb out of the holes and over the broken tree limbs on your path and keep going. These failures are never as significant as your eventual success. . . . Failure is just another word for quitting.

—*Cynthia Whitcomb*

Writing is like sex; you don't have to wait until you're an expert to begin doing it.

—*Student in a UCLA Writers' Program class*

Writing is a form of therapy; sometimes I wonder how all those who do not write, compose or paint can manage to escape the madness, the melancholia, the panic fear which is inherent in the human condition.

—*Graham Greene*

I am apt to let something simmer for a while in my mind before trying to put it into words. I walk around, straightening pictures on the wall, rugs on the floor—as though not until everything in the world was lined up and perfectly true could anybody reasonably expect me to set a word down on paper.

—E. B. White

We are what we repeatedly do. Excellence, then, is not an act, but a habit.

—Aristotle

Until one is committed, there is hesitancy, the chance to draw back, always ineffectiveness. Concerning all acts of initiative there is one elemental truth, the ignorance of which kills countless ideas and splendid plans: that moment one definitely commits oneself, then Providence moves, too.

All sorts of things occur to help that would never have otherwise occurred. A whole stream of events issues from the decision, raising in one's favor all manner of unforeseen incidents, meetings, and material assistance which no man or woman would have dreamed could have come his way.

Whatever you can do, or dream you can do, begin it.

Boldness has genius, power, and magic to it.

Begin it now.

—Johann Wolfgang von Goethe

Bibliography

Writing

WRITING IN GENERAL:

Coles, Robert. *The Call of Stories: Teaching and the Moral Imagination.* Boston: Houghton Mifflin, 1989. An outstanding study of the importance of stories and storytelling in our lives.

Cowley, Malcolm (ed.). *Writers at Work.* New York: The Viking Press, 1958. Interviews regarding the writing habits of authors, useful in helping you understand the process of creativity.

Egri, Lajos. *The Art of Dramatic Writing.* New York: Simon & Schuster, 1972. Lajos's concept of the "premise" should be understood and applied by all writers of drama and fiction.

Keen, Sam, and Anne Valley-Fox. *Your Mythic Journey: Finding Meaning in Your Life through Writing and Storytelling.* New York: Jeremy Tarcher / perigee Books, 1989. A colleague of Joseph Campbell helps you analyze your own guiding myth and shows how it can find expression through writing.

Mack, Karin, and Eric Skjei. *Overcoming Writing Blocks.* Los Angeles: J. P. Tarcher, Inc., 1979. Practical advice and inspiration about what writer's block is and why it happens; preparing to write; business writing; student writing; technical, academic, and professional writing; and personal writing.

Noble, June and William. *Steal This Plot: A Writer's Guide to Story Structure and Plagiarism.* Middlebury, VT: Paul S. Eriksson,

1985. Required reading for writers of fiction and drama, this is a handbook of the most important plots and the basic elements from which they are structured; also provides a working distinction between plagiarism and artistic "stealing," as in T. S. Eliot's comment, "Immature poets borrow; mature poets steal."

Pearlman, Mickey. *Listen to Their Voices.* New York: W. W. Norton, 1993; Houghton Mifflin, 1994. Twenty interviews with women who write.

Poets and Writers Magazine. 6 times annually. New York: Poets & Writers, Inc. A support publication, listing resources for writers, including current magazine and book publishing editorial needs, contests and awards, conferences, and jobs for writers.

Polti, Georges. *The Thirty-Six Dramatic Situations.* Trans. Lucille Ray. Boston: Writer, Inc., 1921. This old-fashioned but fascinating book presents the most common plot patterns in drama and fiction.

Ross, Elizabeth Irving. *How to Write While You Sleep.* Cincinnati: Writer's Digest Books, 1985. Uses dream incubation and visualization techniques to assist the writer with getting organized, dealing with distractions and obstacles in your writing life, writing better fiction, writing nonfiction, and marketing your work.

Rothenberg, Albert, M.D. *The Emerging Goddess: The Creative Process in Art, Science, and Other Fields.* Chicago: University of Chicago Press, 1979; paperback, 1982. A groundbreaking study of the psychology of creativity in all realms of human endeavor.

Steinberg, Sybil (ed.) *Writing for Your Life: Ninety-Two Contemporary Authors Talk about the Art of Writing & the Job of Publishing.* Wainscott, NY: Pushcart Press, 1992.

Sternburg, Janet (ed.). *The Writer on Her Work.* New York: W. W. Norton, Volume I, 1980; paperback, 1981; Volume II, 1990, 1991. Women writers of fiction, nonfiction, and poetry discuss their work and their influences.

The Writer. Monthly. 120 Boylston Street, Boston, MA 02116. Over 100 years old, includes in-depth articles as well as market, conference, and contest listings.

Writer's Digest. Monthly. 1507 Dana Street, Cincinnati, OH 45207. How-to information designed to help writers write better and sell more.

Ziegler, Isabelle. *The Creative Writer's Handbook: What to Write, How to Write It, Where to Sell It.* New York: Barnes & Noble, 1968 / 75. A comprehensive introductory guide to the genres and markets for fiction and drama, including chapters on short story, novel, novella, science fiction and fantasy, "the people in fiction," and tone.

FICTION:

Bickham, Jack M. *Scene & Structure.* Cincinnati: Writer's Digest Books, 1993. How to construct fiction with scene-by-scene flow, logic, and readability.

Braine, John. *Writing a Novel.* New York: McGraw, 1975. A commonsensical approach, complemented by novelist Braine's insight into the psychology and social function of the writer.

Brande, Dorothea. *Becoming a Writer.* Foreword by John Gardner. Reprint of 1934 ed. published by Harcourt, Brace, New York. Los Angeles: J. P. Tarcher, Inc., 1981. Powerful advice, and inspiring recommendations about coming to grips with your desire to write and putting it to the test.

Cerasini, Marc A. *How to Write Horror and Get It Published.* Brooklyn Heights, NY: Romantic Times, 1989. Includes a brief history of horror fiction, "the monsters of myth and legend," religious horror fiction, a chapter on *Weird Tales* magazine, spicy horror and the weird menace genres, and interviews with horror authors Dean R. Koontz, James Herbert, H. P. Lovecraft, and Robert McCammon.

Falk, Kathryn. *How to Write a Romance Novel and Get It Published.* New York: Crown, 1984 / 89. By the publisher of *Romantic Times,* with intimate advice from the world's most popular romance writers.

Forster, E. M. *Aspects of the Novel.* New York: Harcourt, Brace, and World, 1927. This book has become a classic for its insight into the fundamentals of novel writing, including character, plot, and setting. It is especially important for its discussion of narrative voice and point of view.

Foster-Harris. *The Basic Formulas of Fiction.* Rev. ed. Norman, OK: University of Oklahoma Press, 1977. A primer on how to write stories that sell. Geared toward sales in the magazine market, this book contains an analysis of fiction plotting that reduces drama to moral-mathematical formulas reminiscent of Aristotelian poetics. Emphasizes the primacy of emotion and character motivation.

Frey, James N. *How to Write a Damn Good Novel.* New York: St. Martin's Press, 1987. Step-by-step, no-nonsense guide to dramatic storytelling.

Jute, Andre. *Writing a Thriller.* New York: St. Martin's Press, 1986. Offers aspiring writers the groundwork for plotting, writing, and selling a commercial novel.

Koontz, Dean R. *How to Write Best-Selling Fiction.* Cincinnati: Writer's Digest Books, 1981. A sound and persuasive insider's view by the prolific best-selling author of horror and science fiction.

Kuehl, John (ed.). *Creative Writing & Rewriting: Contemporary American Novelists at Work.* New York: Appleton-Century-Crofts, 1967. The book is invaluable for presenting authors' rough and final drafts to give you insight into the process of revision.

Lowery, Marilyn M. *How to Write Romance Novels that Sell.* New York: Rawson Associates, 1983. Lowery's book has helped hundreds of romance writers understand the elements of the genre.

Seidman, Michael. *Living the Dream.* New York: Carroll & Graf, 1992. Useful and inspiring primer for the new writer. How to create a successful career as an author of fiction.

Shaughnessy, Susan. *Walking on Alligators: A Book of Meditations for Writers.* San Francisco: Harper, 1993. Brief essays explore everything from the pitfalls of perfectionism to loneliness.

Stern, Jerome. *Making Shapely Fiction.* New York: W. W. Norton, 1991; Dell, 1992. A clear-headed, a-to-z approach to the basic thematic concepts and structural elements required in every fiction writer's arsenal.

Tobias, Ronald B. *20 Master Plots (And How to Build Them).* Cincinnati: Writer's Digest Books, 1993. Discusses and analyzes plots that recur through all fiction, no matter what genre. Teaches how a successful plot integrates all elements of a story and how to use these effectively in your work.

Wolfe, Thomas. *The Story of a Novel.* New York: Scribner, 1936. A book about the difficulty of approaching a second novel.

NONFICTION:

American Entrepreneurs Association. *Free Lance Commercial Writing Business.* Los Angeles: AEA, 1984. A loose-leaf guide, for easy updating, to the business aspects of writing—from organization of your time, to marketing, to taxes. The approach is hard-headed and practical.

Barzun, Jacques. *On Writing, Editing, and Publishing: Essays Explicatory and Hortatory.* Chicago: University of Chicago Press, 1971. Though out of print, this book still provides insight into the literary profession. Includes contributions by respected editors in every realm of publishing.

Tarshis, Barry. *How to Write Like a Pro: A Guide to Effective Nonfiction Writing.* New York: NAL, 1982. Especially useful for its thoughts on "reader sensitivity," keeping the reader on track, and "a new look at description."

POETRY:

Ciardi, John, and Miller Williams. *How Does a Poem Mean?* Boston: Houghton Mifflin, 1975. The opening chapters provide the necessary first steps for an aspiring poet. No one should submit poetry for publication before reading and applying the principles outlined eloquently here.

Deutsch, Babette. *Poetry Handbook: A Dictionary of Terms.* 4th ed. New York: Barnes & Noble, 1981. Deals with the craft behind the art of poetry, with comprehensive, lucid discussions of such matters as meter, rhythm, and rhyme. In alphabetical order, and cross-referenced, poetic terms are concisely yet clearly defined.

Jerome, Judson. *Poet's Market: Where & How to Publish Your Poetry.* Cincinnati: Writer's Digest Books, 1990. In addition to 1,700 market listings, clearly defining editorial needs, this book contains insightful interviews with poets like Frederick Turner, Elizabeth Searle Lamb, and Tess Gallagher, and with poetry editors including Philip Fried *(Manhattan Review)*, Joan Donovan *(Prime Times)*, and Karen Bokram *(Seventeen)*.

Johnson, Burgess. *New Rhyming Dictionary and Poets' Handbook.* New York: Harper & Row, 1931, 1957. A must for every poet's reference library, this is both a dictionary of rhymes and a guide-book to prosody.

Norman, Charles. *Poets on Poetry.* New York: The Free Press, 1962. A fine collection of prefaces and commentaries, essays and addresses, on the art of poetry, the imagination, and writing.

Turco, Lewis. *The Book of Forms: A Handbook of Poetics.* New York: E. P. Dutton, 1968. A complete manual of poetic forms, essential to all who wish to master prosody and poetics.

FILM AND TV:

Brady, Ben. *The Keys to Writing for Television and Film.* 4th ed. Dubuque, IA: Kendall / hunt Publishing Co., 1982. Valuable primarily for including the entire screenplay of *The Price of Tomatoes,* an outstanding model for action deriving directly from character.

Brown, Les. *Les Brown's Encyclopedia of Television.* Detroit: Gale Research, 1977. Profiles thousands of television actors, executive producers, writers, programs, and companies from the birth of the industry to today. Covers timely technological developments, significant mergers and acquisitions, important events, and landmark regulatory and legal issues.

Coe, Michelle E. *How to Write for Television: A Primer for the Creative Writer Covering Commercials, Interviews, Narratives, Newscasts, Serials, Musicals, and Institutional Promotion.* New York: Crown, 1980. Includes chapters on hard- and soft-sell commercials, sequential commercials, situation commercials, interviews, news, institutional commercials, as well as serial and episodic writing, music, and "how to get a job."

Field, Syd. *Screenplay: The Foundations of Screenwriting.* New expanded ed. New York: Delacorte, 1982; Dell, 1984. The foundations of screenwriting: a step-by-step guide from concept to finished typing.

———. *Selling a Screenplay: Screenwriters Guide to Hollywood.* New York: Dell, 1989. How to pitch, sell, and market your screenplay.

———. *The Screenwriter's Workbook.* New York: Dell, 1984. Exercises and step-by-step instruction for creating a successful screenplay, a workshop approach.

Gianakos, Larry James. *Television Drama Series Programming: A Com-*

prehensive Chronicle. Volumes: 1947–59, 1959–75, 1975–80, 1980–82, 1982–84. Metuchen, NJ: The Scarecrow Press. Featured programming arranged in chronological sequence with a list of series regulars and episodes and overview of the years indicated.

Goldberg, Lee. *Unsold Television Pilots, 1955 through 1988*. Jefferson, NC: McFarland & Co., Inc., 1990. Flopped pilots for prime-time network TV with emphasis on the concepts, the continuing characters, and the stars.

Goldman, William. *Adventures in the Screen Trade*. New York: Warner, 1984. A major screenwriter's inspiring look at the typical turbulence and irrationality of the most challenging of all industries, beginning with the now-legendary observation, "No one knows anything."

Hollywood Agents Directory. 3000 Olympic Boulevard, Suite 2413, Santa Monica, CA: tri-annual. (310) 315-4815. A listing of talent and literary agencies (indexed by type): "1,300 agents and their titles, addresses, phone numbers, and faxes."

Hollywood Creative Directory. 3000 Olympic Boulevard, Suite 2413, Santa Monica, CA: tri-annual. (310) 315-4815. A listing of producers and production companies, with credits, addresses, phone numbers, and fax numbers for the major creative personnel in each company (by title).

King, Vicki. *How to Write a Movie in 21 Days: The Inner Movie Method*. New York: Harper & Row, 1988. Describes what King calls "the inner movie method," from "random draft" to "rewrite draft" and including "Zen and the High Art of Getting the Thing Done"; "How to Pay the Rent While Paying Your Dues"; and "Should I Have a Writing Partner and How Do I Get One?"

Nash, Constance, and Virginia Oakey. *The Television Writer's Handbook: What to Write, How to Write It, Where to Sell It*. New York: Barnes & Noble, 1978. Includes useful information on terminology; teleplay styles; "concept, story line, synopsis"; reasons for rejection; "three-camera, one-camera"; script title page and format; "format for treatments and outlines"; legal and marketing tips; and excerpts from teleplays and treatments.

Seger, Linda. *Making a Good Script Great: A Guide for Writing and Rewriting*. New York: Dodd, Mead, 1987. An entertainment industry inside view by a noted script consultant, Seger here provides guidance on story structure, idea development, character development, and a case study (the rewrite of *Witness*).

Terrace, Vincent. *The Complete Encyclopedia of Television Programs 1947–1979*, Volumes I & II. New York: Barnes & Co., 1979. Complete information on 3,500 network and syndicated programs, story lines, cast lists, credits, running dates, and times.

————. *Fifty Years of Television: A Guide to Series and Pilots, 1937–1988*. New York: Cornwall Books, 1991. Network, syndicated, and cable programming story lines, dates, running times and extensive cast listings.

Whitcomb, Cynthia. *Selling Your Screenplay*. New York: Crown, 1988. An outstanding, inspirational guide to selling to television by a successful and respected Movie-of-the-Week writer.

Wolff, Jurgen. *Successful Sitcom Writing*. New York: St. Martin's Press, 1988. The complete guide to the craft, and business, of writing for TV's most popular format.

REFERENCES

Writing:

Bernays, Anne, and Pamela Painter. *What If? Writing Exercises for Fiction Writers*. New York: HarperCollins, 1990. Helps writers to solve common problems (story beginnings, point of view, and so forth) and increase creativity.

Fenza, D. W., and Beth Jarock. *The AWP Official Guide to Writing Programs*. Norfolk, VA: Old Dominion University, 1992. Program descriptions for 328 writing programs in the United States and Canada, and information on 129 writers' conferences, colonies, and centers. Also consider subscribing to the *AWP Chronicle*.

Fowler, H. W. *A Dictionary of Modern English Usage*. 2nd ed. Revised by Sir Ernest Gowers. New York: Oxford University Press, 1965, 1983. The most authoritative source for questions of usage and style.

Horowitz, Lois. *Knowing Where to Look: The Ultimate Guide to Research*. Cincinnati: Writer's Digest Books, 1984. A listing of librarian and reader's handbooks and manuals, providing solid foundation for research methodology.

Jordan, Lewis (ed.). *The New York Times Manual of Style and Usage: A Desk Book of Guidelines for Writers and Editors.* New York: Quadrangle Books, 1976. Advice on spelling, punctuation, English usage, and overall writing quality, as well as guidelines on basic aspects of journalistic responsibility.

Polking, Kirk (ed.). *Writer's Encyclopedia.* Cincinnati: Writer's Digest Books, 1983. A comprehensive one-volume reference for writers, editors, poets, students—gathering together facts, figures, definitions, and invaluable information from hundreds of sources. Contains samples of scripts, book contract highlights, tax forms, query letters, song lyrics, and head sheets.

Strunk, William, Jr., and E. B. White. *The Elements of Style.* 3d ed. New York: Macmillan, 1979. Mandatory reading for refreshing your sensitivity to bad writing, this book is still the best available on clear, powerful, and direct style.

University of Chicago. *The Chicago Manual of Style.* 14th ed. Chicago: University of Chicago Press, 1969, 1982, 1993. Tells exactly the way to prepare your manuscript—if you prepare your manuscript with "Chicago," it's ready for publication nearly everywhere. Divided into: Bookmaking (the parts of a book; manuscript preparation; proofs; rights and permissions); Style (punctuation; spelling and distinctive treatment of words; names and terms; numbers; foreign languages in type; quotations; illustrations, captions, and legends; tables; mathematics in type; abbreviations; notes and footnotes; bibliographies; citing public documents; indexes); and Production and Printing (design and typography, and glossary of technical terms). Everything you can know about the craft of writing, editing, publishing, and printing books, including proofreaders' marks.

Watt, William. *An American Rhetoric.* 5th ed. New York: Holt, Rinehart, and Winston, 1980. Read this book from cover to cover—it's the best work on rhetoric of the American English language. It tells about the different levels of writing, how to choose your style, how to remain consistent. Divided into "A Guide to Good Writing" and "A Review of Mechanics," with subdivisions that make the finer points of the written language easy to comprehend.

The Writer's Yellow Pages. Dallas: Steve Davis Publishing. Annual. Includes 24,000 entries, including directories of agents, book clubs, book producers, publishers, reviewers, distributors, software publishers, contests and awards, data bases, manuscript analysts, newspapers, printers, typists.

EDITING:

Adler, Mortimer, and Charles Van Doren. *How to Read a Book*. Rev. ed. New York: Touchstone Books, 1972. Everyone who loves reading and writing should read this book about the most productive relationship between a reader and a book.

Baskette, Floyd K., Jack Z. Sissors, and Brian S. Brooks. *The Art of Editing*. 4th ed. New York: Macmillan, 1986. A comprehensive textbook for copy editors, with invaluable examples and information on every step of the editorial process. Impress publishers with manuscripts that need as little copy editing as possible.

Berg, A. Scott. *Max Perkins, Editor of Genius*. New York: Pocket Books, 1983. Insight into one of the century's most influential and admired editors, providing you with a model for the relationship every writer dreams of having with an editor who understands his or her vision and psychology.

Gross, Gerald. *Editors on Editing: What Writers Need to Know About What Editors Do*. 3rd rev. ed. New York: Grove/Atlantic, 1993. Forty of America's most distinguished editors discuss the art and craft of editing.

Lanham, Richard A. *Revising Prose*. New York: Charles Scribner's Sons, 1979. An excellent step-by-step guide to revising that enables you to become your own editor. Lanham's principle of the "lard factor" alone is worth the price of the book because it allows you to cut through theory to instant perspective on your writing.

O'Neill, Carol L., and Avima Ruder. *The Complete Guide to Editorial Freelancing*. 2d ed. New York: Barnes & Noble, 1979. The best guide to the business and practice of editing, essential to anyone entering publishing and any writer who wants to understand a publishing house editor.

Ross-Larson, Bruce. *Edit Yourself*. New York: W. W. Norton, 1982. A brief, precise, and very useful review of editorial principles and practices.

Marketing:

Ballou, Melinda-Carol, Marie Keifer, and John Kremen. *Specialty Booksellers Directory*. Fairfield, IA: Ad-Lib Publications, 1987. Over 2,100 bookstores specializing in one or more specific subject areas, such as children's books, computer or business books, health, crafts, art, travel, science fiction.

Books in Print. Annual. New Providence, NJ: R. R. Bowker. 10-volume set. Available in libraries and major bookstores, this annual directory, arranged by author, title, and subject matter, lists books currently in print from thousands of publishers. Can also be accessed through computer interlink networks such as Internet, Compuserve, and Prodigy.

Carpenter, Lisa (ed.). *Children's Writer's & Illustrator's Market*. Cincinnati: Writer's Digest Books, 1993. In addition to being a complete directory of book, magazine, audiovisual, audiotape, special, and scriptwriter's markets for children's writers, includes chapters on first books, inappropriate submissions, formats for submission, agents, negotiating contracts and royalties, rights, taxes, insurance, and in general "the business of children's writing and illustrating."

The Children's Magazine Market. Redding Ridge, CT: Institute of Children's Literature, 1981. Analysis of hundreds of magazines where free-lance writers can submit their manuscript. Must contact the Institute for copies.

Cool, Lisa Collier. *How to Write Irresistible Query Letters*. Cincinnati: Writer's Digest Books, 1987. Practical marketing advice, and precise instructions on constructing effective query letters for fiction as well as nonfiction.

Deimling, Paula (ed.). *Writer's Market*. Cincinnati: Writer's Digest Books, updated annually. Gives information similar to that in the *Directory of Publishing Opportunities*, but has become the marketing bible of the free-lance industry. Has notes on free-lance writing and marketing fiction and nonfiction. Tells how and where to sell, what editors are looking for. Gives "backyard" markets, regional markets, etc. Provides instructions on preparing and submitting manuscripts, how and what to submit to whom, and directions for copying and mailing as well as postage information. Tells how long you should wait for a reply. Covers copyright law. A must.

Dessauer, John P. *Book Publishing: Basic Introduction.* New York: Continuum, 1974/89. Describes the publishing process in detail, from manuscript preparation through design, printing, marketing, and distribution. Gives full coverage to the small-press phenomenon, along with conventional information on publishers' contracts, the business of bookstores, analysis of employment conditions for newcomers to the business, and a detailed discussion of publishing accounting practices.

Directory of Publishing Opportunities in Journals and Periodicals. 4th ed. Chicago: Marquis Who's Who, Inc., 1979. If you have a list of article ideas, you still need immediate incentive and direction. This book helps you find your incentive and direction. Look under the category which fits your idea. Tells about contracts, copyrights, permissions, reprints; gives names of magazines, addresses, what they want, length, frequency of publication, circulation, rates, published by, name of managing editor, "contains articles on— with emphasis on—." An extremely useful tool for distribution, giving mailing-list information and prices on every imaginable cross section of American society.

Fulton, Len, and Ellen Ferber (eds.). *International Directory of Little Magazines and Small Presses.* Annual. Paradise, CA: Dustbooks. An invaluable annual for the person who writes poetry and short stories. The big magazines take only about twelve short stories per year, mostly from name writers. On the other hand, little magazines, which pay next to nothing, are constantly looking for short stories. This is a good way to start being published.

Gee, Robin (ed.). *Novel & Short Story Writer's Market.* Cincinnati: Writer's Digest Books, 1990, 1993. How and where to get your fiction published by mainstream commercial book and magazine publishers; as well as small presses, literary and small circulation magazines.

The Guide to Writers Conferences: Writers Conferences, Workshops, Seminars, Residencies, Retreats, and Organizations. 4th ed. Coral Gables, FL: SHAWGuides, 1992. A directory of great usefulness for planning your next outing to meet with other writers and with editors.

Halpern, Frances. *Writer's Guide to Publishing in the West.* New York: Pinnacle Books, 1982. Filled with useful reference information about book publishers, magazines, newspapers, syndicators, how to get an agent, how to research photographs, self-publishing, the library, one way to write short fiction, conferences and seminars, contests and awards, grants and scholarships, professional organizations and societies, magazines and newsletters, books for writers.

Henderson, Bill (ed.). *The Publish-It-Yourself Handbook: Literary Tradition and How-to without Commercial or Vanity Publishers.* Rev. ed. Yonkers, NY: Pushcart Press, 1979, 1987. Contains inspiring essays by women and men who started their own presses for various reasons, under various conditions, and explains how one goes about doing it. An excellent comprehensive bibliography gives access to directories, and works on bookbinding, copyright, manuscript preparation, paper, printing, production and design, advertising and promotion, and publishing.

Herman, Jeff. *Insider's Guide to Book Editors, Publishers, and Literary Agents 1994–1995.* Rocklin, CA: Prima Publishing, 1994. The names and specialties of more than 1,000 acquisitions editors at 325 U.S. and Canadian publishers, plus invaluable information about how to make unagented/unsolicited submissions.

Herman, Jeff, and Deborah M. Adams. *Write the Perfect Book Proposal.* New York: John Wiley & Sons, Inc., 1993. Ten proposals that sold and why. Provides examples of market research that will strengthen your query.

Herron, Caroline R. *A Writer's Guide to Copyright.* New York: Poets & Writers, Inc., 1979. Comprehensive discussion of copyright laws, writers' rights, definition of terms, and guidelines for working with the copyright office.

Horning, Kathleen T. *Alternative Press Publishers of Children's Books: A Directory.* Madison, WI: Cooperative Children's Book Center, 1988. An "underground and small press" directory, covering the United States and Canada.

Katz, Bill, and Linda Sternberg (eds.). *Magazines for Libraries.* 4th ed. New York: R. R. Bowker, 1982, 1992. Lists all magazines. This is different from the *Directory of Publishing Opportunities* because it's published for librarians, helping them decide whether or not to subscribe. It tells more about the quality of the magazine.

Literary Agents of North America: Complete Guide to U.S./Canadian Literary Agents. New York: Author Aid/Research Association

International. Annual. A complete guide to over 1,000 U.S. and Canadian literary agencies, including information on how to approach them, whether they charge fees, and what kinds of books they represent.

LMP (Literary Market Place). Annual. New York: R. R. Bowker, updated annually. Includes names and numbers of book publishers, all current markets, editors, proofreaders, and anything else a writer might wish to know. Compiled by surveying the trade. Sections on associations, book trade, courses, conferences, contests, agents, agencies, services, suppliers, direct-mail promotions, illustrators, reviewers, radio, TV, wholesale book manufacturers, newspaper publishing, etc. Tells not only what they are and who they are, but the kinds of things they do. For specifics on magazines, consult the MIMP (Magazine Industry Market Place), below.

Miller, Peter. Get Published! Get Produced! New York: Shapolsky Publishers, Inc., 1990. A highly charged and focused guide to getting your work published and produced (for film as well as television) at the most lucrative levels by a master salesman, executive producer, and literary manager. Includes examples of queries, synopses, treatments, and series pitches.

MIMP (Magazine Industry Market Place). New York: R. R. Bowker, updated annually. The magazine writer's encyclopedic counterpart to the LMP, listed above.

Paltis, S. William. Opportunities in Magazine Publishing Careers. Lincolnwood, IL: VGM Career Horizons, 1992. Shows job opportunities for both writers and editors, as well as information for free-lance writers on how to approach the magazine marketplace.

Publishers Weekly: The International News Magazine of Book Publishing. New York: Cahners/R. R. Bowker. In-depth weekly news about the book industry, including reviews of forthcoming books as well as information about dramatic and ancillary rights sales, the state of the industry, the foreign market, and editors and agents.

Richards, Gillian, and Peter Burton (eds.). Dramatists Sourcebook: Complete Opportunities for Playwrights, Translators, Composers, Lyricists and Librettists. New York: Theatre Communications Group, 1990. Complete opportunities for playwrights, translators, composers, lyricists, and librettists, this book includes over 850 listings, as well as submission guidelines, a calendar of contests and awards, information on script preparation, on workshops, agents, playwright colonies and residencies.

Shaughnessy, Roseanne (ed.). *Guide to Literary Agents & Art/Photo Reps.* Cincinnati: Writer's Digest Books, 1993. 500 listings of agents who handle novels, short stories, nonfiction, scripts, etc.

Whiteside, Thomas. *The Blockbuster Complex: Conglomerates, Show Business, and Book Publishing.* Middletown, CT: Wesleyan University Press, 1981. Insights into the business mechanics of the industry, including information on author tours, chain stores, agents, the "deal fabric" of Hollywood tie-ins, entrepreneurialism, and book auctions.

Time

Lakein, Alan. *How to Get Control of Your Time and Your Life.* New York: New American Library, 1974. A classic on time management, this book is practical and informational on topics such as working "smarter, not harder"; avoiding "the overdoer"; understanding the choice-making process; why deciding is so difficult; how to discover what you really want to do—and do it; and learning "to stress the benefits."

Mackenzie, Alec. *The Time Trap.* New York: American Management Association, 1990. Includes "Why Is Time Management Still a Problem?"; "The Real Purpose of Time Management"; "Making Changes: Start with Where You Are"; and "The Twenty Biggest Time Wasters and How to Cure Them."

Schlenger, Sunny. *How to Be Organized in Spite of Yourself: Time and Space Management that Works with Your Personal Style.* New York: New American Library, 1989. Innovative, personalized solutions that provide ten different systems to match ten basic personality types; aimed at helping you find the approach to getting organized that suits you best.

Taylor, Harold L. *Making Time Work for You: A Guide Book to Effective & Productive Time Management.* New York: Beaufort Books, 1982. Includes useful insights on goals, "quiet hours," the "to do" list fallacy, the information explosion, overcoming absentmindedness, avoiding the paperwork game, travel time, controlling interruptions, family organizers, and keeping the household organized.

Motivation

Atchity, Kenneth. *The Mercury Transition: Career Change Empowerment through Entrepreneurship.* Stamford, CT: Longmeadow Press, 1994. Useful information about dealing with money, "your mind/body asset base," people, and "your troublesome Type C Personality," for those making a commitment to a creative career.

Clance, Dr. Pauline Rose. *The Impostor Phenomenon: When Success Makes You Feel Like a Fake.* New York: Bantam Books, 1985/86. When you start cringing at the question, "What makes you think you're a great novelist?" this book helps you understand that all creative people live in a constant state of self-questioning as they pursue things they've never done before.

Covey, Stephen R. *The Seven Habits of Highly Effective People: Restoring the Character Ethic.* New York: Simon & Schuster, 1989. Covey's treatment of "proactivity" and "interdependence" in the context of principles and right living makes this book one of the most solid and inspiring available.

Delaney, Gayle. *Living Your Dreams: Using Sleep to Solve Problems and Enrich Your Life.* San Francisco: Harper & Row, 1979. Shows how the ancient practice of "dream incubation" can still be useful in working out problems. By analogy, the same principles can apply to the gestation process for your writing.

Peck, M. Scott. *The Road Less Traveled: A New Psychology of Love, Traditional Values and Spiritual Growth.* New York: Simon & Schuster (Touchstone), 1978. Based on the observation that "life is difficult," Peck's insights into the growth of character help provide a solid foundation when all around you is crumbling.

Robbins, Anthony. *Awaken the Giant Within.* New York: Summit Books, 1991. The self-motivator's handbook, presenting Robbins's high-tech and updated view of the power of positive thinking.

Sinetar, Marsha. *Do What You Love, the Money Will Follow.* New York: Paulist Press, 1987. Everyone engaged in a "creative" occupation should read this down-to-earth and spiritually uplifting manual to finding the lifestyle that suits your dreams and the courage to pursue it.

————. *Ordinary People as Monks and Mystics.* New York: Paulist Press, 1986. Draws fascinating and inspiring parallels between people pursuing nonconventional creative careers and monastic religious orders.

Storr, Anthony. *Solitude: A Return to the Self.* New York: The Free Press, 1988. If you're wondering about the uses of solitude, this book will make you feel at home with other creative people.

Viscott, David. *Risking.* New York: Simon & Schuster, 1978. Provides insight into the psychology of risk and reward in an inspiring and accessible manner.

Zdenek, Marilee. *The Right-Brain Experience: An Intimate Program to Free the Powers of Your Imagination.* New York: McGraw-Hill, 1983. Includes discussion of the "logical brain" and the "intuitive brain"; biofeedback training; other-hand writing; dreamwork; fantasy; guided visualization; as well as "success stories from the right brain."

Kenneth Atchity welcomes letters and calls from writers, which should be directed to him at:

AEI's Writers' Lifeline
9601 Wilshire Boulevard, Suite 1202
Beverly Hills, CA 90210
(213) 932-0321

Index